BUILDING FOR JUSTICE

The Historic Courthouses of the Maritimes

James W. Macnutt, Q.C.

SSP
PUBLICATIONS

Halifax, Nova Scotia

Library and Archives Canada Cataloguing in Publication

Macnutt, James W., author
    Building for justice : the historic courthouses of the Maritimes /
James W. Macnutt, Q.C.

Includes bibliographical references and index.
ISBN 978-0-9868733-3-1 (paperback)

    1. Courthouses--Maritime Provinces--History. 2. Justice, Administration of--Maritime Provinces--History. I. Title.

NA4475.C32M37 2015   725'.1509715   C2015-903276-8

Printed in Canada
Designer: Gwen North
All photos by Kevin Farnsworth, unless otherwise noted.

SSP

Box 2472, Halifax, N.S. B3J 3E4 Canada
sspub.ca
sspub@hotmail.com

DEDICATION

This book is dedicated to the Chief Justices of the Provinces of Nova Scotia, Prince Edward Island and New Brunswick in recognition of their commitment to an open, independent, inclusive and impartial interpretation and application of the law in their jurisdictions.

The Pictou County Court House was constructed between 1856 and 1859 in the Town of Pictou to architectural plans prepared by Scottish born architect David Sterling, whose practice was principally conducted in the Maritime Provinces. This architectural composition was one of Sterling's first commissions and is unique in Canada and England in its exterior design. It applies the Victorian use of several historicist styles in one building. It includes styles such as Flemish, Gothic Revival and Renaissance Revival. The building was destroyed by a fire set by an arsonist in 1987. This historic photgraph was taken in 1896.

ACKNOWLEDGEMENTS

The concept of a book on the historic courthouses of the Maritime Provinces was developed by the publisher SSP Publications. Scott Smith, the proprietor, a successful author and commentator in his own right on the architectural history of the Maritimes kindly approached me to write the book. I entered the project with interest but with only a rudimentary knowledge of the historic structures in Nova Scotia and New Brunswick. Writing the book has been an exceptional learning experience for me and one that was possible only because of the great help and enthusiasm I received from many people, only some of whom I am able to identify in the acknowledgements. I approach this task with caution fearing I shall omit someone who should be identified here. If I do, I apologize in advance.

My first acknowledgement must be to the Chief Justices of the three provinces for granting my request that they prepare a foreword for the book. Their forewords are received not as an endorsement or sponsorship of the opinions or interpretations offered by the author; they were provided by the Chief Justices as a contemporary statement of their judicial approach to and practice in the performance of superior court judicial duties.

The Law Society of Prince Edward Island and the Law Foundation of Prince Edward Island both made financial contributions to the author to assist in meeting expenses incurred in the development of the book, particularly in relation to photography. Their contributions enabled the author and the photographer to undertake their tasks.

The extent to which this book shall receive acceptance and a readership shall, in large measure, be the result of the exceptional photography of Kevin Farnsworth and the graphic representations of courtrooms and courthouses prepared by Prince Edward Island architect Philip Jefferson. I have worked with both in earlier books of mine. It has been a joy to work with them and to benefit from their collegial approach to the preparation of the aspects of the book assigned to them. Mr. Farnsworth accompanied me as we toured the Maritimes to visit, document and photograph each courthouse profiled in the book. His photography and observations were of immense help to me in preparing a clear understanding of the buildings we visited.

Each of the Departments of Justice (or equivalent) was cooperative in making its officials available to assist Mr. Farnsworth and me and to facilitate access to the buildings under their administration. I was amazed at the degree of enthusiastic interest in and commitment to the appropriate conservation and preservation of the courthouses expressed by officials who accompanied us as we visited the buildings.

Some of the historic courthouses no longer in active use as courthouses have been adapted by the communities in which they are situated as courthouse museums. I thank the administrators of those buildings for access and for providing me with documentation, information, stories and legends related to the buildings. Their assistance and conversations were a highlight of the process of developing the research for the book.

I wish to express gratitude as well to Mr. Justice Patrick A.A. Ryan, Q.C., Mr. Justice Charles E. Haliburton, and Mr. Justice Clyde F. Macdonald for their valuable contributions including historic information, old photographs and clarification of certain facts. Valerie A. Moore, Q.C. was a valued editor in reviewing parts of the appendix. Bill Hyde who was the principal architect on the planning and construction of the Halifax Law Courts was of particular assistance in editing my profile of that building. David Bergmark, a senior practising architect in Charlottetown, was similarly helpful in relation to the Sir Louis Henry Davies Law Courts in Charlottetown on which he was engaged during successful renovations.

I was also assisted by Pamela Borden, the librarian in the Barristers' Library located in the Law Courts building in Charlottetown. Her enthusiasm for the project resulted in each of my several requests for obtaining publications on my inter-library loans being promptly attended to. I was also assisted by the library staff at the Royal Institute of British Architects on Portland Place in London, England who were unfailingly helpful with research and dealing with sophisticated technology that was beyond my ken. I have visited the Palace of Westminster, the new Supreme Court of the United Kingdom building on Parliament Square in London and the Royal Law Courts building on the Strand in London and received access and assistance from officials there.

I was particularly fortunate to benefit from the editorial assistance of my friends Dr. Jack Whytock and his wife Nancy. Their insight and skills as editors and authors in their own right have led to a text that is consistent in language, style and clarity. I am deeply appreciative of their time, patience and encouragement. The book is stronger for their contributions.

I have benefited greatly from the unflinching and patient support of my law partner Daphne Dumont, Q.C., and members of our office staff. Ms. Dumont has generously turned a blind eye to our staff being usurped for book purposes more often than was reasonable. Inez Somers, a highly valued member of our law office staff has typed, proofread and maintained drafts of various parts of the book and coordinated between author and publisher. Her enthusiastic participation of the development of the book has been a great comfort to me and added greatly to the final result.

While many people have contributed to and supported development of the book they are not responsible for the accuracy of the analysis or opinions I offer. Although several people vetted the text, any remaining inaccuracies are there through my ability to defeat their best efforts.

TABLE OF CONTENTS

FOREWORDS

THE HONOURABLE J. MICHAEL MacDONALD
Chief Justice of Nova Scotia

There is a very good reason why courthouses stand prominently in the hearts of our Maritime communities. They are where our citizens go to peacefully resolve their disputes. They are where independent judges fairly and impartially uphold the rule of law, day in and day out. This is so, whether the outstanding dispute is between individual litigants (civil law) or between an individual and the state (criminal law).

Courthouses are, therefore, important symbols of justice. In fact, by housing the rule of law, they stand as beacons of democracy. As such, they must stand stately, as emblems of strength and dignity. They must stand alone as emblems of independence and impartiality. They must stand with their doors open so that citizens can observe justice in action. They must stand in the heart of the community, so as to be accessible, not just to litigants, but to everyone. In essence courthouses remind our citizens and inform our visitors that justice and democracy reside within.

Mr. Macnutt, therefore, serves us all by highlighting the history of our Maritime courthouses. By doing so, he reveals much more than the details of the selected structures. With equal importance, he reveals the history of our justice system and how it, along with our other institutions, slowly but surely, travelled the winding road to democracy.

THE HONOURABLE DAVID H. JENKINS
Chief Justice of Prince Edward Island

Courthouses portray our view of justice. They reflect our collective aspiration to live in a free and democratic society in which the personal conduct of all citizens and social interactions between citizens are subject to the rule of law. The prominent location and stately appearance of courthouses demonstrate respect for the law and legal institutions, public confidence in the administration of justice, and the paramountcy of these community values.

Courthouses in Canada are public buildings, both in name and in practice. They belong to the public, and cases are heard and decided in open courtrooms under public scrutiny. Exterior and interior design and function generally accentuate that access to justice is for everyone, and the dignity of the Crown will be honoured. This persona promotes public confidence that court proceedings will be conducted by independent judges acting impartially and deciding fairly according to law. Whether the matter heard within is a civil or family dispute, a personal challenge against the exercise of state authority, or the trial of a person accused of a criminal offence, the courthouse stands as a visual symbol assuring due process.

All lawyers and judges undertake to uphold the reputation of the law and the courts. Through this work, *Building for Justice*, lawyer and author James W. Macnutt, Q.C., makes an especially commendable contribution. He presents the results of his exploration and discovery into the history and development of the law in the three Maritime Provinces. His interpretation by depiction of courthouse styles employed over 215 years – first as three British colonies and then as Canadian provinces - provides for a creative and insightful presentation, by which the reader is informed about our system of law, along with some local influences and idiosyncrasies in the development of the law. The author deserves enthusiastic applause for his initiative, scholarly research, and entertaining and informative presentation. If I may say, the author has admirably captured the essence of the Sir Louis Henry Davies Law Courts in Charlottetown. This modern courthouse was named in honour of a renowned Island jurist who became the Chief Justice of Canada (1918 - 1924). Purpose-built, this building exhibits a depth of architectural quality and purity that promotes the core aspirational values of law and justice. It visually signifies the place and role of the courts of civil and criminal justice in our society.

THE HONOURABLE J. ERNEST DRAPEAU
Chief Justice of New Brunswick

Pathway to Justice: our infrastructures are tributaries of manifold influences. Chief among those is the surge of pioneers in the creation of the Province of New Brunswick, a territory carved out of l'Acadie's Nova Scotia during the American Revolution against the English Crown. This rush of colonists loyal to the Crown brought sophisticated men and women, their households, followers and slaves.

The new colonists displaced others who had settled here in earlier times. They brought with them a different approach to institutions of government, education and the administration of justice. In the result, a pathway to justice emerged.

One of the most notable segments in this pathway to justice was the construction of tried and proven courthouses designed in the English style. The functionality of these courthouses had long since proven their utility in England, its overseas colonies including those as modified in New England.

In this educational book, the courthouses built in New Brunswick are architecturally described and ably assisted by the visual buttressing of accompanying photographs provided by the author.

In New Brunswick, as successive governments sought to modernize the pathway to justice, the imposing old structures lost favour. What was also lost was the strict physical division between levels of courts, now housed in the same structures, a state of affairs conducive to concerns over the proximity between courts and judges of different levels, and its impact on the public's perception of judicial independence and impartiality. The current attitude of governments across our country driven, perhaps, by the exigencies of economics, efficiency, or even a backward nod to history, encourages the bundling of all levels of courts in one structure now known as the Law Courts.

The courthouses of our country, from majestic to inelegantly simple, are beacons on the pathway to justice and are, and are intended to be, reassuring to the public.

Within the portal of the court is the judge who will render a decision designed to do right according to law. The courthouse at the end of the pathway is merely the forum; justice according to law is rendered within.

PREFACE

The administration of justice has been one of the principal functions of governments starting with the earliest cohesion of civilized societies. Whether government was in the form of an absolute autocracy or some form of democratic authority, conflict resolution among citizens and between government and its citizens was and continues to be a necessity.

Why a book on courthouses? One of the most significant duties of every level of Canadian government is the maintenance of peace, order, and good government. The buildings constructed to house the exercise of justice must reflect the role performed within them and reflect the dignity of the Crown. Secondary only to the vice-regal residence of the lieutenant governor and the building housing the legislature, courthouses were accorded high status in the design, layout and landscape architecture of the principal communities of a British colony and subsequently a Canadian province.

This book aspires to be a textual introduction to and graphic illustration of the functions performed in courthouses, the official participants in courthouses and an interpretation of the architecture and history of courthouses in the Maritime Provinces of Canada. In my view there is no more effective interpretative device than a courthouse for explaining the Canadian legal system. Each aspect of its internal design is rendered to reflect the legal traditions and heritage to which it is an heir; its layout illustrates the functions of the courts and the roles of those individuals who are principal participants in the drama of dispensing justice in Canada.

The judicial system in Nova Scotia, New Brunswick and Prince Edward Island was one of the first administrative systems created by colonial governors in the British pre-confederation era. The first continuing court system in the British colonial period was established in Nova Scotia in 1721 while the centre of British administrative authority was in Annapolis Royal after the Treaty of Utrecht in 1713. However, the first exercise of judicial authority was conducted not by judges but by the Governor and Council in all three provinces. The establishment of structured courts and appointment of judges occurred later.

The necessity for systems to resolve conflict is self-evident as a practicality given the inherent pre-disposition of humanity to fractious disagreements and physical aggression. The priority for establishing a system of laws and a judiciary is inexorably linked to the role and the function of the Crown in the British judicial system in both its colonial and post-colonial eras.

The British Crown, as represented by the current reigning monarch, Queen Elizabeth II, is the origin and fount of justice in the Westminster System of Government, which is the current term applied to parliamentary government based on the British model. The nexus between the Crown and justice resulted in buildings being constructed to facilitate the dispensation of justice that reflected traditional British cultural and legal values. Courthouses formed one of the core elements of government administration in built form. That connection in early British colonial government necessitated a court being physically proximate to the Crown as represented by the symbolic presence of the Crown – namely the throne situated in the Legislative Council Chamber in the legislative building.

To illustrate that point, until 2011 the highest Court of Appeal in the English court system, the judicial members of the House of Lords, known as the Judicial Committee of the Privy Council, remained physically situated in the House of Lords in the Palace of Westminster and heard cases there. The monarchial connection with its role in the dispensing of justice required the judicial committees' symbolic proximity to the throne.

The symbolic presence of the monarch in the location of the highest court's activities demonstrated the principle of a fair, impartial and balanced administration of justice. In 2011, the Judicial Committee of the Privy Council was renamed the Supreme Court of the United Kingdom and was physically removed from the House of Lords to a new building located across Parliament Square but not far from the Palace of Westminster and adjacent to Westminster Abbey in London. In his Foreword to *The Supreme Court of the United Kingdom: History Art Architecture* published in 2010 to commemorate the move to the new facility, the Right Honourable Lord Phillips of Worth Matravers, President of the Supreme Court, stated

> *"no better location could have been found for the court than opposite the United Kingdom Parliament and next to Westminster Abbey in Parliament Square".*

Therefore, as we explore courthouses in the Maritimes, it is fundamental to bear in mind both that courthouses have an immediate connection with the Crown and that the exercise of judicial authority is conducted on behalf of the Crown. Maritime courthouses reflect that connection in their appearance, form of spacial arrangements, and decorative elements, particularly in their interiors. Also, the connection between the Crown and the dispensation of justice is manifest in the colonial legislative buildings constructed in the Maritimes, as elsewhere in the British colonial system. Each colonial legislative building contained the legislative council chamber (the equivalent of the House of Lords, in which the throne was located), the Legislative Assembly Chamber, and the Supreme Court. While courthouses retain traditional values, they have been increasingly modernized, made accessible to the public and the media, and refocused to demonstrate that they are a service to the public and open for conflict resolution in various forms.

The choice of courthouses which should be featured in the book was almost inevitable: those that are National Historic Sites together with those on the separate Provincial Heritage Places lists. The most recent Supreme Court buildings on Prince Edward Island and in Nova Scotia and New Brunswick are too new to be on those lists. However, as they are the principal courthouses in those provinces, they too must be added as they form part of the historical continuity in the dispensation of justice. Hence these are correctly included in the expression in our subtitle "The Historic Superior Court Courthouses..." A total of twenty-five buildings will be illustrated and described.

There are several levels of superior courts in Canada. In descending order of precedence and importance, they are:

> The Supreme Court of Canada
> The Supreme Court of Appeal of each province and territory
> The Supreme Courts of each province (Trial level) and parallel to the Provincial Courts of Appeal and the Supreme Courts (Trial level) are
> The Federal Court of Canada, Appellate Court, a statutory court of limited jurisdiction
> The Federal, Trial Division, a statutory court of limited jurisdiction
> There are numerous specialized federal courts such as the Tax Court of Canada.

There is a remarkable dearth of analysis relating to the development and principles applicable to the layout and design of English courthouses. The most comprehensive, and the one on which I relied is "*Ordering Law: The Architecture and Social History of the English Law Court to 1914*" a book written by Clare Graham published in 2003. I acknowledge the origin of the term describing separation of the principals in a courthouse as "segregation", is hers. The facts that support the principle of segregation are historical. Other terms could be used, but Ms. Graham's is the most descriptive and helpful.

Above: Carleton County Court House, sculpted masonry detail of an owl denoting wisdom, contained in the decorative elements of the entrance to the courthouse.

For the purpose of this book, the courts that will be illustrated and described are those courts located in the three Maritime Provinces having superior court justices appointed by the national government in Ottawa. The nationally appointed judges, also known as federally appointed judges, are referred to as "justices" and will be so identified in this book, whereas provincially appointed judges are "judges". The term "judges" will be referred to as a generic general term where it is appropriate. Provincial courts and magistrates' courts are not within the purview of our analysis. The purpose of the book as a description and illustration of the Canadian justice system as practised in the Maritime Provinces is most effectively reflected in considering the superior courts of those provinces.

INTRODUCTION

"Good order is the foundation of all things". This quotation from eighteenth-century British philosopher, lexicographer and political commentator Edmund Burke (1729-1797) summarizes effectively the necessity and rationale for a legal system comprised of laws, courts, judges and lawyers whose function and objective it is to maintain legal order in society.

Good order through the creation of laws, a judicial system with attendant courts, and accessibility by the public to those laws and courts has been a fundamental tenet of the British legal system to which the Maritime Provinces as British colonies are heirs. Remarkably, this inherited legal system survived the colonial period into Canadian Nationhood, virtually unchanged.

The concept of order has its most enduring Canadian declaration in the *Constitution Act of 1867* which contains the defining phrase "peace, order and good government" as one of the constitution's primary objectives. The concept of good order has been expanded considerably from its eighteenth-century meaning. Laws and court procedures have been and continue to be created through a prescribed legislated and judicial process. Laws and court procedures are accessible to all citizens in printed and computer-generated digital format for their scrutiny and provide a source of reliable rules to assist in their defence should they fall into disagreement with the state and into litigation with others in society. Citizens are considered to know the fundamental principles of the law (ignorance of the law is no excuse as a defence in court), so access to the law is essential in the Canadian legal system.

The laws and procedures governing the authority of British and Canadian courts are created by or are under statutes enacted by democratically elected governments. The creation of laws and procedures enables both to reflect the values and requirements of the citizen. The laws that are applied and enforced by superior court justices include both laws passed by Parliament or the legislature of the Province in which the superior court has jurisdiction, as well as the common law.

The judicial system in Canada, of which the Maritime Provinces are a part, continues to develop and expand in performing its role. Technology and continuing re-evaluation of purpose and objectives by all elements of the judicial system are continually driving that process. An educated and critical public including a highly engaged and educated judicial and academic community are also catalysts for change. While the principles of good order (as demonstrated by the rule of law) and a fair, open and impartial judicial system have been a constant in the British legal tradition, its modern application continues to open many more doors to public scrutiny, accountability and due process.

Our analysis of the courthouses and the judicial function performed in them will be developed starting with the origins of English law as received by the three Maritime colonial administrations and as applied and expanded by the legislatures and judiciary of the three colonies (subsequently as provinces of Canada). A substantial body of received law and tradition remain operative as part of the legal systems of the three provinces. Colonial and post-confederation courts have also been significantly influenced by jurisprudence and court procedures developed in other common law jurisdictions such as Australia and New Zealand. There is also increasing influence from American judicial practice, theory and decisions and courthouse design standards. An understanding of both the laws of the three provinces and the buildings in which the laws are applied can only be understood if their origins and purpose are understood.

We then move into a description of the origins and configurations of courthouses in the pre-colonial period in England and the adoption of those principles of design by the three colonial administrations. The nature of the administration of justice in colonies with a small population such as each of the three had when they were established necessitated simplicity and adaptations. These adaptations influenced subsequent forms and traditions in courthouse design and use.

The administration of justice was a component of the over-all colonial administration. Its significance and development over time was a major influence in the development of courthouses, the role of the judiciary, and access to justice. This theme will be explored as an influence on the configuration and use of courthouses.

The most important component in the administration of justice is the judiciary. We will examine the origins of its role, appointment, authority and traditions as received by the colonial administrations of the three colonies and as subsequently developed within the colonies, and later as provinces of Canada.

The judiciary cannot function effectively without support systems and personnel. The various officials will be identified by title, function and those traditions associated with each, particularly as they relate to the layout and performance of judicial duties in courthouses.

Could the judicial role function without lawyers? Lawyers have been both reviled and admired, depending largely on their success or failure for the person whose opinion is expressed. Nevertheless, lawyers have been an integral and substantial part in the administration of justice. The origins and traditions associated with them as developed in England and adopted in the three colonies will be explored. The role of lawyers has changed dramatically over the past three hundred years and a summary of those changes will also be considered. One of the notable recent developments in the judicial process is an affirmative answer to the question. An increasing number of persons appearing before courts in Canadian provinces are self-representing. That means that they are appearing before courts without legal counsel. This imposes special and often very difficult challenges and duties on the judge hearing the matter.

It is a well established principle that the public has access to the judicial process. The origin and development of that right will be explored. Few areas of administration of justice have seen more dramatic changes than in this area of the law.

Having explored the history, traditions and principles embedded in the administration of English common law and those responsible for implementation of the system, the buildings in which justice is administered will be examined in detail. We start with the earliest extant courthouses in the Maritimes Provinces continuing with changes to them made to accommodate societal, legal and democratic principles. Courthouses came to be created as separate structures with spaces designed and dedicated to the carrying out of the judicial function and the enforcing of the rule of law. In fact, as stated in the preface, courthouses are an excellent interpretive device for discovering the principles of Canadian justice and the roles and traditions of those involved with the administration of justice, particularly those most responsible for it, namely the judiciary.

In *Building for Justice* we will examine twenty-five courthouses in the Maritime Provinces of Canada, listing those provinces in the sequence in which they became separate British colonies – and therefore separate legal jurisdictions with their own as well as received laws. In so doing, the result will be a description and illustration of the workings of three similar Canadian judicial systems as performed in courthouses. The courthouses in each province will be listed chronologically starting with the oldest building and moving forward to the most recently constructed. Cross references will be made between courthouses in one province having similar characteristics or architecture in another province.

Under the Treaty of Utrecht (1713), the colony of Nova Scotia comprised the continental portion of British North America in what is now the Maritimes. The territorial limits included all of what had been the continental portion of Acadia and resulted in all of what is now New Brunswick and continental Nova Scotia becoming British. The islands in the Gulf of St. Lawrence, including Isle Royal (Cape Breton), Isle of St. Jean (Prince Edward Island) and others in the Gulf, remained French territories until later in the eighteenth century. Newfoundland had been founded as a British colony and was never lost by the British until it chose to join the Canadian Confederation in 1949.

After the Battles of Louisburg (1758) and the Plains of Abraham at Quebec City (1759), Isle Royal and Isle St. Jean were ceded to Britain by the Treaty of Paris (1763). Both Isle Royal, which was renamed Cape Breton Island, and Isle

St. Jean, which was anglicized to St. John's Island (later renamed Prince Edward Island) were joined as constituent parts of Nova Scotia. Therefore between 1763 and the creation of the Island of St. John as a separate colony in 1769 and New Brunswick as a separate colony in 1784, both territories formed part of the administration of the colony of Nova Scotia and were subject to the courts of Nova Scotia. The first Supreme Court that had jurisdiction in what is now Prince Edward Island and New Brunswick was the Supreme Court of Nova Scotia, created in 1754 – on Prince Edward Island between 1763 and the creation of its own supreme court on September 24, 1770 and in what is now New Brunswick, between 1754 and 1784. The three Maritime Provinces have had an unbroken continuity of British legal and judicial tradition since 1763 on Prince Edward Island and in Nova Scotia and territorial New Brunswick since 1713.

What was the source of the authority to create the three supreme courts? We are brought back to the nexus between the Crown and the administration of justice referred to in the Preface. The powers of the monarch under the Royal Prerogative conferred on the monarch absolute personal authority to create new colonies and provide for the administration of those colonies, including the creation of courts. The mechanism for exercising that monarchial power was in the form of documents known as a Royal Commission and Instructions granted by the monarch to a person selected by the monarch to be governor of the colony. The governor's commission and instructions contained the legal authority to constitute the administration and governance of the colony.

The role of the governor in exercising the Crown's Royal Prerogative in the administration of justice was further made real and apparent in the authority vested in the Governor and his council to serve initially as the judicial arm of government of the colony. Each of the three colonies went through a brief period of judicial activities by governor and council. The judicial activities exercised by the governor with his council, included sitting as judge on all trials and making judicial decisions and handing down verdicts and sentences. In addition, the governor was empowered to exercise the monarch's authority under the Royal Prerogative of pardon and commutation of sentences. The consistent and blatant lack of objectivity, professionalism and legal knowledge of a governor and council led to the appointment of chief justices and other superior court justices as need required. The first justice, designated as chief justice, was appointed in 1763 in Nova Scotia.

Above: *Argyle Township Court House & Gaol, Tusket, Nova Scotia – Coat of Arms of King George III in whose reign the original segment of the building was constructed.*

During the Representative Government period in each of the three colonies (from the date of the creation of the supreme courts to Responsible Government in the mid-nineteenth century) all judicial appointments were made by the Crown. The linkage between the Crown and the administration of justice and exercise of judicial authority was profound and is continuing.

The supreme courts in each of the three colonies were confirmed in legislative form after the creation of a legislature in each of the colonies. The unbroken continuity from the exercise of judicial power by governor-in-council to that of a statute-based supreme court with justices appointed by the Crown was ratified and confirmed by the statutes enacted to create the three supreme courts.

Until laws were allowed by the Parliament of Great Britain to differ from the received law of Great Britain, the received law from England in the form of

Above: *King's County Courthouse, Kentville, Nova Scotia – the scales of justice, one of the oldest and most prevalent symbols of justice.*

common law and statute law applied in the three colonies of Nova Scotia, Prince Edward Island and New Brunswick. New laws passed by colonial legislatures during the Representative Government era (of each colony) were subject to disallowance by the United Kingdom Parliament. The exercise of disallowance, while parliamentary, was in fact part of the role of the colonial secretary, a Minister of the Crown. The primary legal authority during the Representative Government era was vested in the vice-regal representative in the person of the governor.

It was not until the advent of Responsible Government as a form of legislative authority in each colony in the mid-nineteenth century that their respective legislatures had broad independent powers to legislate. Even after Responsible Government was achieved by the three colonies their legislative authority had substantial limitations. For example, colonial legislatures could not enact laws contrary to the laws of Great Britain that were adverse to Britain's economic, military or foreign policy objectives or its fundamental laws. Furthermore, even under Responsible Government the colonial legislatures were required to conform to the British parliamentary system of government including the creation and functioning of the courts.

After Confederation the three Maritime colonies continued to be subject to significant legislative and legal restrictions as prescribed by the constitution

of the Government of Canada. Nova Scotia and New Brunswick were among the first of the British North American colonies to join the new Canadian Confederation in 1867. Prince Edward Island at that time enjoyed a period of exceptional prosperity, confidence and independence. It held out from joining until 1873 when, having almost bankrupted itself in overbuilding a railway, it was forced to join the Canadian Confederation to bail itself out.

As noted in the Preface, the fount of all justice in Canada is the monarch: Queen Elizabeth II is successor to numerous British monarchs, and predecessor to future monarchs, who have embodied or will continue to embody the concepts and precepts of justice on which the Canadian judicial system functions. While this is a largely theoretical proposition in the twenty-first century, the symbols of that connection form part of the day-to-day operation of courts, and the roles actually played by judges, court officials and lawyers in courthouses.

The symbols of monarchy and the over-riding objective of openness and fairness in the pursuance of justice are constituent and important components of the decoration of courthouses. Many of those symbols have been constant in form over the centuries but others have been modified with shifts in the principles and emphasis of the judicial system.

Certain of the principles of courtroom layout and the relative positions in the courtroom of judges, lawyers and litigants have their origins in medieval British history. It was in the nineteenth century that the concept and practices of the justice system and administration of law became formalized in a way we would recognize today. Courthouses functioning in the early twenty-first century have the English courthouses of the late nineteenth century as their primary model.

We will examine the symbols and the traditions dictating placement of the participants in a courtroom and the layout of courtrooms as themes as we examine each of the twenty-five courthouses. We will also consider their origin and the ways in which they have developed or changed over the period of time covered by the buildings we examine. Viewing a courtroom, particularly one actively engaged in a legal proceeding explains graphically how the Canadian judicial system works. The building and its spaces are visual evidence of the roles, functions and privileges of all who are participants or visitors to the courthouses.

Responsibility for the construction of pre-Confederation courthouses followed two distinct models in the Maritimes. The first model was that applied in the Provinces of Nova Scotia and New Brunswick and the second in the Province of Prince Edward Island.

The first model was the delegation of regional administrative authority to county councils (shires). These administrative units were vested with extensive authority to develop and manage the necessary planning and structural requirements for local governance in the county. They included the design and construction of a courthouse. In smaller communities the traditional role of the courthouse was combined with other administrative functions such as jails, county council chambers and registry of deeds. Because it was incumbent on the county councils to raise the money to pay for the courthouse, they had discretion in the selection of the designer and builder of the courthouse. Some courthouses constructed under this system failed to follow the traditional standards of English courthouse layout, particularly with respect to segregation. Those courthouses constructed by county councils varied considerably in the architectural styles employed. The decision as to the style of the building was often left to the master-builder or the architect selected by the county council to choose. That decision would be influenced by the experience of the designer with similar buildings or simply on personal preference. Buildings constructed under this model varied widely in their external and internal design but were required to conform to some degree to the received standards of the nineteenth-century English courthouse use, although many were based on American designs which in the eighteenth century were also heavily influenced by the English standards but modified to meet local requirements.

The second model was that applied in the Province of Prince Edward Island. In that province, while the province was notionally subdivided into counties, there was no delegation of administration to county councils. The administration of justice in all its aspects was directed from the provincial capital, Charlottetown. This led to a greater degree of control on cost, consistency of courthouse planning and those activities that were carried on or within the courthouses. County Courts were established in 1873 after the Island joined Confederation. The County Court judges were appointed by the provincial government. They had a limited jurisdiction which dealt primarily with family law issues and enforcement of provincial statutes. The County Courts were administered and controlled by the Department of Justice and Attorney General (or equivalent). The County Courts were merged with the Supreme Court in the 1970s. After the establishment of County Courts, courthouses in the province served both Supreme Court and County Court functions.

After Confederation in 1867, the administration of justice was left with the provinces. However, there was a much greater degree of standardization in the internal configuration of spaces in courthouses, particularly as it related to segregation of the justices from the participants in a court proceeding, from the lawyers and from the public. Nevertheless the selection of architectural styles and internal configuration of space remained with the authority responsible for paying for the building.

We are fortunate in the Maritimes to have a number of courthouses of very early origin. As we examine all twenty-five courthouses the theory and practice of law enforcement and the role of judges, court officials and lawyers between the early nineteenth century and the twenty-first century will be manifest as expressed in the form, architectural design, layout and decorative elements of the courthouses. For that reason, courthouses are chosen as an interpretative device to demonstrate the rule of law as it has developed in Nova Scotia, Prince Edward Island and New Brunswick since they became independent British colonies, and subsequently, provinces in Canada.

The significance of architectural form and style in the design of courthouses was well expressed by G.A. Bremner in his commemorative book *The Supreme Court of the United Kingdom: History Art Architecture*.

> *"Architecture has played a distinguished role over the years in symbolizing ideas of law and justice. A 'good' or 'bad' court building can make all the difference to the way the law is perceived and respected in any given context. This is the lesson one might take from looking at how the notion of justice has been fabricated in court architecture through the ages. If a court of law could not administer justice practically, then it at least had to look as though it could in theory."*

This is a primary theme that will be explored in the context of the historic development of courthouses in the Maritimes.

THE DEVELOPMENT OF ENGLISH AND CANADIAN LAWS

To understand the respective roles of judges and lawyers and the format in which the public participates in the judicial process in courthouses, a brief description of the development of English law and courts is essential. It is required as this development is manifest in both the laws of the country and in the buildings in which the laws are enforced and applied. This description will include the various courts that developed over the centuries, the laws that were applied in those courts and the courthouses in which justice was dispensed.

As noted earlier each of the Maritime colonies received English law, judicial dignities and procedures. Also received were the rules and formalities governing the participation of lawyers and their clients in the courtroom. All of these formalities were ostensibly for one purpose: the open, fair and accessible administration of the rule of law for all citizens and those subject to the authority of the courts. While a preponderance of the European settlers of the Maritime colonies were of French, Scottish, English, Welsh, or Irish origin, it was English law and procedure that applied in the colonies. France had ceded its claim to govern the territory we know as the Maritimes by the Treaty of Paris of 1763 to Great Britain thereby establishing English legal supremacy.

It was the English law that applied in the colonies because the conquering authority was England. It was the Parliament of the United Kingdom that had sole authority to govern the colonies. Scottish law on most civil and all criminal matters after the *Act of Union* of 1707 was retained in Scotland as a separate body

of law and tradition. Scottish law and courthouses had no influence on British colonial law and administration.

The law received from Great Britain was divided into basically two forms: one was the English common law, the other was statute law created by the British Parliament. There was also a substantial legal authority vested in the monarch exercisable by the monarch through the Royal Prerogative and through it delegation to the monarch's representation in the colony, the governor; and, as a subordinate to the governor, through the lieutenant governor.

The English common law was so known as it applied to everyone in England. Common law was a body of law that developed empirically from local customs and usages over centuries in the monarch's courts by judges appointed by the monarch or persons delegated to do so on behalf of the monarch. Its general application in the country was unique in Europe at that time. The interpretation and application of the common law was found in judicial decisions which were recorded; specific cases were decided by judges based on precedent. That is, the subject matter of the dispute, whether civil or criminal, would be decided on the law as interpreted in similar cases decided in the past.

The common law was not static. Being based on precedent and on similar factual and legal situations, as new cases were adjudicated it was inevitable that new factual situations would create legal principles that would expand or restrict the existing common law. Logical extensions of those established common law principles would be created which in turn formed part of the common law. The English common law differed fundamentally from European continental practice which from the late eighteenth century forward was based on a comprehensive legislated code, the Napoleonic Code of France, which required consistent interpretation and application. Because of the fluid nature of the development and interpretation of the common law, it continued to grow and proved to be one of the great strengths of the British legal system as applied in Great Britain and in its colonies.

The common law as received in the Maritime colonies in the eighteenth century had also been received earlier in virtually all of the original American colonies. Indeed, the English common law as modified and expanded by judicial decisions and statute law continues to be applied in many American states to this day. One interesting aspect of that result is that courts in England, Canada and other countries which received and continue to apply common law may refer to interpretations of the common law in other countries; for example, courts in Canada occasionally refer to and rely on decisions made by courts in other common law jurisdictions such as England, New Zealand and Australia. English courts also refer to and adopt as authority decisions made in Canada, Australia or New Zealand. But it is also the case that Canadian courts will consider American decisions on similar laws.

While reference is made to the judicial decisions of the common law of other jurisdictions, the interpretations that bind a judge to a certain decision are those made within that court's own jurisdiction. Similar decisions made by a court in Nova Scotia are binding on subsequent courts in its jurisdiction considering the same issue. While binding, subsequent courts may distinguish or alter the earlier decision if by more modern standards the result would be inappropriate and unjust. The principle of one court relying on common law decisions and being bound by earlier decisions is called *stare decisis*. It must be emphasized that the overriding duty of the judiciary is to ensure fairness to the citizen while not jeopardizing the interests of the state. The principle of precedent, known as *stare decisis* is recognized as one of the highest achievements of the rule of law

Right: Annapolis County Court House, Annapolis Royal, Nova Scotia – a wood carving of Lady Justice holding brass scales of justice polychrome, 1795. Originally a decorative element in an earlier court house in the town.

and application of the law to achieve a just result. Its retention and continuing use by virtually all former British colonies is proof of its adaptability and success.

Statute law is law passed by a legislature having express authority to pass it. All statute laws passed by colonial governments before they attained Responsible Government were subject to disallowance by the Parliament in Westminster. Local matters were seldom disallowed. However, matters in which the colonial authorities in London took an interest would be considered for disallowance. For example, something as seemingly local as the renaming of St. John's Island attracted the interest of British colonial authorities. The first legislative attempt on the Island to rename the Island was to "New Ireland." This was considered appropriate as many of the earliest settlers and land owners were Irish, from what are now both the North and South of Ireland. This statute was disallowed as there was already an island called "New Ireland" within the British Empire, albeit in the South Pacific. The name change that was allowed was as a result of a statute passed by both the Legislative Assembly and the Legislative Council of the Island legislature but became effective only when the statute renaming the Island, Prince Edward Island, was formally approved by the British Parliament in 1798.

Some matters which were considered to have both a British colonial interest and a local interest resulted in direction from Westminster for a statute to be passed by the colony to complement a statute passed by the British Parliament. An example is the abolition of slavery by the Westminster Parliament in 1833. A statute having similar intent was passed in Prince Edward Island in 1825, but the colonial statute did not have full effect until the primary statute was passed by the British Parliament.

With the advent of Responsible Governments in the three colonies, for which there was a protracted and sometimes violent struggle particularly in Nova Scotia, the breadth of legislative authority was considerably broadened. However, no statutes were to be allowed that conflicted, as noted, with the fundamental laws of Britain or that disrupted Britain's economic, military, or foreign policy interests.

Statute law differed and still differs in its interpretation and application from the common law. Statute law is to be interpreted and applied as expressed in the statute. Judicial interpretation does not have the flexibility open to the judiciary as it has with the common law. It is a fundamental premise going to the basic tenets of the rule of law that the voice of the legislature expressed in statutory form takes absolute precedence in the interpretation of the statute. That proposition has been somewhat diminished where the national parliament in Ottawa passes a statute having an application that overrules all other statutes. Judges are required to apply a uniform and consistent interpretation deferring to parliamentary expression, but they frequently must decide the application of the overriding statute. In summary, while judges interpret, apply and expand common law, they do not have authority (except in very rare situations) to override statute law or individual provisions in statutes unless there are clear conflicts in the statute law requiring judicial intervention and decision.

Another source of law subject to review and enforcement by judges are decrees and proclamations issued by the monarch under the residual powers continuing to be vested in the monarch under the Royal Prerogative. These are exceptionally rare and while they have infrequently arisen in the United Kingdom, none have been issued in Canada in many years. The Royal Prerogative, however, retains significant authority exercisable by the monarch in Canada, as Canada remains a monarchy. Constitutional conventions and political reality have effectively extinguished or greatly limited most of those residual powers. Continuity of government and the selection of a prime minister in the case of a deadlock in parliament is one example of where the monarch has clear personal duty and authority to act and issue an order ensuring that the country is never without a government.

While the sources of laws applicable in Canada are clear, there is one aspect of the constitutional structure of Canada that requires frequent judicial consideration and occasional decision. That aspect is the interpretation of the legislative powers of the two primary levels of legislative authority. The first level is the Government of Canada's parliamentary authority to make laws which is expressed in section 91 of the *Canada Constitution Act*, (enacted in 1867 and revised on several occasions – its most significant revision being in 1982). The other level is the legislative authority of the provinces found in section 92 of the *Canada Constitution Act*. Laws passed by either legislative level are subject to judicial review to determine whether the statutes passed are properly within the authority (jurisdiction) of that legislative body. Furthermore, some statutes passed by parliament can have a direct impact on the interpretation and application of provincial statutes. The constitutional history of Canada has witnessed shifting emphasis in the dominance of the legislative power of parliament with that of the provinces. The shift in constitutional dominance as between parliament in Ottawa and the legislatures in the provinces is created by judges responding to the prevailing jurisprudence and current political philosophy at the time of the decision. Some of that shift has arisen from the political and legal realities of modern Quebec, and increasingly, the economic power of Western Canada, particularly Alberta. Judges make these decisions based on the best available evidence and the incremental development of judicial interpretation.

Out of the common law specific laws related to criminal activities have been codified in statute form. Criminal law is within the legislative authority of the Parliament of Canada. *The Criminal Code of Canada* (a statute of the Parliament of Canada) specifies what activities are deemed criminal and prohibited, and prescribes sanctions for those violations.

In addition to *The Criminal Code of Canada*, both parliament and the provincial legislatures have authority to enact laws that create offences that are not criminal in nature but for which sanctions apply. These are referred to as quasi-criminal offences. The clearest examples are the laws enacted by the provinces with respect to traffic violations, the registration and use of vehicles and the governance of professions. The Parliament of Canada similarly has created numerous offences, non-criminal in nature, which imposes penalties. The most well known in this category are several offences created by the *Income Tax Act* of Canada, for example for failing to file an income tax return or falsifying a return.

Criminal law and the quasi-criminal offences are enforced in the courts and by judges after a charge has been laid. All charges are laid and prosecuted in the name of the Crown reflecting the prerogative of the Crown to maintain peace and order. The judges on hearing charges laid by the Crown consider the evidence and the law in making a decision. There is an important exception to that statement: if an accused has the choice and chooses to be tried by judge and jury, the jury makes findings as to the facts. Once the jury has decided the facts, and if the decision is against the accused, the judge or justice decides the sentence.

Not all statutory requirements imposed on the public are heard by courts. Matters which are considered administrative in nature are customarily dealt with by administrative tribunals. Numerous tribunals have been created by both the Federal and the Provincial governments. Great care is taken to try to avoid an overlap in the authority of a federally appointed tribunal with that of

Above: This tripartite painting depicting traditional symbols of justice, and a regnal coat of arms, was originally mounted in the New Brunswick Court of Appeal in a former courthouse. The painting dates to the reign of King George IV (1820-1830). It is the finest historical composition of its kind in any courthouse in the Maritimes, and possibly in Canada. The figure on the right is Lady Justice, holding a sword symbolizing authority and a scales of justice symbolizing fairness in the exercise of justice. The figure on the left is Prudence one of the four cardinal virtues, a Roman representation of wisdom, frequently combined with Lady Justice as the objectives of judicial authority.

a provincially appointed tribunal. It is the case however, that some federally appointed tribunals and provincially appointed tribunals deal with much the same subject matter, but the federal tribunal enforces laws and standards applicable to the country as a whole whereas the provincial tribunal deals with aspects of the subject matter within provincial legislative authority having a local interest and application. Decisions made by provincial administrative tribunals are subject to review by the Supreme Court of the province in which the tribunal functions. On review, a Justice of the Supreme Court has authority to cancel the decision, vary it, or confirm it as issued.

Conflict resolution occurs in many forms in Canada including magistrates or provincial courts, administrative tribunals, the Supreme Court, the Provincial Court of Appeal, the Federal Court trial level courts, and various federal tribunals which occasionally convene outside Ottawa in a province. The nature of the dispute, or issue for resolution, determines which forum is at entry level.

THE DEVELOPMENT OF ENGLISH AND CANADIAN COURTS

In order to understand the current operation of the traditions of the Canadian judicial system, symbols, and the configuration of spaces found in courthouses, it is necessary to understand their origins in England as many of the historic uses and traditions developed there over several centuries.

The connection between the administration of justice and the head of government has been viewed from time immemorial in most societies as a religious duty to be performed by law enforcers such as a monarch: to do good and to see justice served. However, in England it was not until William I (the Conqueror) that the king began to be viewed as the fount of justice and became personally responsible for the administration of justice. The Biblical duty of administering justice by the ruler was recognized by William as an opportunity to make money while he reorganized England after the conquest. The skillful administrators engaged by William established fees for each phase of activity in the judicial process, from filing documents through to and including a fee to be paid to the judges hearing a matter. The king and his advisors observed that the more the administration of justice was embedded in the duties and prerogatives of the Crown the more effective became the collection of those fees. With the passage of time, identification of the king as the fount of all justice became immutable and fixed in the English legal system and in Canada by inheritance.

Medieval courts established the fundamental principles of the rule of law which we would recognize as relevant and appropriate today. They include: 1) Laws that have uniform and general application; 2) fixed procedures in terms of documentation to start and continue a proceeding in the courts; 3) the right of the participants in a proceeding to give evidence and to be heard; 4) consistency and predictability in the conduct of the proceeding including the role of the judiciary and lawyers representing the participants; 5) the reality and appearance of openness, impartiality and fairness in the conduct of a judicial proceeding and resultant decision; and 6) a recognized public and fixed place for the conduct of the proceeding.

Before the creation of settled court spaces in fixed locations in the thirteenth century, courts were itinerant. As the king was frequently on progress through his kingdom to shore up his authority, justice was administered where he was physically present and by the king personally.

After a period of chaos in the governance of England and discontentment among the nobles, King John was required to sign the Magna Carta in 1215 at a place near Windsor Castle called Runnymede. Magna Carta is recognized as a foundational document in the British constitution. In the year 2015, the year of the publication of this book, the eight-hundredth anniversary of the signing of the Magna Carta is celebrated. It is part of the received law of the Maritimes. It established some of the key elements of English liberty, law and democracy. Clauses 39 and 40 are highly significant to the law the Maritimes received from England:

> *"No free man will be seized or imprisoned, or stripped of his rights or possessions, or outlawed or exiled, or deprived of his standing in any other way, nor will we proceed with force against him, or send others to do so, except by the lawful judgement of his equals or by the law of the land. To no one will we sell, to no one deny or delay right or justice."*

Another of the terms of Magna Carta is that the courts of common pleas were to be held *in certo loco* meaning in a certain fixed place where litigants would readily find it. This was highly significant because the court of common pleas dealt with most of the disputes and litigation between citizens. Without that guarantee, a litigant would never know with certainty where to start, continue or appear in the judicial resolution of conflicts.

The fixed location for courts became established in the thirteenth century. The first fixed place, other than those in which itinerant judges who travelled from town to town heard cases, was Westminster Hall. Westminster Hall has been, since its construction in 1099 by King William Rufus, a significant component of the Palace of Westminster in the City of Westminster which forms part of the greater London conurbation. In the next century there were three courts in Westminster Hall located in fixed locations each with settled boundaries within the hall: the Court of King's Bench and the Court of Chancery were separately located on a dais at the south end of the hall and the Court of Common Pleas referred to above against the west wall. A fourth court, the Court of Exchequer was outside the hall but access to it was through the Court of Common Pleas.

The courts that conducted their business in Westminster Hall did so simultaneously with the other courts. The hall was a melée of the judges, lawyers, litigants, and the curious. Trials have always been a popular entertainment for certain elements of society.

The principle of courts being required to be in a fixed location, which seems so obvious to us in the twenty first century, could however, be carried to the extreme. In the 1660s it is reported as factual that the then Lord Chief Justice of Common Pleas, Sir Orlando Bridgman, whose court was located in Westminster Hall, refused to allow the boundaries of his court to be moved even a few inches to avoid a draught because of the provision in the Magna Carta that the court must be held in a certain (fixed) location. Apparently he gave as his decision on the issue that if he allowed the boundaries to be moved even a little, he would lose jurisdiction and the authority of the Court of Common Pleas would be in jeopardy.

Why were all the principal courts located in Westminster Hall? It was because the hall was the primary seat and location of the king and the king's administration. The king was deemed to be continuously present in the Palace of Westminster because of the presence there of his throne. He, as the fount of

all justice, represented in his person the administration of justice and therefore the courts and judicial functions had to be performed proximate to him in order to have the King's authority and legitimacy.

That concept of proximity to the king as a foundation for the legitimacy of courts and judicial decisions was also embedded in the design and layout of colonial legislatures. In both Prince Edward Island and Nova Scotia, the original layout of spaces in their legislative buildings assigned the Supreme Court to a prominent location near the vice-regal throne in the Legislative Council Chamber. Similarly, the Legislative Building in Fredericton, New Brunswick completed in 1882, also contained the primary Supreme Court courtrooms.

It was not until 1826 that the courts were removed from Westminster Hall. But they were removed to a location adjacent to the hall where a purpose-built courthouse was constructed to accommodate the various courts. It was designed by the neoclassical, somewhat mannerist, Regency architect, Sir John Soane. To ensure the legitimacy of the courts in the new building, access was gained through Westminster Hall.

With the growth in the complexity of the economy, the marketplace and the population, the demands on the courts grew to the point where they could not be accommodated in the Soane building.

In 1882 a new building designed by G.E. Street in a Gothic Revival style was built on the Strand (a street that lies outside the precincts of the Palace of Westminster). That building houses virtually all superior courts in London except the Court of Appeal to which reference will be made. While the Law Courts Building on the Strand was the location of the principal courts in the capital, there were numerous other courthouses in the capital dedicated to specialized purposes, such as criminal courts. The "Old Bailey" criminal courts lie to the east of the Law Courts Building on the Strand, almost half way between the Law Courts Building and St. Paul's Cathedral. There are numerous other courts such as the Divorce and the Admiralty Courts and even courts to adjudicate on heraldry matters.

There has been life, confrontation, and litigation outside London. Therefore, there are courthouses in virtually every major urban area in the United Kingdom, and virtually every significant-sized community had a magistrate's court which usually dealt with minor criminal matters and municipal law infractions.

In addition to the courts located in Westminster Hall, there was an

Left: Halifax County Court House, in the 1881-1882 wing. Stained glass image of Lady Justice created by Robert McAusland in 1883, holding the scales of justice in her right hand and a sword in her left. The crown is that of St. Edward. She wears a wreath of mayflowers, the floral symbol of the province.

exceptionally important court also located in the Palace of Westminster. That was the Judicial Committee of the Privy Council which met in the House of Lords. This committee was comprised of persons, invariably highly accomplished barristers or existing justices, who were ennobled for their lifetime to sit in the House of Lords as judges of the last resort effectively as a Court of Appeal. The Statute of Westminster 1931, a statute of the Parliament of the United Kingdom, prescribed that the judicial committee of the Privy Council ceased to be Canada's court of last resort for criminal matters in 1933 and in 1949 for non-criminal matters. The Statute of Westminster vested final appellate authority in the Supreme Court of Canada thereby severing all judicial connections with the United Kingdom.

Tradition in the courts is extraordinarily fixed; thus it was not until 2009 that the United Kingdom parliament created a court of appeal, styled the Supreme Court of the United Kingdom. The judicial committee ceased to exist except for appeals from former colonies which have not yet conferred final judicial authority on their own supreme courts such as Australia and New Zealand. All judicial duties and functions in the United Kingdom became vested in an appellate court which vacated the Palace of Westminster, specifically the House of Lords, and relocated to a building remodelled to accommodate it.

However, the Supreme Court of the United Kingdom did not travel far. The new Supreme Court of the United Kingdom is located in the former Middlesex Guildhall, formerly the principal administrative centre for the City of Westminster, directly across Parliament Square from the Palace of Westminster and adjacent to Westminster Abbey. The nexus between Crown and the highest court in the United Kingdom has continued and the tradition has been preserved.

In the Prologue to G.A. Bremner's commemorative book published contemporaneously with the opening of the new United Kingdom Supreme Court in the former Westminster Guildhall, then Lord Chancellor and Secretary of State for Justice Jack Straw expressed his opinion on the significance of the reconstituted court and the new courthouse:

> "On 1 October 2009 the new Supreme Court took its place at the pinnacle of the United Kingdom's system of justice. Its opening was a constitutional landmark... The Law Lords have served the United Kingdom and many Commonwealth jurisdictions with great distinction over many decades. But while they were based in the House of Lords, the highest court in the land appeared beyond the reach of a great number of the British public, and people were misled into thinking that judges also act as legislators. As Walter Bagehot argued nearly a century and a half ago, a Supreme Court should be 'a great conspicuous tribunal' and 'ought not to be hidden beneath the robes of a legislative assembly.' The creation of the United Kingdom Supreme Court (UKSC) marks the culmination of a long process of separation of the judiciary from the legislative and executive."

THE FOUNDATION OF COLONIAL COURTS

The courts established in the colonies of Nova Scotia, Prince Edward Island and New Brunswick gradually expanded their jurisdiction from that initially conferred under the Governor's Commission and Instructions. As in England, one or more statutes governed the constitution and jurisdiction of the courts; the primary statute in each of the three Maritime Provinces is the *Judicature Act*. Each colony enacted a *Judicature Act* and in it prescribed the courts that would be constituted, the range of judicial authority conferred, the empowerment given to the courts to make rules governing the commencement and processing of litigation, as well as the necessary legal technicalities to enable courts to effectively perform their duties.

Courts initially established as separate courts with their own prescribed jurisdiction were as diverse as the Court of Common Pleas, the Court of King's (or Queen's) Bench, the Probate Court and Admiralty Court. Those separate courts in the twentieth century were consolidated into a single jurisdiction in the Supreme Court of each province.

There is an exception to that statement (as at law there inevitably is): the trial-level courts in New Brunswick have retained the old English name of the Court of King's (or Queen's) Bench, thereby closely adhering to British legal tradition.

Judicial powers initially exercised by Governor-in-Council in each of Nova Scotia, Prince Edward Island and New Brunswick were conferred by legislation on a supreme court with a professional judiciary – in Nova Scotia in 1754, in Prince Edward Island in 1770 and in New Brunswick in 1784.

COURTHOUSES AS PART OF COLONIAL ADMINISTRATION

Courthouses can only be understood in the context of their origins and their significance in the governance of monarchial England. In medieval England *de facto* (in fact) administrative authority, as well as *de jura* (legal authority) were vested in and flowed from the monarch. The development of parliamentary democracy in England has resulted in the monarch's role as the head of state and apex of the governmental structure being reduced largely to one of symbolism but with a few vestigial powers retained in the Royal Prerogative.

Governance in medieval England was conducted by and administered in the name of the monarch. It constituted a triangle comprised of distinctly separate administrative units but interconnected largely through the monarch. That triangle had Parliament at the apex and below at one corner of the base was the judicial system representing the maintenance of law and order and at the other corner the church.

Parliament passed laws called statutes which, together with the common law, constituted the law of the land. Parliament by statute created the monarch's courts and made laws prescribing the procedure for appointing superior court justices and identifying the qualifications for persons who could be appointed justices of the superior courts of the country. The courts and justices appointed to interpret and apply the law were independent of parliament but subject to changes in their jurisdiction (authority) by parliament. The courts and the justices who performed the role defined for them by statute were an equal one third of the governance of England, together with parliament and the church.

The third element of medieval governance was the church. In medieval England the church was the Roman Catholic Church in Rome presided over by the pope. The power of the church was continually in flux with challenges and strains between monarch and pope. It was not until King Henry VIII in England that the relative strength and ultimate power of the monarch and the church was settled. Henry for rather personal reasons broke with the church in Rome and declared that the church in England would be both independent of Rome and subject to his personal direction and control.

To this day, the monarch makes the personal appointment of the principal cleric of the Church of England, the Archbishop of Canterbury – albeit the appointment coming at the end of a long church-conducted selection process which results in recommendations to the Prime Minister who in turn makes a recommendation to the monarch. It would be within the legal authority of Queen Elizabeth II to decline to make a particular appointment.

The Church of England, also known as the Anglican Church, is still the established church of England meaning that it forms an element of the governance of the country with certain powers and privileges not accorded to other religions or other Christian denominations. The Anglican Church in Canada has no special role or privilege not accorded to other churches or faiths.

When the colonial governments were created in Nova Scotia, Prince Edward Island and New Brunswick, the privileges of the Anglican Church were entrenched in the statute law of the colonies. One of the several elements of control exercised by the United Kingdom Parliament was to prescribe that only members of the Anglican Church could hold public office. That meant that no Roman Catholic, Presbyterian, Methodist or Baptist, for example, could be appointed to any public office, which included that of a justice of a superior court. The standards, traditions, precepts, and theology of the Anglican Church were a constituent element of the administration of justice in each of the three colonies until the end of the first quarter of the nineteenth century when the laws were amended to permit non-Anglicans to hold office.

The connection between church and state, as represented by the courts, continues. In a radio interview in 1957, Lord Denning summed up the connection with his characteristic succinct language: "without religion there is no morality, and without morality there is no law". That expression reflects a highly traditional understanding of the connection, but modern jurisprudence has ventured well beyond that simplistic expression to formulate the premises on which the legal system in the modern Canadian courts operates.

The connection among parliament, the church and the courts in the administration of the British colonies had a visible presence in the capital cities of each colony. The capital of each colony was laid out in a prescribed form with a street plan and civic squares having their origin in the ancient world of Greece and Rome but adapted and applied by the British colonial administrators.

The civil design of the capital was to recognize and give appropriate deference to the monarch. The principal site of the monarch's administration was the legislative buildings also variously known as the colonial building, and later Province House (in New Brunswick, the Legislative Building). The legislative building was preeminent as it contained the symbol of monarchial presence in the colony: the throne in the Legislative Council chamber. The legislative building also contained the lower house comprised of persons elected from the citizenry called the House of Assembly or the Legislative Assembly. This chamber was subordinate to the Legislative Council chamber which in the eighteenth and until the middle of the nineteenth

Above: Halifax County Court House, in the original 1861 segment of the building. The non-jury courtroom ceiling medallion carved to create a rosette of acanthus leaves surrounded by geometric and foliate patterns. Part of an elaborate decorative scheme.

century was comprised of men having a minimum value of assets and land and who were appointed by the monarch's representative in the colony, the lieutenant governor.

The colonial legislative buildings also contained the judicial component of government in the form of the Supreme Court. The Supreme Court was in a prominent location in the legislative building continuing the nexus between monarch, the legislature and the interpretation and enforcement of the law. In the Nova Scotia legislative building built in 1819, the Supreme Court chamber was on the principal floor lying between the Legislative Council chamber and the House of Assembly chamber. In the Prince Edward Island legislative building closely modelled on the Nova Scotia building, the Supreme Court was located on the ground floor for reasons particular to the legislature of that province. The symbolism of the location of the Supreme Court in the two legislative buildings was deliberate and highly significant.

The significance of the location for courts extends beyond its presence in the colonial legislative buildings. The legislative buildings were constructed in that part of the capital that was laid out and identified for civic ceremonial purposes as the centre or the core of the urban design of the capital. As the courts became more complex with the growth in the economy and population, purpose-built courthouses were required.

The core urban planning of a colonial capital included a zone or area in which the colonies' principal buildings would be located. Buildings that would define the quality of the economic and political achievements of the colony were located in that core area. Buildings that would reflect the sophistication of the leaders of the colony were established in the architectural and decorative elements of the principal buildings such as the Supreme Court. The Supreme Court and other principal buildings were designed in styles that embedded symbolism of the mother country, the United Kingdom, and of the people of the

Above: *Queens County Court House, Liverpool, Nova Scotia. The Coat of Arms of King George III taken from the late 18th century courthouse located in the town. It was customary to mount the Coat of Arms of the monarch reigning at the time of construction, as part of the symbols and decorative elements of a courthouse.*

The location of the Supreme Court was also significant in terms of the principle that justice must not only be done, it must appear to be done. It was essential that as one of the principal elements of governance of the colony the courthouse must be in a prominent, highly visible and accessible location. The building was a symbol of the importance of law and order in the colony, the presence and dignity of the justices, and the work of the justices and their officials in maintaining peace and justice.

colony. These descriptive terms may appear obsolete in the twenty-first century but records of the legislators responsible for the design and construction of the buildings expressed themselves in precisely those terms. The symbolism remains relevant and significant.

The design of colonial capitals was intended to allow for creation of the most important civic buildings in the province and provided space for expansion and new buildings. Hence, when the Supreme Court required more space for courtrooms, justices, officials and records, larger stand-alone courthouses were constructed. The courthouses so constructed were functional in meeting the contemporary needs of the justices and their staff. They were also designed to enhance and dignify the capital cities.

THE JUDICIARY AND PRINCIPLES OF ADJUDICATION; ENGLISH LEGAL TRADITIONS

Adjudication is rendered by a superior court justice in a civil or criminal trial after hearing the evidence and submissions of counsel (or a party personally if unrepresented), and in a jury trial, after hearing the jury's decision on the facts. There are principles governing the justice's adjudication. Those principles in a civil matter are established by the Rules of Court and by earlier court decisions. In a criminal matter the principles are prescribed by *The Criminal Code of Canada*, policies adopted by the judiciary or requested of them by the Government of Canada. If the latter, they are discretionary only.

Decisions of superior court judges are called judgments, or reasons for judgment. Judgments inform the litigants of the outcome of a legal proceeding and they are also part of law of the land. As such it is a tenet of the English legal system that the judgments must be available to the public. Once released, the judgments become part of the precedents guiding judges in subsequent decisions.

In the seventeenth and eighteenth centuries the distribution of judgments could be delayed in circulation throughout England. Consistency in judicial decisions was frequently compromised arising from difficulties in distributing judgments. For example, a standard of sentencing, in London could, and often did, differ in the provinces. One has only to consider Mr. Justice George Jeffreys, a judge who presided during the reign of James II, to illustrate how personalized judgments could be. He sat in rural courts in Wales and Southwest England in the seventeenth century. He gained the moniker, if not the reputation, of "the hanging judge". His somewhat simplistic but consistent sentence to most criminal offences was the hangman's noose, even though judges in London and

in many other parts of England applied a more balanced and less draconian sentencing. To give some context to his reputation, it should be noted that his reputation was gained following the Monmouth Rebellion, and the sentences that gave rise to his reputation were given to persons charged relating to that rebellion. His reputation, however, did not adversely affect his career as James II ennobled him, and Lord Jeffreys moved on to become Lord Chancellor. Clearly, he complied with the judicial standards of the monarch who appointed him.

A significant element of English legal tradition is the judicial attire worn by judges. The nature and standards of design of the gowns worn by superior court justices was established by 1635. The robes, as a garment, originated in earlier medieval ecclesiastical gowns but were modified to create a distinctive design that identified the wearer as a superior court justice. Black was the colour chosen by Charles I as most suitable for justices, but as various separate courts and complexity of layers within the courts developed, elements of the gowns were designed to identify the particular superior court and level of court to which the judge belonged.

The adherence to tradition in the courts is preserved to this day. The robes worn by judges of a Provincial Court are black with some highlight coloration and similar in design, including length, to those prescribed in 1635. Trial level superior court justices in the three Maritime Provinces wear similar robes but with more colour and with distinguishing sashes. Court of Appeal justices wear relatively simple full-length black gowns similar to those worn by lawyers having the honourific of Queen's Counsel. Formal gowns for ceremonial use differ from those of courtroom usage for Court of Appeal justices.

Wigs were worn from and after the seventeenth century by superior court justices. Tradition holds that wigs were introduced into England by Charles I on his assuming the throne having taken the fashion for wigs from Paris, where he lived prior to ascending the British throne. Their initial use as a Parisian fashion was adopted into the general upper class British population. The wigs were made originally from human hair and later from horsehair and some had a ribboned pig-tail at the back. The top and sides of the wig were made to have tightly twisted curls, always in an off-white colour, and worn simply perched on top of the head of the wearer. Trial level superior court justices in the United Kingdom into the twenty-first century continue to wear wigs while in the courtroom. The wigs in current use include the full-bottomed, bar, and bench or tye-wig. With the modernization of the former Judicial Committee of the Privy Council into the United Kingdom Supreme Court, justices on that bench no longer wear wigs but continue to wear black robes, very different from those they had worn

Above: Coat of Arms of King George III originally located in a late 18th century courthouse located in Fredericton, New Brunswick. Now located in the vestibule of the former supreme court building, currently used as a bar and restaurant.

in the House of Lords. Justices of the Supreme Court wear robes similar to those worn by Queen's Counsel; black silk ankle-length gowns with a vest that extends into full sleeves terminating in buttoned broad cuffs. In the House of Lords their gowns were bright red with ermine dressings and highly decorated with gold-plated buttons.

In Nova Scotia, New Brunswick and Prince Edward Island superior court justices have not worn wigs for at least one hundred and fifty years. There is no accurate record of whether they were ever used in Prince Edward Island. They were used in Nova Scotia into the nineteenth century. It is likely they were used in New Brunswick but there is no record of when their use was discontinued.

The question arises, why would justices wear wigs? Why would judges and justices today wear costumes that have an ancient origin? Tradition is one answer. Change could jeopardize the appearance of authority. However, there are more pertinent reasons: dignity, obscurity, visibility and identification.

Dignity – A court is powerless and ineffectual if it does not have dignity; without dignity it cannot assert authority. A superior court justice irrespective of

his or her physical size must appear to have a commanding presence in the courtroom. Courtrooms are theatres in which emotions, arguments and inter-personal relations are frequently strained to a breaking point. To control the drama of the courtroom the presiding justice needs all the panoplies and devices available to control the courtroom. The gowns emphatically declare the dignity of the presiding justice, the long tradition of the office the justice holds, and the power vested in the justice in the conduct of the courtroom over which the justice presides. Standardized gowns also ensure uniformity of attire by the justices themselves.

Obscurity – Think of Mr. Justice Lord Jeffreys – would he wish to be identified on the street, in his club or in his church the week after ordering the hanging of a member of the local populace? One of the reasons for both wig and gown is to mask the identity of the justice and thereby provide some degree of obscurity when outside the courtroom. In small communities in the Maritimes this reason carries little weight where superior court justices are prominent well known citizens in their own right; however, the gowns sever the link between their private personas in the community from that of the justice in the courtroom.

Visibility – Until the nineteenth century the conduct of courtrooms was less controlled than it is today. Think of Westminster Hall with several courts functioning in a confined space with numerous justices, members of the public, lawyers and litigants milling about often searching for the right court or commenting on the proceedings. The presiding justice must be visible. There can be no room for doubt as to who is in control while many litigants and many more lawyers would like to be in control of the courtroom. During a trial there would be chaos in the courtroom if the presiding justice does not have absolute control. For example, during medieval trials lawyers and the parties to the criminal or civil proceeding could walk around the courtroom with few restrictions which resulted in the courtroom becoming a free-for-all in terms of noise management of the proceedings and the orderly introduction of evidence. The gowns and other devices available to a presiding justice, give the justice the visibility necessary to control the courtroom. The visible elements of a justice's attire may appear old-fashioned and unimportant; they are not. From the moment the superior court justice enters the courtroom gowned and ready to preside, all present in the courtroom rise and the justice bows slightly to those facing him or her and in return led by the lawyers at counsel tables everyone else in the courtroom bows back. Visibility and control have been established.

Identification – There are many levels to the courts in the United Kingdom, and while there are fewer in Canadian Courts, the identity of the presiding justice, as a justice in a particular court, is essential. It is also essential to the litigants and their counsel who need to know the personal identity of the justice. The court officials who are the support resources enabling the justice to carry out judicial duties must also be certain of the personal identity of the justice. The gowns identify the individual entering the courtroom as the justice and, importantly, as a justice of the court the parties intend to be in. Why is the personal identity of the trial justice important to the litigants and counsel? One compelling reason is to know from whom to appeal the judgment to the appellate court. I express this as a practicing barrister. It is also essential for courtesy and civility in the courtroom. Proper and formalized address is required at all times.

The lawyers are referred to by surname, Mr. Smith, Ms. Jones by the justice; the lawyers address superior court justices as "Milord" or "Milady" as the case may be. Lawyers refer to each other in the courtroom as "my learned friend" if one Queen's Counsel refers to another, reference is made to junior counsel as "my friend". If there are more lawyers present than representing the plaintiff and the defendant, courtesy requires reference to another lawyer present representing a party as "my learned friend representing Mr. third party litigant". (actual name used). This anachronistic use of language by lawyers addressing each other is a reminder of the order and civility that must prevail in the courtroom. Lapses in decorum are usually quickly, if not forcibly, corrected by the presiding justice.

Superior court justices upon appointment, even before swearing-in, have the dignity and standing of a superior court justice. If the person appointed held a job or was in private practice, that person immediately stops all further work except that which is necessary to transfer files. This is one of the procedures adopted by governments to avoid the appearance or reality of a conflict of interest, and it demonstrates the elevation of the justice to a unique position in the administration of justice.

Justices are independent. They are independent of the government that appointed them. They must be independent of all business, political or financial interests they may have had prior to their judicial appointment. They are also independent within the court in which they participate. For example, trial level justices are one of several justices in that court presided over by a chief justice. Each justice on the court is independent of the other justices and is duty bound to be independent in their decisions. Justices will confer with each other informally asking advice from their peers, but that is advice only and as requested.

The chief justice is an administrator and leads by example and influence at a personal level, and when necessary, in matters of the conduct of the justices functioning in the chief justice's court. No one tells a justice what to decide, except as is prescribed by law. Governments occasionally establish policies they would like the courts to adopt in terms of sentencing; for example, in relation to drunk driving. The policies are requests only. The courts can adopt the policies but individual justices are free to reject the policies. An individual justice can reject the policy even if approved by the chief justice, if in the justice's opinion there are substantive reasons for rejecting the policy in a particular case.

A fundamental and essential element of the legal system in Canada is the independence of the judiciary; without that independence courts would be awash with special interests, conflicts of interest and unpredictability all of which are anathema to courts in Canada.

Above: *This 1890s English stained glass panel is from the central window of a tripartite window configuration forming the backdrop of the judge's dais. Rescued from the Pictou courthouse during the 1987 fire, it was restored and mounted in the new Justice Centre. The image is of Lady Justice, a classical symbol of justice.*

COURT OFFICIALS

The judicial system would cease to function if it did not have the necessary officials to enable it to perform effectively. Superior court officials are employees of the provincial government, and paid by it, even though the superior court justices are appointed and paid by the Government of Canada.

The principal official and the person responsible for the administration of the courthouse staff and facilities is the chief clerk of the court. In Prince Edward Island the chief clerk is styled the "Prothonotary", a term established in England in 1447. The term comes from the Greek "*protonotarios*", which translates as "first scribe". It was a term applied to the principal clerk of a superior court in the Byzantine Empire. To facilitate the performing of the duties of the Prothonotary in the courthouse, the provincial department responsible for justice appoints a liaison officer who coordinates with other provincial government departments in the staffing needs, building maintenance and repair requirements of courthouses. The Prothonotary has limited quasi-judicial powers which enable the removal of some procedural matters from the judiciary.

Each superior court justice has an assistant (formerly known as a legal secretary) assigned to the justice who clerks for the justice while in the courtroom, during court proceedings, and who is responsible for typing and office management for the justice. Communications between lawyers and justices usually are conducted through the office of the justice's assistant. This ensures arm's-length dealing between justices and the practising bar and it also ensures that both justices and lawyers are informed of developments before there is direct contact between the justice and the lawyer.

Registration of documents, particularly in civil litigation is an important component in the processing of litigation. Each courthouse has an office open to the public for the registration of or filing of documents and staff expertly trained to receive and file or register documents. The courthouses also have facilities for storage and retrieval of court documents.

With the substantial growth in family law litigation in the courts of the Maritime Provinces, officials dedicated to the task of providing support for family law litigants and for recovery of money ordered to be paid by a parent have been appointed. Family Court officials are a separate administrative arm of a modern courthouse and are an essential part of providing efficient service to the public in this very difficult area in the administration of justice.

The sheriff is the principal enforcement officer in the judicial system. The term is again English in origin and goes back to medieval British monarchial tradition in which the sheriff was a direct appointee of the monarch and one of the monarch's principal officials in enforcing law and order. The modern role of the sheriff has been substantially curtailed from its medieval origins, but the sheriff remains an important officer in the administration of justice.

Threats to the security of the public and persons required to perform services in courthouses have required the presence of new officials. They are the security personnel. After entering a courthouse one must first go through a screening device similar to those at airports and then one must pass the vigilant interrogation of a security officer before being permitted to enter any part of the courthouse, even areas traditionally open to the public.

Courthouses have been designed to accommodate the needs of all who are required to be in them to provide an effective operation of the judicial system. As we explore the layout and design of superior courthouses and courtrooms, the role and presence of all staff working in the courthouse will be made clear from the layout and design of the buildings.

THE LAWYERS

Lawyers are persons trained in the law having academic credentials from a recognized school of law. Until the 1970s in Prince Edward Island and earlier in Nova Scotia and New Brunswick, it was possible to attain admission to the provincial Law Society by simply articling with an experienced lawyer for several years and proving competence through bar exams. Now a degree from an accredited law school is a prerequisite to admission. Before admission to the bar, a lawyer aspiring to be admitted to practise law must article with a qualified senior lawyer and pass bar admission exams set by the Law Society. The period of articles is one year, part of which can be spent as a clerk of the Supreme Court. Upon admission to the bar the lawyer becomes qualified to practise law. "Qualified to practise", means being able to hold oneself out to give advice on legal matters to the public and being entitled to charge a fee for that advice.

Lawyers admitted to the bar of one province and considered to be in good standing by the Law Society of that province are entitled, as a right, to a limited practise in another common-law based province or territory of Canada (that excludes the Province of Quebec which has a provincial legal system based on the Napoleonic Code). The limited practise is best described as "occasional appearances". Each law society is an independent self-regulating association but all law societies in Canada belong to a "Federation of Law Societies", an informal body comprised of representatives from each law society in the country. The federation serves as a forum for discussing and making recommendations to the individual law societies and to a limited extent to provincial and federal governments on public policy issues.

A body established to represent lawyers in matters affecting the legal profession such as on ethical and public policy issues including human rights is the Canadian Bar Association. Membership in the association is discretionary but most lawyers in private practise at some stage in their career become members and serve on committees or related governance bodies. The principal public voice of lawyers in Canada is expressed by the Canadian Bar Association.

Until very recently, in the United Kingdom lawyers were divided into two distinct groups with their own governing bodies: solicitors and barristers. Solicitors generally did not go to court but would engage a barrister for a client who is engaged in litigation. The barrister devoted his or her practice to appearing before criminal or civil courts. The barrister traditionally dealt with the client only through the solicitor. The distinction between the professions in Britain has now been blurred with some solicitors being eligible after specialized training to appear in superior courts as solicitor-advocates. Most lawyers in England choose to conduct their practices as solicitors or as barristers only.

In the Maritime Provinces, from the beginning of the judicial system in the colonial era, no distinction existed between the role of the solicitor and that of the barrister. In the early days of colonial society, legally trained lawyers were scarce; the governor-in-council simply invited "gentlemen" to apply to the lieutenant governor-in-council to act as lawyers. Any lawyer admitted to the bar in any of the Maritime Provinces and in good standing with the law society of the province has the authority to appear and argue in any court in the province. However, as a matter of aptitude, interest and opportunity many lawyers choose to limit their practice to one focussed on either a solicitor's or a barrister's role.

There is a distinction within the legal profession that does not relate to the role of a lawyer as a solicitor or a barrister. That distinction is the honourific referred to as Queen's Counsel. Sir Walter Raleigh was the first lawyer to have had this honour conferred on him; it was for services rendered to Queen Elizabeth I. Since then, the

Left: Sir Louis Henry Davies Law Courts, Charlottetown, Prince Edward Island. A portrait in oils of Sir Louis Henry Davies, after whom the Law Courts in Charlottetown, is named. A copy by Robert Hyndman of an original in the National Collection in Ottawa.

distinction has been continued in many jurisdictions following English legal traditions. All three Maritime Provinces have passed statutes that authorize the appointment of Queen's Counsels.

A Queen's Counsel is a lawyer qualified in law as a competent and experienced practitioner. The standard until recently was experience and expertise in the courtroom, but that has now been broadened to apply to achievement generally as a leading member in good standing of the Law Society of a province. Queen's Counsels are conferred by order of the Lieutenant- Governor-in Counsel thereby continuing the monarchial origin and dignity of the honourific. The selection of individuals to receive the honourific is made by a committee formed by the provincial Law Society comprised (on Prince Edward Island) equally of superior court justices, and existing Queen's Council with a representative of the Department of Justice and Attorney General. Both Nova Scotia and New Brunswick also confer Queen's Counsel designations on meritorious members of the bar and follow a procedure similar to that followed on Prince Edward Island. If there are qualified candidates, the appointments are made annually, usually in December. Queen's Counsels are given slight deference and priority in scheduling cases and on ceremonial occasions involving bench and bar. Otherwise, this title stands as a recognition of professional achievement and an honour to those who receive it.

Only a relatively small number of those graduates of law schools in Canada practice law in a private fee-for-service law office. The training received by students in law school is also exceptionally effective in preparing the graduate for a career in government and as corporate counsel. Of those lawyers who choose to practise law in a private fee-for-service setting, very few perform the role traditionally referred to as that of a barrister: representing the plaintiff or the defendant in a courtroom involving litigation or in answering criminal or quasi-criminal charges. A sub-speciality in law is acting for the Crown in prosecutions under *The Criminal Code of Canada* or other statutory offences. Lawyers performing this role are called "Crown Counsel" although the older term "Crown prosecutor" is occasionally used. Another specialized area of law deals with the drafting of legislation; lawyers performing this highly specialized function are employees of the Department of Justice of a province and are identified as "Legislative Counsel".

Specialization within the legal profession is continually growing with increasing complexities in the law, the nature and rules of the many federal and provincial courts, and the extensive array of regulatory tribunals. Another specialization in the profession involves non-judicial conflict resolution. Collaborative law, mediation and arbitration are all forms of non-judicial conflict resolution practised by specialized lawyers who are increasingly finding favour with the legal profession and the public. Lawyers, therefore, perform an extensive variety of professional roles reflecting the requirements of their employers – whether those employers are public bodies or private citizens.

Lawyers in any field must practise to a high ethical standard. The standards to be followed by lawyers are prescribed in a Code of Ethics initially developed by the Canadian Bar Association and now adopted by each province (other than Quebec which has its own code of conduct). The standards of practice establish the duty of the lawyer to his or her client (governmental, corporate or private), to the courts and equally important, to their peers. Due diligence, avoidance of conflict of interest, competence in the area of law in which the lawyer practises and the exercise of good judgement in the client's best interest are all part of the very high ethical standards addressed in the Code of Conduct.

Failure to adhere to the standards of practice, whether that failure is real or perceived by a client, can be addressed by the client filing a complaint with the provincial Law Society. As a self-regulating profession, each Law Society has a statutory and professional duty to investigate and make a finding on each complaint. The finding by the Law Society on a complaint is subject to judicial review. Protection of the client, the integrity of the profession and avoidance of bringing the profession and administration of justice into disrepute are all objectives of the self-regulation of the legal profession through the provincial Law Society.

The entitlement of the legal profession to self-regulate and the obligations of the Law Society as the regulatory body are prescribed by statute. Each province in Canada has a statute establishing the provincial Law Society, empowering its self-relegation and creating offences prohibiting non-qualified and unlicensed persons from practising law. The standards to be applied by the Law Society are a matter of public policy and are periodically reviewed and result in amendments to the governing legislation. As one of the oldest self-regulating professions, lawyers have a well established tradition of behaviour, attire, community service and ethics.

One of the most notable ethical standards owed by lawyers called to the bar and practising in the courts at any level is that owed to the courts. All members of the legal profession appearing in a Canadian court of law are deemed to be officers of the court. They are officers not in the sense of being employed or paid by the court, but in the sense that they owe the courts a very high ethical standard of truthfulness, ethical and courteous behaviour, and have a duty not to mislead the courts in making representations on the law. This is not the least of the duties of a lawyer engaged in court work, but it is one that is infrequently expressed and often not fully understood. The corollary to the relationship with the court as an officer of the court is the right to be in the court with or on behalf of a client, the right to be heard by the court, and the right to be addressed in court with courtesy, respect, patience and when required, tolerance.

Gowns are worn by lawyers when in open court before a superior court justice. The basic gown now worn by lawyers in court was established in 1685. It was established as a mark of respect at the time of the death of King Charles II. Having been established, as with virtually all other aspects of the justice system, it quickly became tradition and fixed. Gowns come in two forms, both gender neutral as there is no difference between the gowns worn by male and female lawyers in court. One form is for Queen's Counsel and the other for those lawyers who do not have the honourific. The gowns look very much alike except to the lawyers themselves: Queen's Counsel robes are made of silk and have subtle increases in decorative detail whereas the common barrister's gown is made of "stuff" a coarse wool fabric. Both gowns and the accompanying vest are black. The gowns are worn with a shirt with a distinctive "wing" collar that has its origins in eighteenth-century fashionable gentlemen's attire. A cravat having two tabs is worn with the collar.

There is a clear procedure to follow when representing a client in court. The Rules of Court established by a rules committee established by the chief justices and their bench (comprising members of the law society and one or more justices) govern the procedure to be followed in court. This is further detailed in practice notes issued by the chief justice of each of the two superior courts found in each of the three provinces. The two courts are the trial level court, for which there is a chief justice in each province and a Court of Appeal for which there is a chief justice who is also styled the Chief Justice of the Province.

In a criminal or quasi-criminal prosecution, Crown counsel leads first. At the conclusion of the Crown's case, the defendant (the accused) has the right to give evidence but is not required to do so because in the British and Canadian system of justice an accused is presumed to be innocent until proven to be guilty. In civil trials the plaintiff's counsel leads. When the plaintiff rests (concludes) its case, the defence then advances its case. In both criminal and civil trials, after each witness has given evidence on direct examination (by counsel for the party for whom the witness is giving evidence) opposing counsel has the right to cross-examine that witness.

There is also a precedence traditionally, but not always followed, as to the location of the lawyers in the courtroom. Crown counsel and plaintiff's counsel are at the counsel table that is on the right of the justices as they face the lawyers (except on Prince Edward Island where Crown counsel often sit to the left of the judge as the judge faces counsel). Counsel for the accused or the defendant sits at counsel table to the left of the justices as they face the lawyers. In some courtrooms counsel tables are parallel to each other: in those courtrooms the Crown/plaintiff is situated at the counsel table closest to the judge and counsel for the accused or defendant at the counsel table behind it. While this is the traditional placement of the lawyers in relation to the justices, the tradition is important as it clearly defines who is who, and what role each plays in the courtroom. It is another device for ensuring order, clarity and form.

Above: *Law Courts Building in Halifax, Nova Scotia. The Coat of Arms of Canada with its motto, in English, "From Sea unto Sea". The Coat of Arms is mounted in virtually every superior court courthouse in Canada, usually in each courtroom.*

In the Court of Appeal, similar standards apply. Counsel for the appellant sits at counsel table to the right of the appellate justices as they face the lawyers, and the counsel representing the respondent (usually the victor in the lower court) sits to the left of the appellant justices as they face the lawyers; or in an appellate courtroom where counsel tables are parallel to each other, counsel for the non-appellant sits at the table closest to the justice, and counsel for the respondent sits at the table behind the appellant.

The lawyers in a courtroom setting must adhere closely to the etiquette and procedure for addressing the witnesses as well as the justice's and fellow counsel.

They must at all times, no matter the provocation or irritation which invariably develops during a trial, treat the witness with courtesy and respect: never first or nick-names – always "Mr.", "Mrs." or "Ms". Children are seldom in court as witnesses, but when they are, they are called by their given names but with a respectful and not a familiar manner.

One of the most effective methods of conflict resolution in a civil (non-criminal) matter where the parties are represented by counsel is a negotiation between counsel conducted on a "without prejudice" basis. The term means that all representations and concessions made by counsel as they negotiate are not prejudicial (cannot be used against them) if negotiations fail and the parties go to trial.

Lawyers engaged in representing clients in criminal and civil litigation are entitled to instruct their lawyer freely, openly and truthfully without fear of their information or admissions being compellable as evidence at trial. Such communications with a client's counsel are styled "privileged". The privilege protection, which is of long duration in the British legal system, is still substantially intact although it is being gradually reduced in recent years. "Privilege" and "Without Prejudice" have been essential and fundamental principles of practice available to clients and lawyers to assist in ensuring fairness and objectivity and in protecting the fundamental right of an accused or a litigant to retain and instruct counsel.

The role of the lawyer in the litigation process where the lawyer is representing an accused was best expressed by the eighteenth-century wit Dr. Samuel Johnson. James Boswell, Johnson's biographer in his 1786 published recounting, of Johnson's tour of Scotland, stated, "a lawyer has no business with the justice or injustice of the cause which he undertakes, unless his client asks his opinion, and then is bound to give it honestly. The justice or injustice of the cause is to be decided by the judge". Justice is determined by the rule of law. Guilt, innocence or liability is determined by the degree to which the actions of the client are found by a judge to be a breach of the law. The role of the lawyer is to advance those arguments at law which can demonstrate innocence or non-liability. It is for the judge to make the determination not the lawyer (or if the matter is heard by judge and jury, by the jury).

A classic and frequently asked question of a trial lawyer is "how can you represent someone you know is guilty?" The answer lies in Dr. Johnson's comment quoted above. I was asked by my six-year old granddaughter how I could represent someone I knew broke the law. My answer demonstrated the principle expressed by Dr. Johnson. I explained that guilt or innocence is based on law and whether a person was guilty within the terms of the law. Morality and ethics, I explained, are not part of deciding guilt or innocence. I knew I still did not have her with me. I asked her whether there were rules at her school that if broken would see her sent off to the principal. Yes, I was told. She said that one of the rules was that students were not to bang their lockers and make a noise. I asked her whether she would be considered to have broken the rule if she tripped over something someone left on the floor and she fell forward banging her head on the locker. Would that break the rule? Oh no, I was told, she would be sent to the principal's office for medical attention to make sure she was alright. I said that is one example of a rule that must be interpreted by the principal to decide whether the rule had been broken. A lawyer, I said, was someone who would help her in explaining the facts and assist in getting the principal's decision that the rule had not been broken.

One of the essential tenets of the English legal system is that every citizen is entitled to defend him or herself to the extent available at law. Lawyers are trained as advocates to enable them to put their client's case most effectively before the decision-maker, the judge (or jury where it is a jury trial).

Lawyers are not essential in the judicial process. Accused and parties to civil litigation may choose to self-represent. A particular accused or plaintiff (or defendant) may choose to appear in court without a lawyer and self-represent, meaning that he or she would personally advance his or her interest/defence in court. Justices at all levels of the judicial system respect the right of parties in a court proceeding to represent themselves and where there is self-representation the presiding judge adapts the proceedings at trial to inform the self-represented accused or litigant of what the rules and practices of the court are. There are, however, situations in which a trial justice has authority to appoint counsel for a party – invariably for a person accused of a very serious criminal charge, a child or a person who appears to have mental or physical infirmities that render them less able to effectively represent themselves.

Notaries in the three Maritime Provinces are usually lawyers. A lawyer, to be a notary, must be sworn in and receive a separate certificate qualifying the lawyer as a notary. The role of a notary in a common law jurisdiction such as we have in the Maritimes is largely one of notarizing documents under oath on the Bible or by an affirmation under the *Evidence Act* for use, or potential use, in courts in other jurisdictions. After signing the notarial certificate the notary affixes the notary's notarial seal. The latter is a hand-pressed metal seal in relief which when affixed to paper over the notary's signature leaves an embossed image of the seal.

Lawyers who wish to take oaths must also be sworn in as a commissioner for taking affidavits. A commissioner for taking affidavits performs the same service as a notary but because the sworn document is for use in the province in which the oath is administered, the notarial seal is not used.

Admission to the bar occurs after the lawyer, as noted, has passed all required bar examinations and has proven academic achievement with the appropriate law degree. Bar admission brings us back to the fundamental nexus between lawyer and the courts. Admission to the bar involves obtaining the qualifications endorsed by the Law Society for admission to the Law Society of the province in the form of a court order. To obtain that order of the court a prospective candidate for admission to membership in the provincial Law Society must make an application to the court proving the candidate's qualifications as endorsed by the Law Society. The application is taken very seriously by all three parties: the presiding superior court justice, the Law Society and the candidate. Any failure of the documentation to prove entitlement to admission results in denial of the order or an adjournment of the hearing until the candidate perfects his or her documentation or qualifications.

Lawyers are one of the primary components of the judicial system. The courthouses in which many lawyers appear are designed to accommodate their role. As we will see when we explain the development of courtrooms and courthouses, lawyers have been and continue to be active parties to the layout, form and style of courtrooms and courthouses. The administration of justice in the English legal tradition of which the Maritimes are a part requires an independent, qualified and responsible bar. A qualified and competent bar has been one of the great achievements of the English legal system; that system has been received and adopted by all Canadian common law provinces. The role of lawyers is also a fundamental tenet of the Westminster system of democratic government of which the Canadian national government and each territory and province of Canada is a part.

THE PUBLIC RIGHT OF ACCESS

Justice must not only be done, it must be seen to be done. This statement of principle is a fundamental and continuing commitment of the judicial system. It has its origins in medieval English courts and continues to this day.

What does this expression mean? It means that the objective of the judicial system is to mete out justice in a fair, objective and competent manner within the terms of the prevailing law. It also means that to garner the respect and confidence of the public, the process of achieving judicial decisions must be open to view by the public.

Public access to the conduct of the courts is so entrenched in the Canadian judicial system that the public has a right to attend all but a very few court proceedings and has a space in the courtroom designated for its use.

The design of courtrooms, following the English courtroom traditions, prescribes space for each of those persons entitled to be there: judge, clerk, lawyers, the accused/litigants, the public, the media and law enforcement personnel.

The right of the public to have access is reflected in the term "the bar". While that term is a colloquialism for lawyers, the term comes from a railing or balustrade that separates the working part of the courtroom (justice, clerk, lawyers, jurors and accused/litigants) from the public. The working part is inside the bar and the participants are entitled to be there on the Court's business. The public, while entitled to be inside the courtroom chamber, is located outside the bar.

Exclusions to access by the public include matters affecting children, national security and matters that on motion by one of the parties before the court are adjudicated to be necessary for exclusion on a public policy basis. There are few exclusions. There are members of the public in every jurisdiction who for entertainment, sentiment or philosophical adherence to justice being seen to be done, attend many court proceedings.

Access to the courtroom however confers no right to participate in the proceedings of the court. Any verbal or physical intervention in the court proceedings would result in prompt removal from the courtroom by a security officer of the court that is usually in attendance at all court proceedings. While a member of the public is not entitled to intervene in Court proceedings, those in attendance in the courtroom must follow courtroom procedure in according deference and dignity to the presiding justice by rising when the justice enters the courtroom and when the justice leaves at the end of the court session that day. Those attending to view the proceedings simply follow the behaviour of the lawyers in this regard.

The right to attend a court proceeding is not based on a personal interest in the matter arising from a familial, economic, religious or public interest issue. It is a fundamental right of the citizen. Even where the public is barred from attending a particular proceeding, the presiding justice must give substantial weight to the right of the public to attend and makes a decision to exclude the public only after hearing submissions from the lawyers representing parties in the proceeding. Arising from the principle that justice must be seen to be done, is the role of the media in the courtroom during proceedings. As with the general public, the media has a right to be present and to report on the proceedings.

Reporting court proceedings in most courtrooms is limited to reporters taking notes and writing or verbally describing the proceedings. Recording devices are permitted in the courtroom with leave (permission) of the court by anyone other than the official recording of all proceedings for court purposes. Television cameras are not permitted in most courtrooms although the Supreme Court of Canada has permitted television cameras in very controlled circumstances. There is a substantial debate in the legal community including justices, lawyers and officials as to whether television cameras should be permitted.

The debate centres on court dynamics. The courtroom is a theatre, in which each participant plays a prescribed role. The justices in exercising their role must occasionally forcibly control the behaviour of witnesses, the accused/litigants and the lawyers. The lawyers, on the other hand, occasionally find it necessary to be somewhat dramatic in their advocacy for their client. Television cameras would change the dynamic in the courtroom. The justice would cease to be the centre of the proceeding, the television camera would, and the participants would shift their focus and style of presentation to the television cameras. This issue is not yet settled.

The media exercises considerable restraint and discretion in what it covers in court proceedings. Family law matters, for example, even if open to the public, are generally not reported. Most issues affecting persons under eighteen years or who suffer some form of mental disability are generally not covered. Virtually all significant criminal and quasi-criminal matters are covered as it is a fundamental premise of Canadian law that the public has a right to know matters affecting law enforcement.

In attending a court proceeding, the public are not required to wear any particular attire but must be dressed in subdued conservative clothing suitable for the dignity of the courtroom. The presiding justice has absolute control over those in his or her courtroom in terms of demeanor and dress; if the justice considers either an observer's attire or demeanor to be inappropriate in terms of court traditions and dignity, the justice may have the individual removed from the courtroom. This also applies to the lawyers; if the presiding justice is not satisfied that a lawyer is properly attired for appearance before the justice, the justice can and will adjourn the proceedings until the fault has been remedied.

Access to the courts by the public has another and very important dimension – legal aid. Increasingly the cost of obtaining qualified legal services is such that some persons required to be engaged in a court proceeding cannot afford to hire a lawyer. Each of the three Maritime Provinces has a full-time legal aid service. The qualifications for receiving the service differ among the three provinces, but the common element is in family law disputes in which the welfare of children is involved. There are also limited free legal counsel services available through some provincial and federal government departments. These are few and arise only where fundamental civil rights are at issue

Above: *Old Carleton County Court House, Upper Woodstock, New Brunswick. Coat of Arms of Queen Victoria painted by John Lee, part of the original furnishings of the 1866 renovation of the courtroom.*

and then only after applying a needs test. Most lawyers consider that they have a professional ethical duty to provide entry level free, or virtually free, legal advice.

The placement of the public and the media in the courtroom will be discussed in more detail when we consider each of the various courtrooms examined in this book. It is clear that the entitlement of the public to observe the administration of justice has guaranteed allocation of space in all courtrooms to ensure that the public's right is protected.

DEVELOPMENT OF ENGLISH COURTHOUSES – MEDIEVAL TO 21ST CENTURY

Introduction: Medieval to Early 1700s

Early English court functions were performed in the space most convenient and accessible to the King and the judges. The courtrooms had no prescribed form or standards of design. As the independence of the judiciary and role and traditions of the courts became more established, courthouses and courtrooms were designed to meet standards of design required to complement and enable those functions within the traditions of the English legal system. Those standards and traditions changed over the centuries and with those changes, changes were made to the design of courtrooms and courthouses.

Courthouses as a distinct architectural structure became necessary as the complexity of the law grew and the administration of the courts required a predictable and visible location. Records of pleadings, trials and judicial decisions also required permanence and accessibility. The move to create a courthouse was highly influenced by Magna Carta which required courts to be in a fixed location. A fixed location and increased civil rights resulted in the redesign of the courtroom and the courthouse. These developments also resulted in additional court documents which the parties/accused were entitled to receive and to have on file in the courthouse as proof of due process. Some commentators have observed that the principal determinant in the reconfiguration of space in courthouses was the increasing volume of documents for storage.

Courthouses as an architectural composition grew outwards from the layout and design requirements of the courtroom. This was influenced by both the judiciary as well as record keeping. Later changes in the design and layout of courtrooms resulted from court procedures and changes in the rights at law of those participating in the courtroom, particularly the parties to a proceeding, the lawyers, the officials and the public.

By the end of the reign of Henry II (1154-1189), a fixed location had been established for most courts, both in London and in English county capitals. By that time the principal participants in the conduct of a trial had been established. Each of those participants had to be accommodated in some fashion within the confines of the structure housing the court.

Judges were the preeminent individuals in a superior court courtroom, followed in priority by the clerk of court, the sheriff (if required to be present), the lawyers and the accused or the litigants.

From the beginning of the development of courthouses the public assumed a right to witness court proceedings, but it was several centuries before that right became entrenched to the degree that there was a specific allocation of space in the courtroom for the public.

What characterized the medieval courts and has continued as a principle to this day is segregation. The earliest courtrooms were designed to conform to a protocol and precedence for those participating in the courtroom; each participant had an allocated space separate from the others.

The judges required a space that was exclusively theirs. This arose from their need to be seen, to be heard, and to have manifest authority. The space had to be both separate and secure. From this space the judge had to be able to control court proceedings and to be above those appearing in the courtroom seeking redress or answering a criminal charge. Segregation for judges in the courtroom required a barrier separating the judge from everyone else: that separation in a medieval court was in the form of a balustrade (or bar) and later an elevated dais with a prominent desk and throne-like chair. The judge alone was entitled to sit during the proceeding.

The next area of segregation in a medieval courtroom was an area allocated to court officials who organized and presented court documents to the judge and who received documents from the lawyers present representing a litigant or an accused. The area for officials was segregated by a balustrade (bar) from the next area of the courtroom which was allocated to the litigants or the accused and their lawyers. The lawyers in turn were segregated from the public by a balustrade. Behind the space segregated for the lawyers, members of the public wandered about vocalizing their support or approbation for particular witnesses or parties.

In the conduct of a medieval trial, the lawyers and their clients moved freely within their segregated area; no designated space was allocated to plaintiff or defendant, nor to the Crown or accused. Chaos was a predictable result of the lack of organization, but this system continued until the end of the 1600s.

Even in a medieval court, rituals became established in the conduct of a trial which became part of legal tradition. Rituals involved styles of address to the other participants in the courtroom including other counsel and their clients, the judge and the clerks. Clothing worn by the principals defined their role and gave them dignity and visibility. Clothing and forms of address became entrenched as a ritual by the thirteenth century.

Segregation as a principle extended to areas of the courthouses other than the courtroom. Judges were accorded their own access to the courthouse, their own private chambers, and a private access to the courtroom. The judge would be physically segregated from the lawyers, for example, unless the judge wished to speak to the lawyers privately in his own chambers, and then only on invitation by the judge. Medieval courthouses had no separate space for the lawyers or their clients. Consultation between lawyer and client was carried out in the general mêlée of the courtroom or public spaces.

Another way of expressing the concept of segregation (which continues to this day) is that spaces were allocated to establish patterns of authority. The role performed by the judge was as an appointee and agent of the monarch. The judge's presence and activity in courthouses was required to demonstrate that pattern of authority. The segregation of the accused or litigant and their counsel was a visible reminder that the lawyers and their clients were subservient to the rule of law and subject to the authority of the monarch as represented by the judge. Layers of authority were clearly defined and made visible in the layout of the courtroom and the courthouse.

The architectural composition of a medieval courthouse was not singular. The medieval courthouse was an important public building for carrying out the work of the monarch. As such, the buildings in which medieval courts functioned were frequently used for other public administrative purposes and lacked any architectural feature on the exterior of the building which identified the function as a courthouse performed within it. That was to change in the eighteenth century.

By the late sixteenth century many of the customs in ritual, protocol and procedure had become established in courtrooms. While many further developments would occur in the eighteenth and nineteenth centuries, the core elements of the English legal traditions had been established. Of particular importance in the development of English law and judicial conduct in court was the establishment of judicial independence in 1701 by the Act of Settlement. That independence meant the judiciary, after appointment, were free from any direction, supervision or duty (at a professional level) to the monarch who appointed them. Also, it meant that the judges were independent of each other and were obligated to follow their experience, conscience and sense of community values in conducting a trial and reaching a verdict.

Eighteenth Century

With changes to courtrooms in the eighteenth and nineteenth centuries, courthouses were reconfigured in their layout arising from new principles functioning in the courtroom. Courthouses became recognizable architectural compositions.

The integration of courtrooms in the English tradition with life in the colonies of what were to become Nova Scotia, Prince Edward Island and New Brunswick became established after the formalized consolidation and integration of geographical areas of mainland Nova Scotia that had formerly been separate English and French areas of influence by the Treaty of Utrecht in 1713. Many of

Above: Kings County Court House, Hampton, New Brunswick. A carved Coat of Arms of Queen Victoria, monarch when the court house was constructed in 1872, forming part of the judicial dais.

the developments in the layout and design of English courtrooms and, later, of courthouses, would be applied in the design of courthouses in colonial British North America. But, as we will see there were to be significant differences between the English buildings and those developed in British Colonial America – in areas we identify today as parts of the United States.

Several factors influenced the development of English courtrooms and courthouses in the eighteenth century. These included increasing literacy and awareness of the entitlement to civil rights and access to the law, and an open, impartial and predictable court process. The chaos and unpredictability of earlier court procedures were largely rejected by a public increasingly assertive of its citizenship and rights that should flow from it. Another significant factor was the economic development of England which saw the citizenry move from peasantry to paid workers not beholden to an overlord. These factors resulted in the development of court procedures more respectful of the individual in society, the need for justice to be done and to appear to be done, and stability

in the marketplace which required a predictable and reliable administration of justice and an objective enforcement of mercantile contracts.

While courtrooms had a predictable form by the end of the eighteenth century and the roles of the judges, litigants and counsel were well established, the formality and rigidity in court proceedings that developed in the nineteenth century were not yet established. In her book *Ordering Law: The Architectural and Social History of the English Courts to 1914*, Clare Graham recounts the relaxed nature of some rural courts in describing an incident that occurred in one particular courtroom. It was not uncommon for a trial to become a social event for the theatre it offered. Graham tells of the trial of a young woman accused of murdering her baby. An aristocratic lady who was a friend of the presiding judge was sitting with him on the bench when the jury handed down a "guilty" verdict. The judge promptly sentenced the convicted woman to death by hanging. The lady leaned over to her friend the judge and dissuaded him from that sentence. The sentence was reduced to imprisonment. This incident reflects the social and theatrical dimension of some trials in the eighteenth century and would not have occurred after the major judicial reforms of the nineteenth century.

Developments in the theory and practice of the law and the rights of the citizen also witnessed a parallel development in the eighteenth century in the form of the role of architecture as a defining element in buildings having prominence in the governance of the people.

Prior to the eighteenth century, interest in the role of architecture as a means of aggrandizing the monarch, an institution or an individual had been well and widely established. It is a characteristic of our species going back to the Neolithic period throughout the world, with few exceptions, that power, status and achievement are expressed in our built environment. It was not, however, until the late seventeenth century and throughout the eighteenth century that the architectural composition of public buildings to identify function as a component of urban design became established as an objective of the state and as a norm in England.

Architecture is an effective device for giving physical expression to the symbolism and principles of the courts: that justice be done openly, objectively and competently, and be seen to carry out those principles with appropriate decorative symbolic devices such as – Lady Justice, blindfolded, holding the scales of justice in one hand and a sword in the other. This symbol was frequently applied in or about courthouses to identify the functions carried out in the building.

The architecture of courtrooms and courthouses was also a means of presenting and controlling the theatre of the courtroom. Trials, both civil and criminal, are usually proceedings of high drama, emotion and conflict – the essential elements of good entertainment. Courtrooms were designed to recognize that dimension of court proceedings but subject to the need to enable judicial control through authority and clearly defined procedures governing the behaviour of the participants in the trial and the orderly introduction of evidence and examination of witnesses. The nineteenth century would bring greater rigidity, formalities and control than were practised in the eighteenth century.

Also, it was not until the early eighteenth century in England that courtrooms as an architectural composition became standardized. With that standardization courthouses became predictably similar and contained design elements that assisted them being distinguished from other public buildings.

Among those standardized design elements that became ubiquitous in eighteenth-century English courtrooms were the following: 1) segregation of the judiciary from the litigants, the lawyers and the public in the courtrooms; 2) the judges desk and chair were positioned opposite the public entrance to the courtroom on an elevated dais – the judges chair being throne-like in appearance; 3) the judge's access to the courtroom was a separate entrance restricted to the use of the judge and court officials; 4) the presence of the monarch was declared in a Coat of Arms of the monarch, usually mounted directly behind the judge; 5) a portrait of the monarch in the courtroom on a wall within the space segregated for the judge, usually positioned to the right of the judge, signifying the precedence properly accorded the monarch; 6) tables and chairs for the lawyers with their position being formalized to counsel for the Crown or plaintiff on the right hand of the judge, and the counsel for the defence or defendant on the judge's left, and the only balustrade or bar in the courtroom being now behind the counsel tables segregating the officers of the court (which by now included the lawyers) from the public; and 7) the precedence accorded to the position of a person or object in relation to another is called handedness.

The principle of handedness which governed the placement of the accused and the litigants and their counsel extended to a Court of Appeal in which the chief justice took precedence in the centre of the panel of judges, with the next most senior judge to his/her right and the junior member of the panel (if three) on the left of the chief justice.

The origin of handedness is both historic and Biblical. Deference and precedence have traditionally been accorded to objects and persons on the right hand of the principal; for example Christ sitting on the right hand of God. The principle pre-dated the New Testament of the Christian Bible and appears to go back to the origins of tradition and custom in the ancient Middle East civilizations such as Mesopotamia and Egypt. While the principle of handedness has no intrinsic connection with the exercise of judicial authority, the practice of handedness is so embedded in British cultural traditions that its relevance and application was subsumed to apply.

The principal element in the design of a courthouse is the courtroom. As noted, the layout and ultimately the external design of the courthouse flow from the courtroom, or courtrooms depending on the size of the population being serviced by the courthouse. The internal configuration of space in a courthouse extended the principles of precedence, segregation and access that developed over centuries in courtrooms. That development was incremental; it was not the work of a particular architect, jurist or planner.

Courthouse design by the mid-eighteenth century included secure and segregated access to the buildings for judges; segregated hallways for court officials, including the judges, to the courtrooms; and space for clerical staff and document storage. Apart from segregation of the judiciary from the public and lawyers, the layout of spaces was a pragmatic response to growth in the clerical staff, court procedures and filing and retrieval of documents. The principles of design changed over time, but only as required by changes in court procedures prescribed by the judiciary, by technology, or by changes in public policy relating to access to courtrooms by the public, including the media. A mid-eighteenth century courtroom would be fully recognizable as such to us today.

Eighteenth century English courthouses in their external architectural form did not have a distinctive "courthouse look". They were identifiable as a substantial civic building. Because of size, importance of architectural features and location, courthouses were one of the two most important civic buildings in a town or city. Occasionally, the eighteenth-century courthouse was signed to identify it as a courthouse. That was frequently the practice in New England;

a practice adopted in early nineteenth century courthouses in New Brunswick and Nova Scotia.

By the mid-eighteenth century, the British Empire had become firmly entrenched in North America, both in what was to become Canada and in the eastern United States. Because the American colonial administrations preceded those in Canada, the colonial administration developed in the American colonies proved to be highly influential on the administration adopted in the colonies that would become Canada.

There is a direct parallel in the influence of American colonial administration on the interior and exterior design and layout of legislative buildings to that of courthouses. As noted, the principal courtroom in an English colony was contained in the colonial legislative building. The connection among eighteenth-century colonial courthouses was substantially influenced by a shared jurisprudence and a judiciary who were moved from one colony to another.

By the mid-eighteenth century, courthouses in colonial America in their simple standardized form had been established. Virtually the same form was adopted and applied in Canada. That is not surprising as there was extensive trade and travel along the eastern seaboard of North America and there was also a movement of colonial officials as well as judges from one colony to another through the Empire before the British colonial possessions were reduced and divided by the American Revolution. Indeed, some of the earliest courthouses in Nova Scotia and New Brunswick are closely modeled on mid-eighteenth century Virginian courthouses, which embody those principles.

The courts developed in North America by the mid-eighteenth century embodied the standards of protocol, procedure, precedent, and ritual that were then prevalent in England. However, after the creation of the standardized courthouse in North America, the courthouses followed their own paths of development only slightly influenced by changes in England. That is largely because many of the changes that developed in nineteenth-century England resulted from factors not as strongly adopted in North America: substantial integration of the Church of England as an arm of the governance, social stratification and resultant class structures of post-industrialization, and complexities in the economy that required numerous specialized courts, many of which were not adopted in colonial America (or whose jurisdictions were integrated into the existing courts).

Architectural style and the integration of courthouses architecturally into the planning of cities and towns became a major factor by the end of the eighteenth century in England but earlier in American colonies. In the American colonies it developed in this way earlier because new towns were being created there from the forests and wilderness; in contrast England had an extensive range of historic buildings that could be modified to accommodate courtrooms. As a result, American town planning required decisions as to the most important public buildings, their location and design. This process resulted in courthouses being accorded high precedence as a component of the concept and built expression of democratic government in the United States of America.

Public policy considerations had to be made as to what received English traditions and customs would be adopted in the new colonies and how the town planning could reflect these considerations. The colonial administration endeavoured to create an England in miniature. However, political, social and geographical differences as well as the existence of older public buildings in England resulted in Americans creating on the whole a more open and democratic society in the colonies. Because courthouses were recognized as among the most important public buildings in England, they were featured as an essential component of the core elements of urban design in new colonial towns. The architectural traditions of the England the colonists left were the guiding standards in constructing courthouses in the United States. The English traditions were modified by local circumstances in the United States resulting in a distinctive American understanding of courthouses and their significance in an urban setting. It is a curious fact that as with the layout and design of legislative buildings in colonial America, courthouses established standardization in layout and design internally and externally before their counterparts in England.

Courthouses were recognized as one of the three most significant structures in the principal colonial cities and towns: those being parliament (or town hall), church and courthouse. The design of courthouses as a part of that configuration of buildings usually conformed with or complemented the styles of the other principal buildings. The North American buildings tended to be fabricated in wood and presented a simplicity reflecting the economic, spiritual and political aspirations of the communities in which they were built.

The architectural styles in which courthouses were built changed with developments in architectural fashion. Buildings specifically designed and built as courthouses in the early eighteenth century were built in the then high fashion for public buildings: Queen Anne or early Georgian with elements in their design of the baroque which was the predominant style of the mid-to-late seventeenth century. The interior decoration of the buildings mirrored the exterior style. But these styles were simply a decorative envelope for buildings based on their core element of a courtroom with prescribed segregated spaces and interior fittings such as a witness box, counsel tables and a dais with the judge's desk and chair surmounting it.

The exterior appearance of courthouses in North America through virtually all of the eighteenth and into the first quarter of the nineteenth century looked very much the same: simple rectangular buildings sometimes with a neoclassical pediment and columns. The scale of the building was dictated by the number of courtrooms. If the building was designed in one of the neoclassical styles, it would usually have a pediment over the front entrance extending across the full width of the building. However, some limited the portico to one half of the width. In the centre of the pediment there was a tympanum (the flat triangular surface in the centre of the pediment framed by the eaves). In the tympanum, either a Royal Coat of Arms of the monarch in whose reign the building was constructed or a symbol of justice in some form would be mounted.

Nineteenth Century

With the accession of Queen Victoria in 1837, a quiet but effective moral revolution occurred in England led by the Queen and by her consort Prince Albert. They married in 1840 and with the marriage the Queen acquired a husband with a strict moral code and high sense of public duty. His moral code was in part a reaction to the apparent absence of morality in the lives of the Queen's uncles, who were also relatives of Prince Albert. While the Queen and her consort were the living embodiment of the new moral code, the public movement for reform started earlier and acquired growing momentum with the endorsement of the Crown. That sense of morality became pervasive by the mid-nineteenth century and it was combined with the efforts/preaching of numerous social reformers advocating economic, social and legal reform. All elements of society and governance were reconsidered and fundamentally reworked by the end of the nineteenth century and were led primarily by social reformers and the churches.

Photo: Scott Smith

Above: *Sherbrooke Courthouse Museum, Sherbrooke, Nova Scotia. Constructed in 1850, one of three similar courthouses designed and built by Alexander MacDonald of Antigonish.*

It was in this atmosphere that several Reform Acts were passed by the Westminster parliament; major reforms occurred in both the laws of the United Kingdom and in the superior courts which were to administer the laws.

Several of these changes that had an influence on the design and functioning of courtrooms and courthouses included: 1) increased segregation of the participants in a courtroom; 2) additional secure and isolated passageways into and around the courthouses for each of the participants; 3) judges, lawyers and litigants/accused would see each other only in the courtroom; 4) Justices might call on lawyers to meet with them "in chambers" (in their private office) but only on invitation and subject to a clearly defined protocol; 5) segregation of juries became firmly established with a dedicated space divided by a balustrade for the jury inside the courtroom; and 6) segregation of juries came to include separate passages within the courthouse so that there could be no contact between jurors and the judiciary, with the lawyers, with the litigants/accused or the public, and the creation of dedicated conference rooms where they could confer in private.

as demonstrated at law by women's property rights becoming essentially those exclusively of husbands or fathers. In the courtroom, and in the courthouse that social stratification resulted in differences in the treatment of litigant/accused while in the courthouse and in the conduct of trials. Women were segregated in seating in the public areas of a courtroom and many trials were not accessible to women because according to the social structures of the time, they were unladylike, or too sensitive for their delicate sensibilities. Few of those restrictions were adopted in colonial courthouses.

An accused would be isolated from others in the courthouse by being given a dedicated passageway from the exterior of the courthouse up to and into the courtroom. The public continued to have a right to view trials and other court proceedings, but space and the hours and conditions of access, as well as the location in the courtroom to view proceedings became much more rigidly controlled. Underlying the legal changes, it must be emphasized, was the moral code as preached by the Christian Churches which became more rigid and confining than in the eighteenth and early nineteenth centuries.

Arising from the vast economic, mercantile and political expansion within the Empire in the nineteenth century, trials and various court proceedings increasingly attained national significance and interest. With the prominence given to many trials, lawyers became much more significant in their own right. Not only were they advocates for their clients, they became in modern terminology, celebrities. As public figures, lawyers sought publicity and public acclaim outside the courtroom to enhance and develop their reputation in it. It was in the nineteenth century that the conferring of the honourific Queen's Counsel attained high status and significance for a barrister and was eagerly sought by them. The legal profession became more segregated and precedence was established. The distinction between barristers and solicitors became a rigid demarcation in the providing of legal services (not to be significantly altered until the twenty-first century). Again, this distinction was not adopted or applied in American/Canadian courthouses.

The increasing interest in the history of architecture and in the use of architecture to express form, function and status resulted in courthouses being built in historicist styles. The eighteenth century use of baroque and Georgian-influenced decorative elements was rejected early in the nineteenth century by what was perceived as the purity and dignity of the Greek Revival style. It was considered to be the most appropriate expression of purpose and dignity for a courthouse.

Photo: Scott Smith

Above: *Alberton Court House, Alberton, Prince Edward Island (1878). While this former courthouse, now a museum, did not serve as a superior court courthouse, its photograph is included as a representative example of numerous county and magistrate's courts located throughout the Maritimes. It is a National Historic Site.*

Segregation in the English courthouse was further influenced and became more rigid with the increasing social and gender stratification of English society. Such stratification resulted largely from the Industrial Revolution and the wealth produced from it which created new classes in society and vast differences in wealth among those classes.

The influence of the church and increasing social and gender stratification had a major influence on the design and functioning of courthouses in the mid-to-late nineteenth century. Among those influences was the isolation of women

In the nineteenth century, architectural styles changed almost as rapidly as ladies' fashions. Gothic Revival as an architectural style was rejected until the 1840s. After that it became the dominant style largely as a result of the influence of architects Charles Barry and Augustus Welby Pugin who created a new interpretation of British Gothic in the design of the Palace of Westminster (1854). The Gothic Revival style became the dominant architectural composition for virtually all public buildings in the United Kingdom for fifty years – to the end of the nineteenth century for churches, courthouses, legislative buildings, town halls and other public buildings.

The profound influence of the British Empire on the colonies resulted in the importation and use of British architectural fashions throughout the Empire as well as in the United States.

The majority of the surviving historic courthouses in the Maritime Provinces are from the nineteenth century and are therefore highly influenced by nineteenth-century British Neoclassicism and Gothicism. In terms of the internal form of courthouses, they were also highly influenced by American colonial courthouses. We are fortunate in the Maritimes to have several courthouses from the pre-Gothic period which are in the late neoclassical Georgian styles. We will explore all the styles currently standing and identify the architectural principles and standards of each.

Twentieth Century

The influence of the British legal system continued until 1933 (when the Supreme Court of Canada became the final Court of Appeal for Canada for criminal appeals) and 1949 for all other matters. The establishment of Canada's judicial independence from Britain resulted from statutes passed in both the Parliament of Canada and the United Kingdom Parliament. The statutory basis of Canadian judicial independence was the culmination of decades of growing cultural, legal and linguistic developments in Canada that prepared the way and ultimately dictated the requirement for that independence.

The changes that led to the independence of the Supreme Court of Canada as the final Court of Appeal did not affect the architectural design or layout of courthouses in the Maritime Provinces. The form, architectural style, layout and decorative elements of courthouses between 1900 and 1949 remained largely static from the late nineteenth-century standards. There was some experimentation in the exterior architectural styles of courthouses, but very little as the number of post-Confederation courthouses (largely in the nineteenth century) were sufficient for the first decades of the twentieth century. New courthouses built prior to 1949 followed prevailing architectural styles. An appropriate exception is the Supreme Court of Canada building constructed in 1938-1940 in a style which could only be described as a fusion of French Chateau (early French Renaissance) and Art Deco styles.

The judicial independence of Canada from Britain did not lead to significant changes to the structures in which justice was administered, but it did lead to a growing sense of independence in the growth, self-confidence and perspective of the Canadian judiciary. Issues such as the relative legislative strength of the provinces in relation to that of the national government were addressed by the Supreme Court of Canada reflecting more sensitively and accurately the reality of the Canadian polity as the issues were addressed. Another substantial issue was the relative position of Quebec law and the French language in Canada. The Supreme Court was well positioned to hear appeals from provincial courts of appeal and to make decisions consistent with a consensus of common law provinces and responsive to the demands of Quebec politics.

Also in relation to changes in the law, one of the most significant was in the human rights field. Canada enacted human rights legislation long before the United Kingdom. Canadian jurisprudence is now influencing the English courts in the interpretation of its relatively new law. A similar result is observed in recent family law legislation in the United Kingdom which is similar to laws enacted in Canada decades ago.

It was with the independence of Canada's highest court from that of the United Kingdom that Canadian law and Canada's Supreme Court justices effectively assumed the definitive and independent voice that enabled Canadian law to mature into a singular identity.

While the second half of the twentieth century witnessed changes in the law responding to public policy issues such as human rights and family law, changes in the administration of the courts and ultimately in the design of courtrooms and courthouses were most profoundly changed as a result of technology. Technology enabled effective auditory recording of trials and other court proceedings. This in turn led to more reliable typed transcripts of

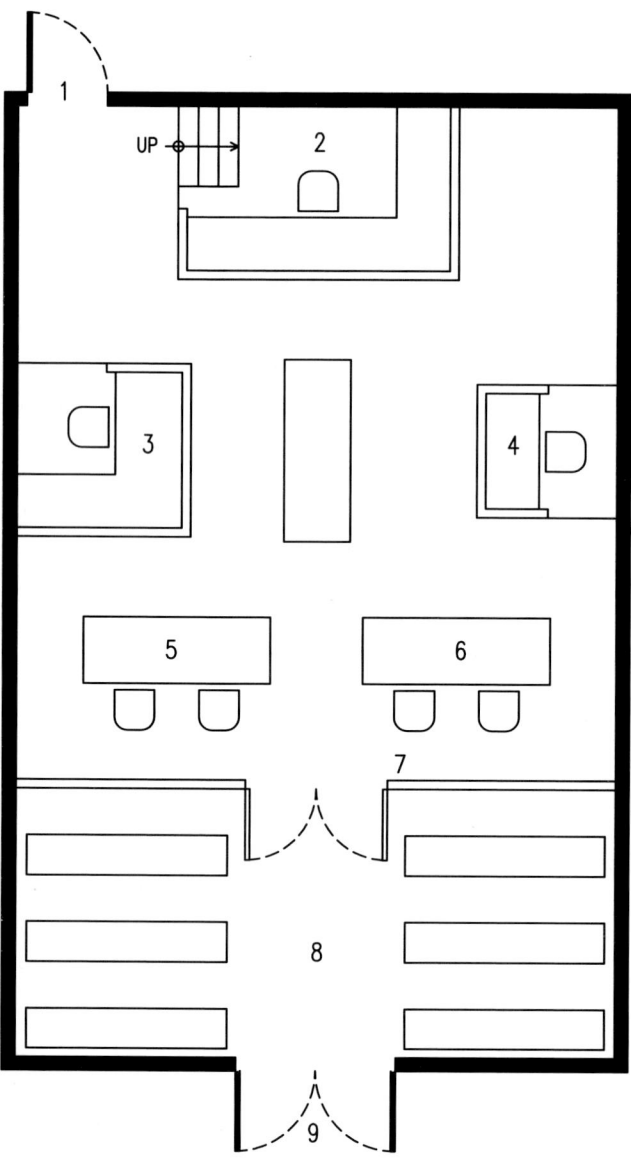

NON—JURY COURT ROOM

1 SEGREGATED ACCESS FOR JUDGE & CLERK
2 JUDGE'S BENCH
3 CLERK'S DESK
4 WITNESS BOX
5 PLANTIFF'S COUNSEL / CROWN ATTORNEY TABLE
6 DEFENDANT'S COUNSEL / ACCUSED'S COUNSEL TABLE
7 BAR OF THE COURTROOM
8 PUBLIC SEATING
9 PUBLIC ACCESS

| 0' | 5' | 10' | 20' |

court proceedings. These enabled justices, in making their decisions, to reassess the notes taken by them during those proceedings over which they presided. Judicial decisions were more reliable in their assessment of the facts as a result. But the courts being, as noted, very traditional and therefore reluctant to accept change have moved little into the visual recording of court proceedings for the public, such as in television coverage. Recordings and documentation are, however, well integrated into the evidentiary process and enable some evidence to be admissible in this form. Developments in technology were accompanied by a growing public demand for access to justice, including access to court processes and judicial decisions.

Courthouses built in the post-Second World War era were primarily constructed in the 1970s and 1980s. Pressures on the courts arising from their expanding caseload and from the public, the legal profession and within the judiciary itself emphasized that the courts had to modernize to accept and integrate the new technologies to make the courts more efficient and to appear to be more open and friendly to the public. Courts built in the latter part of the twentieth century reflect a philosophical trend to demystify the law and the judicial process, in an attempt to make the courts more accessible and relevant to the public. The second half of the twentieth century saw the single most rapidly growing area of law, namely family law, making demands on time, resources and space on the judiciary and court facilities.

With the growth in the demands on the courts to accommodate the rapidly increasing family law sector, access by unrepresented litigants increased substantially. Demands for court-supported child support recovery and accountability have also put extraordinary demands on the courts or their officials which has resulted in the growth of a wide range of new facilities and officials to accommodate those demands.

Courthouses built in the mid and latter part of the twentieth century were in architectural terms almost uniformly banal and uninviting to the public. There are a very limited number of exceptions, one of which is the Sir Louis Henry Davies Law Courts in Charlottetown. This was the case notwithstanding a change in the philosophical approach by the courts which required the opposite. The principle of a courthouse as one of the three key public buildings in the community in which they were located was relegated to the least significant consideration by urban planners. Most exteriors were designed to look like every other, usually standardized, government office building. They failed to give evidence of the dignity of the law and those who perform their duties within them including the judiciary,

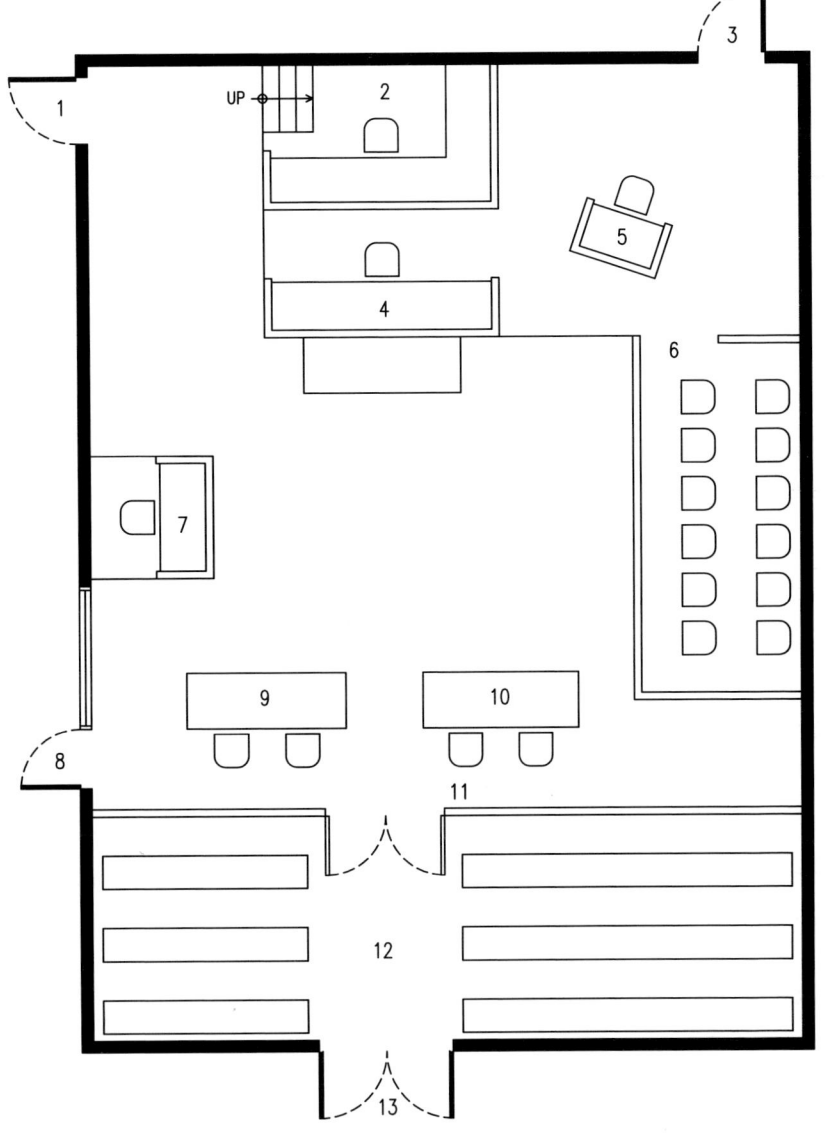

JURY COURT ROOM

1 PRIVATE ACCESS FOR JUDGE & CLERK TO SECURE CHAMBERS AREA C/W SEGREGATED ACCESS TO EXTERIOR
2 JUDGE'S BENCH
3 PRIVATE ACCESS TO SECURE JURY AREA C/W SEGREGATED ACCESS TO EXTERIOR
4 CLERK'S DESK
5 WITNESS BOX FOR NON-ACCUSED
6 JURY BOX
7 WITNESS BOX / ACCUSED'S DOCK
8 CONTROLLED ACCESS FOR ACCUSED FROM SECURE DOCK AREA C/W SEGREGATED ACCESS TO THE EXTERIOR
9 PLANTIFF'S COUNSEL / CROWN ATTORNEY TABLE
10 DEFENDANT'S COUNSEL / ACCUSED'S COUNSEL TABLE
11 BAR OF THE COURTROOM
12 PUBLIC SEATING
13 PUBLIC ACCESS

0'   5'   10'   20'

COURT OF APPEAL

1 SEGREGATED ACCESS FOR JUDGES & CLERK
2 JUDGES' BENCH
3 CLERK'S DESK
4 ADDITIONAL COUNSEL TABLE
5 PLANTIFF'S COUNSEL / CROWN ATTORNEY TABLE
6 DEFENDANT'S COUNSEL / ACCUSED'S COUNSEL TABLE
7 BAR OF THE COURTROOM
8 PUBLIC SEATING
9 PUBLIC ACCESS

0'   5'   10'   20'

the officials and the lawyers. Passing a courthouse constructed during that period gives one no sense whatever of the functions performed within it.

On the other hand, the interiors of courthouses constructed very late in the twentieth century have changed significantly. Both the air and light quality have improved considerably. The fittings for the judiciary, officials, lawyers and litigant/accused have been made more efficient, comfortable and compatible with the functions being performed in them. Also, seating for the public and for the media including folding desk-like surfaces are improvements in courthouses. The key to the late twentieth century changes was efficiency. Aesthetics were of little influence in the design of the courtroom; simplifying for the purpose of efficiency and functionality a space was created that was spartan – usually with a predominance of light coloured wood in the fittings.

During the same period judicial gowns saw some simplification and addition of colour, but the basic garment was still traceable to its medieval origins. Gowns worn by officials (those who required them such as the prothonotary or chief clerk) remained much the same as was the case for the lawyers. No changes of a perceptible nature have been made to barristers' gowns in the

Maritime Provinces for over one hundred fifty years. If there were changes since courts were established in the Maritimes, they appear not to be significant.

The demands of the public for affordable legal services particularly in criminal and in family law matters resulted during the last quarter of the twentieth century in the development of provincial government legal aid systems. All three provincial governments have hired lawyers to provide free legal services for certain persons requiring access to justice. The range of services has had to be limited to keep costs manageable; the qualifications for access to legal aid are based on a means test and on the service required being one offered as a priority by the legal and staff lawyers. The priority is for children and women at risk in domestic disputes and in certain criminal law situations. In addition to the government funded legal aid program, the law schools at Dalhousie and the University of New Brunswick also offer free legal aid clinics which have the added benefit of offering excellent training for student lawyers. The legal profession itself has traditionally recognized an ethical duty to assist those who cannot afford legal services. Most lawyers offer some form of free or limited-fee service at the preliminary enquiry stage of a client's need for information and direction.

Twenty-first Century

The twenty-first century has witnessed dramatic changes to courtrooms and courthouses in the Maritimes and elsewhere in Canada. Those changes have occurred because of security and public relations issues. In many ways the delivery of judicial services is being revisited and reoriented.

Security has always been a significant issue in courts as noted earlier in relation to the reasons for judges and barristers in the United Kingdom being segregated and wearing wigs and medieval gowns. The need to protect the personal security and privacy of the participants in the judicial process has been a continuous priority in the delivery of judicial services both in the United Kingdom and in Canada.

The security issue in the twenty-first century has become one of the primary concerns because of numerous shooting rampages in recent years in the United States in which judges and lawyers have been the target of attack by the deranged or unhappy accused or litigants. It is believed that what happens in the United States will follow into Canada in due course. The firearms threat for example is exacerbated by the terrorist experiences in the United States.

Canada has not had many similar experiences to those in the United States, but the United States/Canada border does not exist in terms of the power of suggestion on the susceptible, insane and delusional. Provincial Departments of Justice which are responsible for the planning, upkeep, renovation and improvement of courthouses, in consultation with the chief justices of the provinces, have taken precautionary steps intended to prevent similar events occurring in the Maritimes to those occurring in the United States. This approach has given rise to various security innovations in the exterior and interior design of courthouses.

A recent incidence on Prince Edward Island will demonstrate the type of security risk that can arise. At the Sir Louis Henry Davies Law Courts Building which houses the Supreme Court of Prince Edward Island and the Prince Edward Island Court of Appeal in Charlottetown, a bizarre situation arose for which no preparation could have been anticipated. An unhappy and angry, perhaps mentally distressed, former litigant in a family law dispute, drove her vehicle one evening after regular court hours (but while security guards were in place inside the building) from the street onto and along the sidewalk leading into the main entrance to the building. She drove through well-built oak doors continuing through a narrow vestibule and through a parallel set of oak doors entering the main lobby of the courthouse and stopped only when the vehicle collided with the wall of the barristers' lounge. She then continued over twenty times to drive forward and backward while inside the courthouse in an apparent attempt to escape. Since that incident, access to the building has been reconfigured, with a substantial barrier separating the street from the sidewalk into the courthouse, and the entrance doors were rebuilt to resist such force.

Virtually all courthouses in Canada now have security screening similar to those procedures at airports or in the Parliament of Canada. Occasionally full body searches are conducted when required. Numerous video cameras are stationed throughout courthouses, including all courtrooms, and on the exterior elements of the building giving a full view of all aspects of the buildings. The security guards on duty are trained to monitor the images from all of the video cameras.

In the last few years it has become customary to have a security officer present in the courtroom during most family law cases, and in criminal trials.

The bench (desk) at which the justices sit also has an emergency device to call for additional security if required.

The second substantial change affecting the operation of courthouses is philosophical. Courtrooms and courthouses in the nineteenth century were designed to overawe and intimidate those of the public who required, or were required, to use their facilities. With the growth in the demands on the courts particularly family law clients, every element of the justice delivery system is rethinking the concepts of access to justice and the role of judges and courthouses.

The judiciary is leading the way in making the courts more user-friendly. The buildings are being opened to guided tours sometimes led by members of the judiciary. The tours are designed to demystify the buildings and the functions carried out in them. The judiciary are also developing information guidelines and giving free public talks on the delivery of justice, the roles of the judges, courthouse, officials and the legal profession. The Chief Justice of Canada, the Honourable Beverley McLachlin, P.C. is quoted as saying "The Courts belong to the people of Canada, and the people have the right to know about this important institution." This book is in part a response to this premise.

Courthouses are now being identified and promoted as public places to be used by the public for conflict resolution. This represents a complete reversal of the nineteenth-century concept of the role of the judiciary and courthouses.

In keeping with that philosophy, courts are developing new pre-trial procedures presided over by a justice enabling pre-trial resolution of conflict. These have proven to be welcomed by the public and viewed as highly successful by the legal profession.

Canada is a bilingual country by law; hence the superior courts of each province are required to provide trials, especially criminal trials, in both French and English when the accused request the service. Most courts also endeavour to facilitate translation services for persons whose working language is not French or English.

The language issue has its built-in place in courtrooms. Courtrooms are now designed to accommodate a translator as an official in court proceedings where translation services are requested involving the French language.

Human rights issues have been an influence in the design of courtrooms and courthouses. They must now be wheelchair accessible and have efficient elevator service to different levels. Courtrooms are notorious for being acoustically limited; most courts now provide an auditory enhancement device to anyone requiring one in the courtroom.

Efforts have been made to improve late twentieth century courtrooms in terms of airflow, temperature, natural light and as noted, auditory enhancement. It is a curious fact that nineteenth-century courthouses were designed to admit light and air into courtrooms and were frequently influenced in their acoustics by well-established precedents in church architecture. However, the absence of such human necessities in courthouses built in the 1970s and 1980s demonstrate that those designing the courthouses were not briefed on or ignored fundamental principles of the design of structural spaces intended to house numerous persons for several emotionally charged hours.

One of the problems related to the acoustics in a courtroom is a change in the training of lawyers and judges. In the nineteenth century and early twentieth century, legal training involved advocacy skills. One of the paramount skills in advocacy is projecting the voice to be heard. Astonishing as it may seem, it is not at all uncommon for counsel and judges alike to be inaudible in the courtroom. All vocalizations in the courtrooms are recorded, but few courtrooms have inbuilt voice amplification systems.

A few new courthouses have been built in the twenty-first century in the Maritimes but it is not yet possible to predict whether the designers of courthouses will revert to the principles of location, prominent architectural design and dignity that characterized the eighteenth and nineteenth century courthouse. Those that have been built are usually styled "justice centres" and have been designed to be inclusive and user-friendly but architecturally are not prominent landmarks. One can only hope that the role of the courts, the judiciary and the legal profession as one of the three primary government functions, as the dispensers of justice, will be revisited and returned to their proper priority, dignity and status in architecture and location.

What is to come?

In conclusion to this chapter, courthouses are the structural embodiment of the duty of governments in Canada, both national and provincial, to facilitate and dispense justice. Courthouses are an effective device for studying and interpreting how the administration and dispensation of justice works in all three of the Maritime Provinces.

We now move forward to textually analyzing the significant historic courthouses of the Maritimes and in so doing illustrate graphically and in words how courtrooms and courthouses deliver the service prescribed for them. An exploration of a functioning courthouse is an excellent interpretative device for explaining the judicial system in Canada.

There are twenty-five courthouses included in this book. As stated in the Preface their selection was obvious: those included are either the principal locations of the current Supreme Court of each province, or are designated historical sites.

In addition to the description of the buildings, a description of a modern civil trial and a description of a criminal trial (significantly different from a civil trial) are added as appendices.

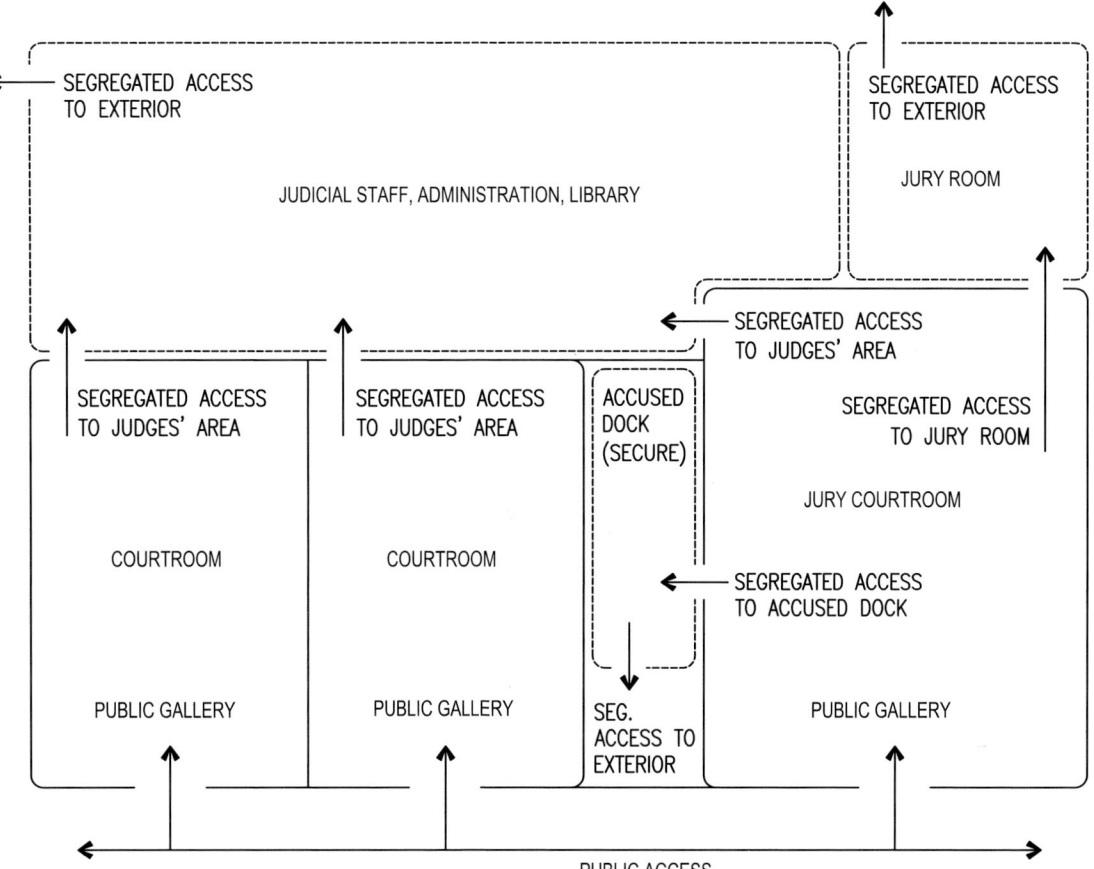

CONCEPTUAL DIAGRAM DISPLAYING THE ALLOCATION OF SPACE IN A MODERN COURTHOUSE

Above: *Antigonish County Court House (1855)*

Photo: Paul Toman

THE HISTORIC COURTHOUSES OF NOVA SCOTIA

ARGYLE TOWNSHIP COURT HOUSE & GAOL
TUSKET, NOVA SCOTIA

Recognized as the oldest extant courthouse and jail in Canada, the Argyle Township Court House, built between 1803 and 1805, is located in the community of Tusket in Southwest Nova Scotia on the Old Main Post Road. It originally served both the Townships of Argyle and Yarmouth.

There was a controversy in 1801 as to where the courthouse should be located. Yarmouth was a modestly prosperous town, as was Tusket, although Tusket was a substantial shipbuilding centre and as a result attracted commercial and mercantile interests. The decision to build the courthouse in Tusket was purely practical: Tusket lay in the middle of the combined boundaries of Yarmouth and Argyle Townships. It was easier to get the principals of any legal issue to and from Tusket than from any other location in the two townships.

The construction of courthouses in Nova Scotia was the legislatively delegated responsibility of each county. In 1801 a resolution of the Court of General Sessions of the Peace which also served as the county administrative body provided that funds were to be raised to construct a "gaol" (jail in current usage). The priority when the courthouse was being constructed was the lock up. Courts had been convened in the area in various buildings and locations prior to this and did not appear to be as necessary to the General Session as the jail. The resolution prescribed that the jail was to be twenty by twenty-five feet

Above: The justice's bench, dais and backdrop.

Opposite page: Argyle Township Court House & Gaol, Tusket, Nova Scotia. The original segment of the building was constructed between 1803 and 1805. It is the oldest extant courthouse in Canada.

Above: Restraining devices in the jail original in kind to the building.

Left: The interior of the courtroom. The grand jury box to the right and the petit jury box to the left. The prisoner's dock in the foreground with counsel table in front of it.

in dimension and thirteen feet high at the ceiling but have six foot clearance only in the six ground floor jail cells below.

The resolution further called for the building to be sheathed on the exterior walls with clapboard, which it continues to have, and the lower ground floor where the lock-up cells were to be located was to be wood-framed. The latter resulted in numerous escapes from the jail. In 1870 additional renovations were made to the courthouse. The jail cells were rebuilt using cement and stone with exceptionally stout iron bars on the iron doors. There are no recorded escapes after the renovations.

The courthouse served both County Court and Supreme Court functions. Between 1840 and 1924 a Supreme Court justice, while on circuit, visited the courthouse once a year. There was no permanent courthouse staff. The justice travelled with his own clerk. The only permanent employee was the jailer, who did not reside in the building but visited it daily when the jail had inmate(s), to provide them with water and food. The only heat source in the building was from wood stoves, none of which apparently were located in the jail.

The courthouse was in continuous use until it was discontinued as a functioning courthouse in 1944 and was then restored as a courthouse museum in 1982. It is currently under the curatorial administration of the municipality of the District of Argyle and the Argyle Municipality Historical and Genealogical society who work as stewardship partners for this building.

THE EXTERIOR

Who designed the courthouse? It was not designed by an architect. Its construction and design were overseen by two members of the Court of General Sessions, James Kelly, Esq. of Yarmouth and Captain Theunis Blauvelt of Tusket. The construction by local master builders, possibly shipwrights, conformed to both the standards prescribed in the resolution and the early nineteenth-century construction practices common in the area. It has substantial New England influences and is a standard New England meeting house in its configuration of spaces and uses. It is a simple rectangular building with a pitched roof, the gable end on the front of the building.

The influence of the New England meeting house in the design of the Argyle Township Courthouse and Gaol is apparent and predictable. The extensive mercantile, trading, fisheries and family connections between this region of Nova Scotia and New England were extensive in the early nineteenth century. Indeed, American influences on the architecture, economy and social norms were particularly profound in the English-speaking elements of the community because of the substantial Loyalist population and continuing trading links with New England, moreso than direct influences from British sources.

New England meeting houses usually included court facilities. The meeting house served virtually all secular community needs. A meeting house model was developed in late seventeenth and during the eighteenth century in Virginia while it was an English colony. The Virginian building was heavily influenced by English prototypes. The Virginian model had a profound influence on the standard New England meeting house.

In his book entitled *The Courthouses of Early Virginia: an Architectural History*, Carl R. Loundsbury put the influence of English architecture on the design of courthouse buildings in Virginia into context:

> *"...the courtrooms of colonial Virginia shared many of the same features as those found in the Beverley guildhall in the East Riding of Yorkshire, the town hall in Bishop's Castle, Shropshire, and the Courthouse in Chester, Pennsylvania, but differences in the arrangement of the magistrates platform, clerk's table, and lawyer's bar testify to the impact of regional or provincial practices on a common legal culture."*

Thomas Jefferson, one of the signatories of the American Declaration of Independence and the third president of the United States, was personally fascinated by architecture and the role architecture can play in the development of a culture and as a unifying force in a newly emerging society. Jefferson was instrumental in establishing a standardized courthouse design in Virginia for both the interior layout of a courtroom and the exterior architectural style that would identify the function of the courthouse. The Jeffersonian standard became the dominant influence in courthouse design in other areas of the United States including New England. The connection between the Argyle Township Courthouse and an American meeting house and English courthouse prototypes was established through the Jeffersonian model for several courthouses in Nova Scotia and New Brunswick.

The front end of the roof of the building has a cupola which provided ventilation and in which a bell was installed. The bell was rung as a call to action for volunteers in the event of fires in the community and as a call to the community for community meetings. The date of the cupola is unknown but probably pre-dates the 1870 renovation. The presence and use of the bell tower reflects the multiple uses to which the courthouse was put. Most nineteenth-century county courthouses in both Nova Scotia and New Brunswick being constructed and paid for by the local county government served the county in various forms as community needs were identified.

The overall dimensions and design of the building were created from the configuration of the interior spaces, particularly the courtroom. They governed the placement of the doors, windows and external dimensions of the building.

The wood-frame building has neoclassical design elements in its external façade, particularly in its fenestration and front entrance which are Georgian by date and style. In the Georgian style, the eave returns on the front are supported by modest modillions. The corners of the courthouse are articulated with Tuscan Doric pilasters.

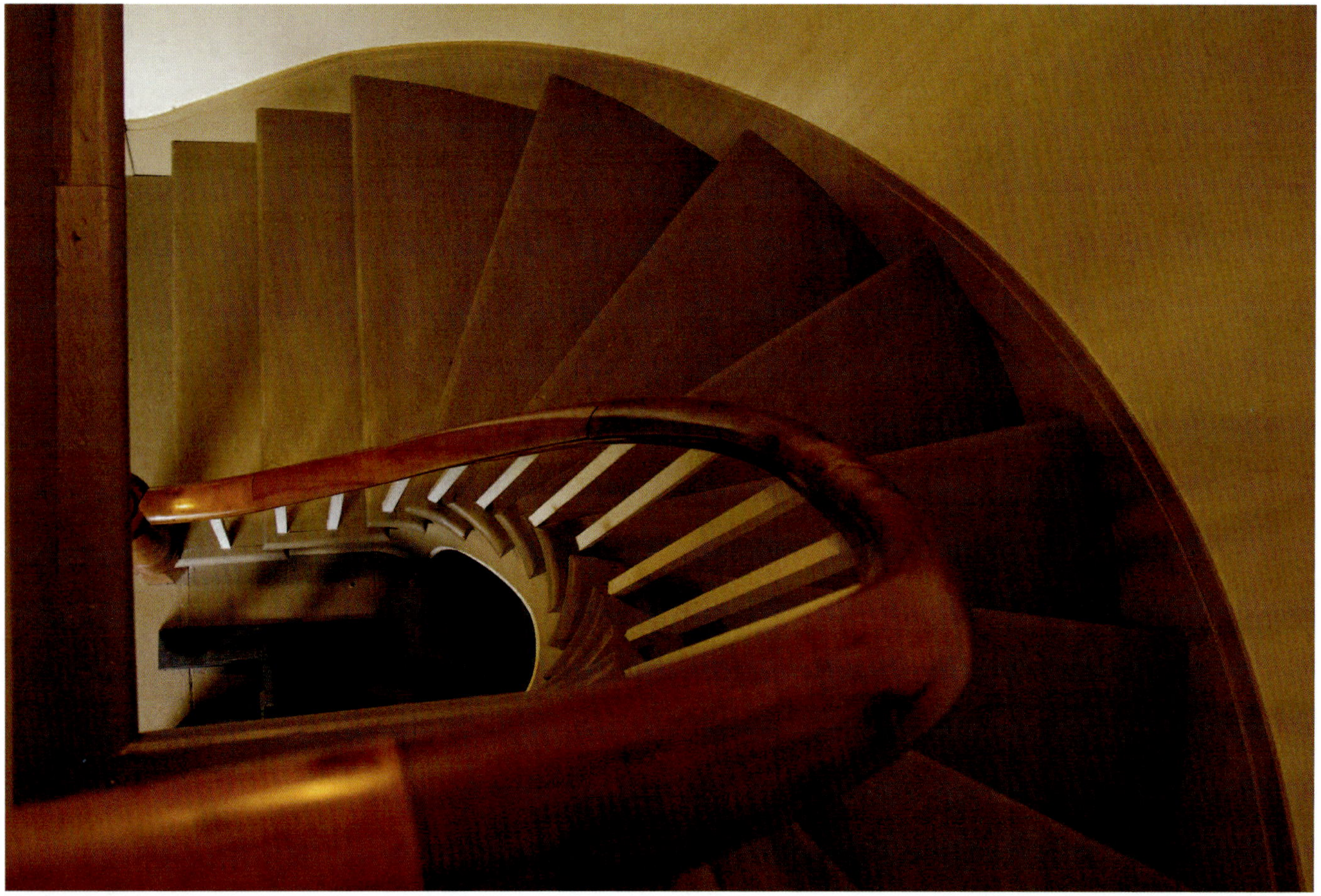

Left: *The curved staircase leading from the ground floor to the principal floor (piano nobile) where the courtroom is located.*

THE INTERIOR

The eighteenth-century English and American principles governing the architectural design of important public or private buildings required the principal room(s) to be on the second floor, the latter being known in classical terms as the *piano nobile*. The builders of the courthouse complied with those standards and installed the courtroom on the *piano nobile*. Subsequent additions to the courthouse included a segregated stairway for the judges, which was installed behind the courtroom and rose from a side entrance on the ground floor to the judge's chambers, located on the *piano nobile*.

There were two periods of reconstruction, 1833 and 1870, which together resulted in the original building being enlarged by one third of its original dimensions. The 1870s renovations were designed by architects, the Yarmouth firm of Kinney & Haley. They were primarily responsible for rebuilding the jail, creating a secure holding area. The ground floor enlargements enabled the installation of municipal services and offices for court officials. The second floor renovations created the judge's segregated staircase to chambers dedicated for his use, a jury room, a barristers' room for gowning and for interviewing clients. The building as it stands now is virtually identical to the building as completed after the 1870 renovations.

It became clear from an archaeological examination of the courthouse that a second floor courtroom was constructed at the same time as the jail. The lower ground floor jail cells were separated into two standards: three cells for those awaiting or convicted of criminal offenses and three cells for those persons imprisoned for debt. The latter were larger and somewhat more commodious. Neither would meet current standards of incarceration.

The stairway opens directly into the public seating area of the second floor courtroom. The public seating is configured as a stepped platform enabling excellent sight lines for all observers. The seating is in the form of extended

Windsor chairs (made locally), seating ten or twelve people. The style of the Windsor chairs is compatible with the date of construction of the original building, but there is no known proof of the actual date of construction. The activities conducted in a courtroom would constitute high entertainment for those members of the community not directly engaged in the court proceedings. It has been a fundamental tenet of the English legal system that justice must be seen to be done as well as be carried out. The public has a fundamental right to attend all court proceedings except those for which an order barring the public is obtained.

There is a balustrade (the "bar") separating the public seating area of the courtroom from its operational area. The justice's bench is opposite the bar, on an elevated dais. The clerk of the court has a desk in front of the justice, facing counsel. The courtroom now configured has the accused's dock in a segregated box against the bar facing the justice. It is believed to be in its original configuration, one aspect of which is noteworthy: the uppermost framing of the dock on the back projects significantly forward to a point at which the maximum discomfort would be experienced by an accused during the trial. The concept of innocence until guilt is proven was not a primary concern of the builders of the courthouse.

Counsel table was between the accused's dock and the clerk. As now configured there is one counsel table, oval in shape, one end chamfered to enable it to directly abut the dock putting it at right angles to the justice's bench. It is not known which side of the counsel table the Crown/plaintiff took and which counsel for the defendant took. In this configuration the accused could manually grasp whichever lawyer displeased him. It is quite possible the table as now arranged is the original location or shape of counsel table. The sharing of one table by both counsel is an early-nineteenth century practice found in several other early-to-mid-nineteenth century Nova Scotia and New Brunswick courtrooms. There are two jury boxes, one on each side of the courtroom enclosed in elevated segregated balustrades. The smaller jury box was for the use of the petit jury which was the trier of facts in a criminal or civil trial and the larger jury box was for the use of the grand jury. The ceiling is ornamented by a rosette that provides access to ventilation from the cupola.

The care and attention given by the local county and court officials in designing and building the Argyle Township Court House are typical of the high regard accorded the building as a component of community life. It corresponded

Above: *The tiered public gallery located at the back of the courtroom with its locally crafted Windsor benches.*

exactly with the objectives and personal interest in such projects by such officials in similar buildings in England at this time. Christopher Chalkin in his 1998 book entitled *English Counties and Public Buildings* stated that

> *"County Halls are intended to provide suitable accommodation for quarter session assizes and county courts. They symbolize the community spirit of the county and esteem of its rulers. This was reflected in dear materials, a splendid facade or palatial rooms, or all of them, similar to larger contemporary country houses."*

The Argyle Township Court House and Gaol was declared a National Historic Site in 2005.

ANNAPOLIS COUNTY COURT HOUSE
ANNAPOLIS ROYAL, NOVA SCOTIA

The Annapolis County Court House located in the town of Annapolis Royal in the Province of Nova Scotia was constructed in 1837 in a neoclassical architectural style known as Palladian. It is one of the oldest courthouses in Canada in continuous service as a courthouse. An earlier British colonial-era court is believed to be the first court in British North America to apply English common law. It serves as both a courthouse and as a jail for short-term incarcerations usually for accused awaiting trial. The courthouse was designed by the Grand Jury of the county with the assistance of the builder Francis Le Cain. Their choice of external architectural style and the internal configuration of the courtroom were heavily influenced by English standards but with American influences as well.

Justice was administered in this community commencing in 1605 during the French colonial period. At that time Port Royale was a French military stronghold and served as the capital of Acadia. Port Royale changed hands on several occasions between the French and the English, with the last of the military battles resulting in continental Acadia becoming British under the Treaty of Utrecht in 1713. After this territory shifted from French to British control, courts of justice were convened and justice administered by the British military governors. The British renamed Port Royale Annapolis Royal and constructed a fort they named Fort Anne. British Fort Anne was constructed by Scots military personnel in 1629 and is still standing contained the earliest courtroom in this area of British North America.

Opposite page: Annapolis County Court House, the courtroom as reconfigured in the Colonial Revival style after a fire in the early 20th century.

THE EXTERIOR

The exterior design of the courthouse closely resembles that of Villa Emo completed in 1565 in the Veneto region of northeastern Italy to architectural plans prepared by Vincenzo Scamozzi. He was a pupil of and adherent to the architectural principles developed by the highly accomplished and influential early Renaissance architect Andreas Palladio. Villa Emo was a private palace-like residence of a nobleman situated in an extensive acreage dedicated to farming and formal gardens.

There is no similarity between the interior of Villa Emo and the Annapolis County Court House – the Palladian architectural standards were applied to a wide range of public and private buildings in the eighteenth and nineteenth centuries. Palladianism became the dominant influence in the development of neoclassical architecture during the Renaissance throughout Europe. That Villa Emo as an external design was choosen as the model for the courthouse attests to the high regard the builders had for the importance of the courthouse in the community it was to serve.

The front elevation is symmetrical and dominated by a projecting porch, called a portico, which rises to a pediment at the roof level. The ground floor level of the portico is infilled to create a ground floor entry bordered on each side by a window having Georgian proportions with nine over six lights. The roof of the ground floor entrance is the floor of the portico. The portico has four well proportioned Tuscan Doric columns which rise from the floor of the portico to support the pediment. Mounted on the face of the building immediately behind the

Above: *The roof-mounted cupola admitted air into the courtroom below.*

columns are "shadows", in the classical tradition known as pilasters. In the flat reduced scale the pilasters have the same width as the structural columns. Centred on the floor level of the portico is the entrance comprised of double doors, each of which contain six bevelled panels in the classic Georgian manner. Access to the entrance is by a pair of exterior granite staircases one on each side of the portico. Wrought iron railings are embedded in the granite staircases. The double doors of the entrance are surmounted by a neoclassical Georgian fan light. The tympanum of the pediment is unadorned, except with the words "court house".

The roof is a hipped roof with a shallow flare as the roof line transitions to the eaves. Four chimneys, two on each exterior wall of the building originally provided an outlet for the wood stoves which were the source of heat for the building. All but one of the chimneys has been removed. The windows on the *piano nobile* contain six over six lights as one would expect in a late Georgian Palladian style.

The first floor level is constructed of evenly dressed blocks of granite on the front elevation and rusticated blocks on the sides and back. The principal floor is wood-framed. The wood surfaces of the *piano nobile* are covered in rough cast – a stucco material which is painted to look like stone giving the entire building the appearance that its exterior walls are constructed of stone.

THE INTERIOR

The principal floor is located on *piano nobile*. The ground floor space in the courthouse contains holding cells for the jail and for administrative support staff. It also contains a door and staircase at the back of the building which provides a segregated entrance to the courthouse and access to the second floor courtroom for the judges, including the superior court justices.

The courtroom is on the *piano nobile* and occupies most of the space on that level. The double front doors lead into a hallway which extends across the interior front of the building. From that entry hall double doors lead into the courtroom.

Most of the original arrangements of spaces in the courtroom remain as configured at the time of construction, notwithstanding an extensive fire which destroyed most of the interior early in the twentieth century. The decorative elements such as the balustrades that created the segregated spaces in the courtroom including the bar of the courtroom, the grand jury box, the petit jury box and the witness boxes are in much the same location as before the fire. The design of these elements is similar to the original but in the Colonial Revival style architecture popular at the time of rebuilding. The prisoner's dock has been altered to create an internal platform enabling it to serve as a plinth for an extraordinary statue of Lady Justice which is dated to 1795. She appears to be carved from wood and is painted to give a marked liveliness to the statue. The wood used in the extensive decorative elements in the courtroom is birch, stained or varnished to look like a more luxurious wood like mahogany.

The judge's bench is predictably on an elevated dais, but with the novelty of a panelled box built into each end of the bench. Each box is approximately three feet in height and comprised of angled panels on each of its four sides which provide a broken line for the judge's bench but one that provides an anchor and visual interest to the composition. The box to the left of the presiding judge is the witness box (where the witnesses in a trial sit or stand to give evidence), and the box to the right of the judge was designed for the use of the accused in a criminal trial.

Counsel tables are aligned parallel to each other in front of the judge and clerk. The counsel table closest to the judge is occupied by the Crown prosecutor in a criminal case, or plaintiff's counsel in a civil matter. The table behind is for defence counsel in a criminal trial or counsel for a defendant in a civil trial. Beside counsel tables are two segregated areas, one on each side of the courthouse. One is for the grand jury box, the other for the petit jury box.

Grand juries have long been abolished, but Nova Scotia was the last to do so in 1984. Grand juries were not part of a judicial proceeding. They were convened for various community purposes, and in criminal matters would serve to review the Crown's evidence to determine whether there was sufficient evidence to have the accused stand trial. The petit jury is the classic jury comprised of the accused's peers who sit in judgment on the facts. In jury trials it is the jury that determines the facts; essentially determining guilt or innocence in a criminal matter and liability in civil matters. The grand jury and the petit jury did not sit at the same time, so why there was a segregated space for both is unknown, although the designers of buildings in neoclassical styles required harmony, balance and proportion which resulted in a visual balance in the composition of the room on both sides. Several other early nineteenth century Nova Scotia and New Brunswick courtrooms have similar interior spacial arrangements.

The ceiling of the courtroom is a deep coved recess in the middle of which there is a grid pattern aperture which rises to a glazed cupola mounted on the roof, now blocked. At one time it provided air and/or light into the courtroom.

The principle of segregation is carefully maintained in the construction of the courthouse – separating the judge from the parties appearing before the judge, the judge from the lawyers and the public from the judge and the parties.

The Annapolis County Court House serves both Supreme Court justices and Provincial Court judges. Judges of both levels of the court system sit occasionally at prescribed times while on circuit from one rural court to another.

The Annapolis County Court House has been the non-military and judicial architectural focal point for the whole of Annapolis County. In 1937 ceremonial bearings of the Dominion of Canada as issued on November 21, 1937 were mounted on a wall in the courtroom. Reflecting its civic importance to the people of the county, in 1994 a special dedication of the courthouse was made.

Above: The exterior design of the courthouse closely follows a 1588 Italian Villa, "Villa Emo", in the Palladian style.

The plaque commemorating the dedication reads:
> *"on behalf of the Municipality of Annapolis County, it is my honour and pleasure as warden to co-dedicate the main courtroom of the Annapolis Royal Courthouse in the name of Micmac (sic) grand chief, Memberton Grand Sagamore of the Micmac, Canada's First Nation Grand Chief."*

The plaque was signed by Ben Silliboy as Grand Chief and Warden Henry R. Delong as Grand Warden.

The Annapolis County Court House was designated as a National Historic Site on the 14th day of August 1994.

RICHMOND COUNTY COURT HOUSE
ARICHAT, NOVA SCOTIA

The Richmond County Court House, located in the Community of Arichat on Cape Breton Island, in the Province of Nova Scotia, was designed and built by Alexander McDonald in 1847. That was eight years before he constructed a similar courthouse in Antigonish and before construction of the Sherbrooke courthouse eleven years later.

In 1847 Arichat, which is located at the eastern entrance of the Strait of Canso, was one of the most prosperous communities in the Maritimes because, during the age of sail, Arichat had a key location on one of the most important shipping routes into the Gulf of St. Lawrence.

THE EXTERIOR

The Arichat courthouse, like its later counterparts built by Alexander McDonald in Antigonish and Sherbrooke, was constructed in the Greek Revival style with a portico and interior peristyle (columned) courtroom in the Ionic style. The exterior of the Arichat Courthouse has been substantially altered with a replacement of the columns (from the Ionic order to pre-fabricated Tuscan Doric), and the windows from storey-and- a-half, double wood sash windows to vinyl windows broken into two parallel units. The original double door entrance has been replaced with somewhat neoclassical modern doors. The building is

Opposite page: Richmond County Court House, the first of three similar courthouses designed by Alexander MacDonald of Antigonish.

an extraordinary early example of a Nova Scotia Greek Revival courthouse; it is much loved and respected by the people of Isle Madame, of which Arichat is the principal community.

THE INTERIOR

The interior of the Richmond County Court House differs significantly from those of Antigonish and Sherbrooke. The courtroom occupies virtually all of the interior, with the exception of an interior entry vestibule (added later) and infilled offices and passageways adjacent to the courtroom. It is similar to the Antigonish courthouse inasmuch it has the Ionic order as the decorative element in the interior columns. The columns are virtually identical to those in Antigonish. The Arichat building does not have second storey galleries similar to the Antigonish courthouse.

The dominant features in the courtroom are: 1) a domed ceiling supported by an entablature in the Ionic order. The entablature is in turn supported by the original Ionic columns; 2) an elevated gallery along the north wall of the courtroom on which the Judge's bench is centred; 3) a pair of stairways on either side of the bench leading from the floor of the courtroom to the elevated gallery; 4) a balustrade along the judge's gallery similar to those installed in the later Antigonish and Sherbrooke courtrooms; and 5) an unusual architectural feature at the south end of the courtroom which is a gallery of similar height and proportions to the Judge's gallery, also fronted by a balustrade. One half lawyers, accused/litigants from the public. The space within the balustraded area followed the New England precedent of a large table at which counsel for the parties would sit facing each other. In making submissions to the court, counsel would stand and face the judge. The photographs also reveal that there were at least two wood stoves in the courtroom with suspended pipes leading to chimneys on the roof. The configuration of the main floor area is similar to other early-nineteenth century courthouses in Nova Scotia and New Brunswick.

The courthouse was combined with a jail. (The cells were constructed contemporaneously or nearly so, with the construction of the courthouse, and are currently remarkable for being little altered since their construction).

The Arichat courthouse has been removed from courthouse service. The floor area of the former courtroom has been cleared of balustrade enclosures and courtroom paraphernalia. It now serves effectively as a council chamber for the local municipality and as a venue for some community activities.

Above: The judge's dais and gallery. The balustrade is original. The Ionic columns supporting the judge's desk are also original.

of the balustrade is designed to be manually removed to create seating for the public, probably for community meetings or concerts, on bleachers that would be installed for public viewing of court proceedings or community events.

The main floor level of the courtroom is substantially altered and bears little resemblance to the original configuration of spaces. From nineteenth century photographs it is clear that the floor level was virtually all a service or functional area for court-related purposes surrounded by a balustrade to segregate the clerk,

As the oldest of the three similar courthouses constructed by Alexander McDonald of Antigonish and having an extraordinary example of neoclassical craftsmanship in the balustrades and Ionic columns, this building deserves to be restored to its external original architectural features including the columns, windows, entrance doors and cladding.

In an historical assessment of the building conducted for the Canadian Inventory of Historic Buildings, a descendant of Alexander McDonald is reported

Above: *A notable feature of this courthouse is the platform at the back of the courtroom on which community entertainments would be staged. The center section of the banister lifts away to create an opening to the public seating in the middle of the courtroom.*

Right: *The fluted Ionic columns are carved from a solid tree trunk. The details of the capitals and the entablature above are technically correct for a building in the Greek Revival style.*

to have informed researchers working on this building that Alexander McDonald travelled to Maine where he obtained plans and modelled the three courthouses attributed to him on a courthouse he observed there. The three courthouses are basically New England meeting houses with a courtroom infrastructure.

The Arichat courthouse conformed to the standards of British Colonial courthouses in its allocation of space for the conduct of court business and the segregation of the principals functioning in the space, but the architectural design had its origins in New England.

QUEENS COUNTY COURT HOUSE
LIVERPOOL, NOVA SCOTIA

The Queens County Court House located in the Town of Liverpool, in Queens County, in the Province of Nova Scotia, was constructed in 1854 to design(s) created by William G. Hammond. Construction was carried out by George W. Boehner, a local carpenter. Both Mr. Hammond and Mr. Boehner were residents of Liverpool.

The Liverpool courthouse is a remarkable architectural achievement. It is an outstanding example of the Greek Revival style of architecture favoured in New England.

This building is a reminder of the close ties and continuing connections between New England and the Maritimes. The designer of the Liverpool courthouse chose as his precedents, or models, the buildings he would have observed and visited in New England. The Greek Revival style in post-revolutionary America was one of its two earliest National Styles. The Greek Revival style had its origin in the ancient world of Greece but was rediscovered after the Ottoman Empire, which governed Greece, opened access to foreigners to Greece in the late eighteenth century. As a specific style it became popular in Britain and other areas of Europe. The Americans adopted the style as theirs and gave it an expression that became identifiably American. In part that singularity arose from

Right: Details of the Doric entablature and fluted columns in the portico.

Opposite page: The architectural details of the Doric order configuration of this Greek Revival building are technically correct and elegantly presented.

the fact that the American buildings were primarily built of wood, whereas the originals in Greece and as reinterpreted in Britain and Europe were in brick or stone. The style was chosen as a deliberate policy by the Government of the United States to give dignity, continuity and authority to the fledgling nation.

The designer and builder were both familiar with the American buildings but so too were many of the residents of the county who had their origins in New England, having emigrated in the 1780s as Loyalists. The availability of wood in the county as a cheap source of building materials also encouraged the adoption of the American style.

THE EXTERIOR

Construction of a Greek Revival building in wood was not inconsistent with the standards of the original Greek architecture. The greatest example of classical Greek architecture is the Parthenon in Athens on the hill known as the Acropolis. It is constructed of stone quarried from a nearby hill.

There is a particular connection between the wood-constructed Liverpool courthouse and classical Greek architecture. It lies in the fact that Greek temples were constructed of wood before the later stone temples such as the Parthenon. The wood frame elements of construction of the early Greek temples were the origin of the design elements of classical Greek architecture. Elements of the original construction of temples like the post and beam framing became the stone pillars which support the portico (a porch) and the corner boards (called pilasters) giving definition to the building. In the Liverpool courthouse there is a correctly proportioned layered frieze which would originally have been lintels connecting to the upright posts forming part of the framing. The frieze contains decorative elements that had their origins in wood frame ancient Greek temples. There are other elements of the design that are similarly parts of the original wood frame construction, namely the metopes and triglyphs. The triglyphs are the vertical blocks with fluting. They were originally the exterior end of the framing of the ceiling on which the roof would have been built. Today we would call these blocks joist ends. The flat areas between the triglyphs, the metopes, were the portion of the lintel continuing the length of the building on top of the posts into which the triglyphs (joists) were inserted in a mortise and tenon fashion.

The Liverpool courthouse accurately represents a classical Greek temple and, being constructed in wood, the architectural elements are true to the original sources of Greek temple architecture.

The front of the Liverpool courthouse is dominated by the portico. The wooden columns in the portico are in the Doric order which is the first of the three classical Greek orders. The columns are correct in an even number (4) and proportioned correctly to the standards of the style. A classical Doric order column has a slight bulge in the middle called entasis, created to correct for an optical illusion that would give a distorted narrowing. There is, also correctly, no base for the columns. The top of the columns have a squared element called

an astragal, against which the flattened circular capital at the top of the column rests. Both are correctly configured. The top of the portico has a forward-facing triangular element called a pediment and between the framing of the eaves of the pediment a simple triangle called the tympanum. On the walls of the building immediately behind the Doric columns are "shadows" of those columns called pilasters which replicate, but on the flat, the proportions of the columns in the round.

The portico has a large entrance into the building with a neoclassical framing in which double panelled doors are located. The doors appear to be original. Great care has been taken in the conservation of this building. That is evident in the new door constructed on the left side of the building to enable wheelchair access. That door exactly replicates the originals in the front entrance.

The front entrance is bordered on each side by a Georgian-styled window, both of which are correctly centred between the columns and proportioned to the space between the columns.

The exterior cladding of the courthouse is designed to give the illusion of being ashlar or dressed stone. The exterior of the building, like that of the Annapolis Royal Court House, is covered in stucco designed to give the impression it is constructed of stone. The attempt to give the solidity of stone is enhanced by the surface application of a paint and sand combination. Therefore, the surface has the feel of sandstone. The colour reinforces that deliberate image. This method of creating a stone-like exterior from wood was used in several prominent buildings in southern England and elsewhere in the Maritimes. Government House in Charlottetown, now known as Fanningbank, built in 1834-1837, originally had a similar finish but it did not age well in our climate and within twenty years was covered with shingles.

The sides of the courthouse have windows of the same size and proportions as those in the portico, thereby providing continuity, balance and harmony in the design.

The roof is a shallow-pitched gable roof. It is sheathed in slate.

The overall external composition of the courthouse is highly accomplished and connected to both the American nineteenth century application of the style and its ancient Greek origins. The use of the Greek Revival style is an allusion to democracy and many of our principles of justice, including the concept of public involvement in trial by jury and access by the public to viewing the judicial process. The right to observe the exercise of justice and justice appearing to be done were Greek principles of justice lost for centuries, until it became reintroduced in the English standards of justice 1500 years later.

THE INTERIOR

The interior of the courthouse, while refreshed and somewhat modernized, retains the fundamental principles of English courthouse design. Upon entering the courthouse one passes from a small vestibule into the courtroom. The judge's bench is on the back wall and rests on a raised dais with a shallow apse-like recess behind it. The jury box is on the left wall. The prisoner's dock has been removed as a gesture to the modern emphasis of an accused appearing to be innocent until proven guilty. The accused in this courtroom sits adjacent to the presiding justice. The court clerk sits in a segregated area in front of the justice – facing counsel and the public. The lawyers are at counsel tables facing the clerk and the justice. Behind counsel is the bar of the courtroom, behind which the public sits.

The ceiling is a recessed cove with an elegant chandelier in keeping with the character of the building.

Few courtrooms in the Maritimes have been so honoured and respected by their keepers. The architectural integrity of the building has been faithfully and accurately preserved. The interior functioning of the courtroom has been

Above: *The elevated Judge's bench and dais are original. The courtroom has been beautifully renovated and decorated in keeping with the style of the building.*

marginally altered except as has been necessary for modern changes in the philosophy of the delivery of justice.

This building is a pleasure to view and inspect. It is one of the architectural treasures of Nova Scotia and Canada.

ANTIGONISH COUNTY COURT HOUSE
ANTIGONISH, NOVA SCOTIA

Many early nineteenth century courthouse designs in Nova Scotia and New Brunswick, in their architectural features and their internal spacial arrangements, were influenced by contemporaneous popular taste in decorative styles prevailing in the provinces at the time of construction. They were also heavily influenced by similar buildings in the New England States.

The Antigonish County Court House, located at 170 Main Street in the Town of Antigonish, in the Province of Nova Scotia, was designed and constructed in 1855 by local master builder Alexander McDonald in the highly popular Greek Revival style. It was the second of three similar courthouses designed by McDonald in northeastern Nova Scotia, the first being Richmond County Court House (see page 65). That style was prevalent in New England and was considered to be a National Style in the United States at the time of the construction of the Antigonish courthouse.

There was a substantial American influence on the arts and culture of the Maritimes in the mid-nineteenth century, particularly in Nova Scotia and New Brunswick. While the Greek Revival style was popular and extensively applied in buildings in Great Britain in the first half of the nineteenth century, no court houses resembling the Antigonish courthouse were built there. The courthouses built in the Maritimes were a colonial expression of the principles of English courthouse standards but in an American-influenced architectural style

Opposite page: Antigonish County Court House, one of the three similar courthouses designed by Alexander MacDonald, in the Greek Revival style, modelled on an American meeting house.

constructed in wood, usually created by a local craftsman such as Alexander McDonald utilizing local materials.

THE EXTERIOR

The front elevation is a symmetrical, well proportioned elegant building with a front-facing gable roof and storey-and-a-half rectangular configuration. It is framed by corner boards, referred to as pilasters, which complement the full Ionic columns supporting the portico. The portico is accurate to the Greek Revival style in having a layered architrave which runs across the full width of the façade below the roofline. The pediment has an unembellished tympanum as one would expect from the Greek Revival style employed in a small scale courthouse. The windows extend upwards a storey-and-a-half; they originally provided direct sunlight into the two storey courtroom. The lower portion of the windows became separated from the courtroom when an enclosed vestibule was created across the interior front of the building. It provided protection from the cold during the winter months, added security and some noise control from the public passageway into the courtroom.

THE INTERIOR

The interior of the courthouse contains one courtroom. It is a remarkable chamber, containing all the elements of segregation, dignity and authority that mid-nineteenth century courthouses required. The courtroom occupies

Above: *Details of the Greek Ionic Order fluted columns and capitals used as the decorative theme in the interior of the courtroom.*

virtually all the interior space of the building with the exception of service areas, passageways and offices on the left and right hand sides of the building, infilling the space below the gallery which extends the full depth of the courtroom on both sides. The courtroom is, in classical language, a peristyle hall, which brings the origins of the design back to Greek architectural principles.

The balconies are accessed by stairs located at the left and right hand end of the vestibule. They are original.

The public entrance to the courtroom is from the vestibule. The vestibule expands into an enlarged entrance hall in the centre of the vestibule in front of the double front doors. There are two doors into the courtroom from this entrance hall, into the left and right sides of the public seating areas of the courtroom.

The choice of the Ionic column as the classical order of the columns, with their finely carved capital, is a remarkable choice; the Ionic column with its volutes is more difficult to fashion than the Doric order which was usually chosen. The choice is a testament to the importance the local community gave to its principal civic building. The Antigonish County Court House was as fashionable at the time of its construction as any in rural Nova Scotia and a testimony to the pride and confidence the people of the county had in their community and its future.

Courthouses in rural areas such as Antigonish in the 1850s were used for many community activities as well as for court purposes. In many aspects, the courthouse and local churches were the primary community centres and attracted a wide range of social and administrative activities.

English courtroom protocols were often altered in the colonies to reflect local traditions for procedures created to meet local needs such as a community hall and administrative centre. Such is the case at the Antigonish courthouse. The courthouse served both the Supreme Court and County Court in Antigonish County.

A unique procedure was followed in this courthouse when the Supreme Court circuit justice sat in the courthouse and there were no criminal trials to be heard: the prosecutor rose and presented white gloves to the presiding justice. Another novelty in this courthouse relates to the use of a gavel. Gavels were not a standard device for establishing order in an English court; a local worthy is reported to have attended a Liberal Convention in Ottawa at which Lester Pearson was elected leader of the Liberal Party in 1958. The enthusiastic local delegate brought back the gavel used at the convention and presented it to the Antigonish courthouse. Thereafter it was used by presiding judges as an instrument for establishing order in the courtroom.

The Antigonish courtroom has been preserved with considerable care demonstrating affection and appreciation for the special role the courthouse has played in the history and the ongoing life of the County – and also demonstrates a commitment to conserve this exceptional example of its built heritage.

There is a plaque affixed to the front of the courthouse erected by the Historic Sites and Monuments Board of Canada after the courthouse was designated as a National Historic Site of Canada, which in part reads "...(the courthouse) is one of the best examples in Nova Scotia of the typical mid-nineteenth century Maritime Courthouse." While internal modernization has occurred to the functional elements of the courtroom, the renovations carefully retain the principles of mid-nineteenth century courthouse standards in its spacial elements.

Similar courthouses to the Antigonish courthouse were designed and constructed by Alexander McDonald in both Arichat, the Richmond County Court House (as noted above) and in Sherbrooke, Nova Scotia.

Above: While the courtroom has been renovated, most of the original layout and decorative details have been kept. Counsel tables in the foreground conform with modern standards not the original.

HALIFAX COUNTY COURT HOUSE
HALIFAX, NOVA SCOTIA

The original configuration of the Halifax County Court House located at 5250 Spring Garden Road in the City of Halifax, the capital of the Province of Nova Scotia, was constructed between 1860 and 1861. It was a replacement for the Supreme Court facilities which formed part of the principal constituent elements of the Provincial Legislative Building known as Province House.

The Halifax County Court House was designed by Toronto architects William Thomas and Son following an invitation for tenders called by the Government of Nova Scotia. At the time of the design and construction of the courthouse, Nova Scotia was a colony of Great Britain, with a form of government known as Responsible Government. Unlike courthouses located elsewhere in the colony, the Halifax courthouse was built under the supervision and direction of the government of the colony and at its cost.

Right: The principal entrance into the courthouse. The vermiculation of the rusticated masonry on the ground floor is one of the defining characteristics of this building.

Opposite page: The Halifax County Court House. Details of the Roman Triumphal Arch are displayed. Note the exceptional carved masonry details in the carvings and rustication.

THE EXTERIOR

The exterior of the courthouse conforms to the standards of courthouse design in the English law courts tradition. It is monumental and in a highly prominent location in the city, intended to be one of its most imposing structures. It was designed to impress, intimidate and assert the authority of the rule of law and the administration of justice. While the courthouse now has one of the most significant locations in the city, at the time of construction its site was considered to be inconvenient by the lawyers and justices because it was some distance from the centre of the business and legal community of Halifax. It was, however, an appropriate location as it was constructed on the lawn of Government House, the residence of the Lieutenant Governor of the Province. The nexus between Queen Victoria as the fount of justice in the person of her representative, the Lieutenant Governor, and the courthouse was significant as it followed the tradition of placing the principal courthouse proximate to the Crown. The former Supreme Court facilities in Province House also expressed that tradition as the Supreme Court courtroom was located on the *piano nobile* of that building between the Legislative Council Chamber (site of the throne symbolizing the presence of the monarch in the colony) and the General Assembly of the colony.

Above: *Each keystone in the Romanesque windows located on the ground floor has a unique carving. This carving is of Neptune, the Roman god of the sea.*

Right: *This is one of two pavilions in the Greek Revival style added at both ends of the original building forming the third phase of its construction.*

The Halifax courthouse was constructed in four phases: 1) the 1860-1861 building in the centre of the front elevation as it is today; 2) a wing at the back of the courthouse constructed in 1881-1882 parallel to the original, joined to the original by a hyphen (a connecting link) 3) the east wing; and 4) the west wing. The latter were constructed in 1908 and 1930. As the size and economic importance of the city grew, the requirement for additional court services and justices also grew, hence the requirements for the additions.

The original element of the courthouse, the central element, as designed by William Thomas is a four storey building of a neoclassical design referred to as Palladian. The Palladian design attribution rises from the exterior front elevation architectural style being based on the architectural principles and construction practices of Andrea Palladio (1508-1580), who was one of the most influential Italian architects of the early Renaissance. Palladio's published pattern books and textual guidelines to other architects and builders served as the primary influence in the creation of eighteenth century British Georgian architecture. The Halifax County Court House can be said to be Palladian in that sense, although the architectural style could be more specifically referred to as Georgian architecture heavily influenced by Romanesque design elements, which had their origins in ancient Rome.

The defining element in the architectural style of the building is the choice of column. The columns are located on the second floor of the front elevation

Right: *The principal staircase leading from the ground floor to the piano nobile where the original supreme court trial courtroom and Court of Appeal courtroom are located.*

(the *piano nobile*, the principal floor). They are in the Tuscan Doric order with prominent horizontal banding. They are engaged columns and in two configurations. The first are in the round and are centred in an architectural composition which resembles a Roman Triumphal Arch. The second are paired engaged rectilinear columns also having prominent horizontal banding. The horizontal banding employed as a design element in all six columns is characteristic of a particularly robust form of Tuscan columns – used in the nineteenth century for courthouses, prisons and public buildings intended to present an emphatic, intimidating and dominant presence in the community.

The Halifax County Court House in its original form as a neoclassical building presents a front elevation containing three stories. Each floor level has windows that are symmetrically balanced on the façade. In addition to the three stories containing windows, there is a basement level in which holding cells are located for prisoners awaiting transfer to a courtroom for trial.

The ground floor of the original building is divided into three segments. The middle segment projects as an applied or flattened portico. It is approximately one half of the width of the building. The whole of the portico is designed, as noted, on the model of a Roman Triumphal Arch. On the second floor, centred between the Tuscan columns referred to above in the *piano nobile,* are three round-headed Palladian windows. On the ground floor below the Palladian windows are three round-headed arches. The central arch contains the principal entrance to the building. The two adjacent arches frame windows giving light to interior spaces.

Above the third level of the Roman Triumphal Arch is an entablature that forms part of the arch which in turn supports the pediment.

Adjacent to the central element of the original building, the Roman Triumphal Arch, are two windows on each of the three floors. The first and second floor windows have round-headed Romanesque windows with broad articulated architraves surmounted by a keystone. Each of the keystones is designed to display the mason's skills in the carving of the decorative details. The building is animated by numerous highly articulated carved decorative

Above: The second floor courtroom located in the second phase of construction of the courthouse. The transverse-beamed ceiling is a highly accomplished example of local craftsmanship.

around the front and sides. Each block of the quoins is individually rusticated. On close examination it appears that few of the quoins have the same pattern of rustication.

One of the most decorative features of the masonry is found in the rustication located on the ground floor of the Roman Triumphal Arch. Each block of the rustication is vermiculated. Vermiculation is a carving on the face of a block of stone used in rusticating a level of masonry. Vermiculation resembles worm holes carved into the stone. The application of vermiculation adds shadow highlights and movement to an otherwise static surface.

The front elevation of the Halifax County Court House is one of the most elaborate and sophisticated architectural compositions of the mid-nineteenth century in the Maritimes. It perfectly represents in its architecture the purpose of the building and the atmosphere the functions conducted within present to the public. It establishes solemnity, dignity, power and authority.

The wings added laterally to the front elevation by contrast with the original building are relatively simple. They are primarily in a complementary Greek Revival style. The architects of the two wings were careful not to attempt duplication of the original design elements and to separate but connect them to the original. The two wings are self-contained pavilions with a hyphen connecting them to the original. The resultant architectural composition of the front elevation, although constructed in three phases, presents an effective and integrated architectural composition.

The building originally had a cupola centred on the roof, located on the ridge line of the roof behind the pediment. The cupola was removed many years ago.

elements. The ground floor level of the Roman Triumphal Arch, the central element of the original building, has keystones carved in the shape of faces resembling Neptune, the Roman god of the sea, with flowing beards that link the faces with the arch below.

Between the round-headed arches of the first floor of the Roman Arch are medallions carved by the highly skilled masons, in the form of lion heads.

The corners of the front elevation are framed by quoins which extend from ground level to the frieze which runs below the eave line of the building

THE INTERIOR

The interior of the Halifax County Court House presently configured is comprised of six courtrooms. All of the courtrooms were used as the principal seat of the Supreme Court of Nova Scotia (trial division) and the Nova Scotia Court of Appeal until 1971. Starting in 1971 the building was used as the Provincial Library, continuing until 1985. It was returned to courthouse use in 1985 as the principal Provincial Court in the province. The Provincial Court has a provincially appointed judiciary and deals primarily with criminal and quasi-criminal matters.

The interior of the building, although it is now a Provincial Court, is relevant to this book as several of the courtrooms are in their original nineteenth century Supreme Court configurations – or have sufficient details to identify the original courtroom.

The principal entrance to the building faces Spring Garden Road and leads into a substantial hall which contains an imperial staircase. At the top of the staircase the two original courtrooms are located. The courtroom to one's right on the second floor, (the *piano nobile*) is the original Supreme Court courtroom.

Left: The original Supreme Court courtroom. The justice's bench and dais panelling are original. The decorative elements of the courtroom are in the Renaissance Revival style fashionable at the time of construction, also original.

Below: Details of the panelling in the justice's bench displaying the high degree of craftsmanship employed.

To the left is the original Court of Appeal courtroom.

The Supreme Court courtroom contains virtually all of its original elements. The most prominent feature of the room is the justice's bench and the elaborate dais paneling mounted on the wall behind the bench. It has a substantial height, terminating in a corbelled cove, giving it definition and dominance and identifying the placement and importance of the judiciary. The bar of the courtroom dividing the functional area of the courtroom from the extensive public seating is original, with its interconnected turned spindles. The second significant element of the decorative features of the room is the ceiling. It is comprised of a wood framed grid pattern, in the centre of which is an elaborate and remarkable medallion. The medallion is constructed of wood, carved to

create a rosette of eight acanthus leaves in spiral form, radiating from a central roundel which in turn has a central foliate design, apparently of a rose. The radiating acanthus leaf configuration is surrounded by three concentric circles of decorative detail.

The windows conform to the design of the exterior windows of the front elevation adjacent to the Roman Triumphal Arch. These are monumental and add to the elegance and dignity of the composition.

The former Court of Appeal has been substantially altered to bring it into conformity with its current use as a Provincial Court courtroom, but the decorative elements of the deeply coved, wood-framed ceiling and dado rail remain intact.

Above: The former Court of Appeal courtroom. Now configured as a Provincial Court courtroom but the wainscoting, doorways and ceilings are original.

Left: Detail of the entablature of the justice's dais panelling in the former supreme court courtroom.

Above: *A newly created courtroom displaying contemporary standards of courtroom design in a non-jury courtroom. This could be either a Provincial court or a supreme court courtroom.*

The 1880s addition to the courthouse located at the back of the building has an exceptionally fine transverse-beamed ceiling. The transverse-beams extend across the width of the courtroom and are supported on longitudinal bracketed beams running the length of the courtroom. The centre of each transverse-beam is further supported by a vertical post tying the ridgeline of the ceiling to the transverse-beam. The transverse- beam has additional support in the form of diagonal bracing between the vertical posts and the ceiling. The configuration of the framing is an elegant and highly accomplished form of joinery and is one of the highlights of the building. It also contains a stained glass window which depicts Lady Justice in the centre bay of a Palladian window located behind the judge's bench. This is the only extant decorative element in the building symbolizing justice and the purpose of the building.

Great emphasis has been given in describing the architectural components of this building and each of the courthouses profiled in this book. The reason is, as referred to in the Introduction, the appearance of a building articulates its relative importance in the community and, in the case of the Halifax County Court House, the moral and philosophical lessons to the citizenry to be taken from the building. The design of a courthouse invariably reflects the prevailing approach and attitude to the rule of law and the duty of the citizen at the time of its creation in the enforcement of law and order. The design of a well conceived public building in any era should convey a message as to its purpose and role. This courthouse does that effectively as an expression of the mid-nineteenth century concept of the law and the role the judiciary and legal procedures play in the Province.

The Halifax County Court House configured as the Supreme Court of Nova Scotia and the Nova Scotia Court of Appeal is the most elaborate and accurate expression of the English Courthouse traditions of the mid-nineteenth century found in the Maritime Provinces.

Above: *Details of the bracketed cornice and pressed-tin ceiling in the original courthouse.*

CUMBERLAND COUNTY COURT HOUSE
AMHERST, NOVA SCOTIA

The Cumberland County Court House located at 50 Victoria Street in the Town of Amherst, Nova Scotia was constructed of local sandstone between 1883 and 1889 as a replacement for an elegant wood frame Georgian style courthouse constructed in 1831 and destroyed by fire in 1887.

The new courthouse was designed by Nelson Beckwith of the nearby community of Baie Verte, New Brunswick. The attribution of the origin of the design arises from an article in the Amherst Gazette dated November 8, 1887 which referred to Mr. Beckwith as an architect who by that date had "... the deserved reputation of being a skillful architect and builder." *The Biographical Dictionary of Architects in Canada 1800 – 1850* confirms the identity of the architect.

THE EXTERIOR

The architectural elements in the neoclassical design of the front elevation of the courthouse include paired Tuscan Doric engaged columns supporting a broken (open-spaced) entablature with dentillation which in turn support an open pediment – all in the nature of a Roman Triumphal Arch. The double front doors are surmounted by a round-headed arch which projects into the tympanum. The

Right: The front entrance with its paired Tuscan Doric columns support a prominent pediment.

Opposite page: Cumberland County Court House; neo-classical in style, the building combines Romanesque and Greek design elements in a free-handed Victorian form.

with an oculus or circular window in the tympanum.

The roof has a hipped platform configuration with a dormer window on each side of the attic. The dormers are framed by fluted Tuscan Doric pilasters and capped by a triangular pediment.

The overall composition, while in varying neoclassical styles, creates consistent themes that unify the composition. It is an elegant and dignified addition to the centre of Amherst and established it, at the time of construction, as one of the most

voussoirs of the arch support the eaves of the pediment. The date of construction is embedded above the round-headed arch.

The entrance projects from the face of the building from the ground floor to the third level of the building terminating at the roof level. This projection creates a shadow line and breaks the front to give visual interest. On each side of the front entrance on the ground floor is a pair of round-headed windows in the Romanesque style, each containing a Renaissance Revival fan motif in the arch and a neoclassical keystone in the centre of the arch.

The decorative detail of the paired ground floor windows is repeated in a pair of windows on the second floor above the front entrance. The two windows on both sides of the central projecting bay adjacent to the paired windows above the entrance also have a neoclassical decorative element, in this case a triangular pediment – which serve as a capital for each window.

The central projecting bay of the front is capped at the roof line by a pediment

significant secular buildings in the town. It remains as such.

Mr. Beckwith also served as the master carpenter and was assisted in the construction of the building by John Weldon of Dorchester, New Brunswick and Jeremiah Embree of Amherst. The contractor was the Rhodes, Curry Co. a prominent building contractor in this area of Nova Scotia.

The Amherst courthouse served, until recently, as a local jail as well as a courthouse and at the back of the building there was a fenced jail yard which enabled the inmates to exercise.

The courthouse has served to house a superior court and a county court. As the complexities of the law developed in the second half of the twentieth century, specialization and separation of court facilities became necessary in Nova Scotia. It continues to serve as a court for matters falling within the jurisdiction of the Supreme Court of Nova Scotia and is serviced by a Justice who travels from courthouse to courthouse as needed.

THE INTERIOR

The Amherst courthouse conforms with the traditional English standards of courthouse use of space in most respects: segregation of the Judiciary, allocation of space for the lawyers representing the parties, public seating and access to trials and an open and accessible courtroom. The courtroom appears to be in its original configuration. The jury box against the front (south) wall of the courtroom is unusual as there is no segregation nor is there a secure passageway for the jury to gain access to the jury box. The jurors must cross the courtroom in front of the public, defence counsel and the accused/defendant. The Amherst courthouse is not unique in this regard as it is a factor dictated by the size of the building, which limits the creation of passage ways standard to a nineteenth century courthouse. It is similar to several other courthouses of this era in Nova Scotia and New Brunswick in its allocation of space and passageways.

Above: The second floor courtroom has been extensively renovated. Many of the traditional standards of courtroom layout have been removed.

VICTORIA COUNTY COURT HOUSE
BADDECK, NOVA SCOTIA

The Victoria County Court House, located at 495 Chebucto Street in the Town of Baddeck in Victoria County on Cape Breton Island, in the Province of Nova Scotia was constructed in 1889 to a design created by a local master carpenter Philip MacRae of Big Farm, Big Baddeck. In its original configuration it was asymmetrical, comprised of what is now the centre projecting element (pavilion) of the building and the recessed extension to the right. In 1967 an extension to the left of the centre pavilion was added. There was a further extension added in 1980.

THE EXTERIOR

The exterior design is neoclassical in its decorative elements. There are neoclassical pilasters dividing the windows on the second floor (the *piano nobile*) which are in the Tuscan Doric order. The pilasters support a layered entablature which extends to the roof line. The roof has a hipped roof configuration in the original building, but the later left wing extension has a simple flat roof. The entablature has projecting modillions; in original classical Greek architecture these were projecting structural beams, but in this case they are decorative only. The second floor windows have a pedimented hood decorative element. Below the second storey windows is a belt course in the nature of a narrow architrave supported by short Tuscan Doric pilasters which align with those above, dividing

Opposite page: The Victoria County Court House has neoclassical design elements on the second floor with its Tuscan Doric pilasters, pedimented window treatments and principal entrance details.

the windows. The lower pilasters rest on a rusticated granite base which also serves as cladding for the ground floor. The cladding on the second floor above the granite base is wood; the spaces between the windows and pilasters are sheathed with clapboard. The single most notable feature of the front is the entrance which is neoclassical in character. The door is surmounted by a fan light and above it a round-headed arch with a fan-like decorative element carved into the tympanum. The door has a galleried hood supported by paired, finely carved corbels.

While the exterior decorative elements are neoclassical in style, in typically Victorian fashion the configuration of the external massing of the building is not neoclassical. Victorian architects and builders liked to mix and match styles without regard to the origins of the styles or the proportions of the classical buildings from which the decorative elements came. However, the building is exceptionally attractive and beautifully maintained on its exterior.

THE INTERIOR

The interior conforms to the late nineteenth century English courthouse design standards respecting segregation, public access and the positioning of the courtroom. The courtroom is on the second floor (the *piano nobile*, the principal floor). There is a monumental stairway for the use of the public, the courthouse staff, the accused/litigants and the lawyers. The courthouse has a separate dedicated stairway intended to be for the exclusive use of the judiciary and the jury. The jury box has a secure access from a passageway behind the Justice's

Above: Courthouses were constructed of the finest materials, with the best available craftsmanship and the most fashionable designs. This 1890 staircase is original to the construction of the Victoria County Court House and combines all of these elements.

turn of the century, the size of the population and the scale and nature of crime led to a requirement for secure jails separated from the courthouse and away from the main urban areas.

The Victoria County Court House is the most significant civic building in a town of international significance, as evidenced by the inscription on the cairn (commemorating the life and achievements of Alexander Graham Bell, the inventor of the telephone) mounted on the front lawn of the courthouse. Numerous civic activities are held in or on the grounds of the courthouse, including Remembrance Day ceremonies. The building is an administrative centre for the town and for certain provincial government services.

Many of the changes to the interior of this highly important building are inappropriate and insensitive to the design and craftsmen-created decorative elements. But they are largely cosmetic. The interior of the courthouse could and should be returned to its original features. It is more than a simple courthouse. It is a symbol of the pride and commitment of the people of this town and county to their history and the buildings that embody that heritage. The staff and volunteers who work in and around the building are committed to its preservation. Restoration of the interior would be a fitting reward to all those who have, over many decades, dedicated themselves to its conservation.

bench and a secure jury room. This passageway is shared with the Justice but a doorway in this passage enables either the jury or the justice to divide the passage providing segregation of the Justice and jury from one another.

The courthouse also contains a jail. It is one of the few courthouses constructed in the late nineteenth century in Nova Scotia with a jail. By the

Above: The redecorated and renovated courtroom on the principal floor. The character but not the function of the room has been altered.

LUNENBURG COUNTY COURT HOUSE
LUNENBURG, NOVA SCOTIA

A courthouse listed 1970-71 on the Canadian Inventory of Historic Buildings is located in the Town of Lunenburg in the Province of Nova Scotia. It was constructed between 1891 and 1892 to architectural plans prepared by Halifax architect, Henry Busch. The courthouse no longer serves as a functioning courthouse. Its facilities have been taken over by the municipal government of the town and county. In fact, the municipal council meets in the former courtroom.

The exterior of the brick-clad building is designed having primarily Italianate architectural elements. The former courtroom retains some of the layout and internal structures of a superior court courtroom; but with the removal of many of its decorative and functional elements, it is difficult to interpret how the room would have functioned as a superior court courtroom.

Right: The double-doored neoclassical entrance into the courtroom.

Opposite page: Lunenburg County Court House. The courthouse is no longer in use as courthouse, but continues to serve the town for municipal purposes. The Romanesque architectural details of the front elevation create a handsome facade.

Passing mention of the building is required as it forms part of what is a World Heritage Site, one of only two urban areas in Canada so designated (the other being the Old Town of Quebec City). It continues to be identified in the town as the Old Courthouse.

Lunenburg contains a remarkable and highly important artifact remaining from the original 1775 wood frame courthouse. The 1775 building remains partially intact. In 1902 it was purchased by St. John's Anglican Church and was extensively renovated and converted into a parish hall. The artifact is a painting on a wall of the parish hall. It remains in its original form and composition and it was discovered during repairs to the wall. The painting formed part of the dais backdrop behind the judge's bench. It has been fully exposed and conserved and is one of the most extraordinary depictions of the principles of justice and the nexus between the administration of justice and the monarchy in the province. The Heritage Trust of Nova Scotia refers to it as a mural composed of oil on plaster, (the painting is believed to date from 1801). The painting is substantial in its dimensions and depicts a neoclassical plinth supporting a coat of arms. The coat of arms and the plinth are each approximately one half of the composition.

Above: *The original courtroom has several of its original decorative and courtroom elements, but serves now as a town council chamber.*

The coat of arms displays the armorial bearings of King George III of Great Britain and the Colony of Nova Scotia. In the centre of the circular shield is the motto of the Order of the Garter "Evil be to him who evil thinks." Below the shield is a ribbon-like banner that contains the royal motto "God and my right". To the left of the shield is the lion which represents royalty and to the right a unicorn, a fictitious beast, also symbolizing the British monarchy. The shield is surmounted by a cap of state, again symbolizing the monarch and the monarch's authority as head of state.

The plinth is sarcophagus-like in configuration emphasizing the neoclassical origins of its design. It also speaks to the dignity and longevity of the royal house whose arms are illustrated. In the centre panel of the plinth are words in Latin, "*Fait Justitia ruat coelum*". An accepted translation is "let justice be done, though heavens fall." The meaning of the expression is that even if, in extreme circumstances, social order is under threat and is in turmoil, justice must be done.

This mural with its message appears to be the oldest Canadian visible expression encapsulating the historic English principles of justice. These principles are found in both the Latin motto on the plinth and in the motto of the Order of the Garter, which is one of the highest honours that can be conferred on an individual in the United Kingdom. The presence of the coat of arms of George III emphatically asserts the inexorable connection between the Crown and the administration of justice and the principles to be applied in that administration. The size of the coat of arms and its placement in the courtroom emphasizes that connection.

That the 1775 Court House was adjacent to the Church of England is not happenstance. In the design and arrangement of British colonial towns, the principles of precedent and the symbols of authority were to be made manifest. The Legislative Building in each colony must be proximate to the vice-regal residence and to the established church, the Church of England, and to the law courts. Collectively they represent the principles of British governance. The current location of the mural proximate to the church in this county capital is therefore fitting and symbolic.

Above: An original Coat of Arms of King George III from the 1775 wood frame Lunenburg Court House, part of which is embedded in the St. John's Anglican Church parish hall. One of the earliest depictions of a monarchial Coat of Arms in any courthouse in Canada.

COLCHESTER COUNTY COURT HOUSE
TRURO, NOVA SCOTIA

The Colchester County Court House, also known as the Truro Courthouse located on 1 Church Street, in the Town of Truro, Nova Scotia was constructed between 1903 and 1904 to architectural plans created by J.C. Dumaresq & Son. The builder was Messer Wilson, a local contractor. The primary exterior cladding is reddish-brown brick of varying tones with door and window details in grey sandstone quarried locally.

The architectural style selected by the architect was a departure from the late nineteenth century customary Romanesque or eclectic Gothic styles. The Dumaresq firm chose the highly fashionable Edwardian Neoclassical style in which to express the decorative elements of the exterior. The Edwardian neoclassical style was part of a sequence of varying expressions of neoclassicism known as Georgian, as they were developed in the eighteenth and nineteenth century. Preceding the Edwardian Neoclassical style were several styles which consciously rejected aspects of the seemingly rigid symmetry, proportions and strict adherence to a vocabulary of Georgian architectural details but continued the overall appearance of the Georgian character.

Right: The interior decorative elements are Edwardian neoclassical in style. The architectural detail is exceptional and in very good repair.

Opposite page: The Colchester County Court House is Edwardian neoclassical in style. It represents a return to more traditional Georgian details from the styles which preceded it. The style would have been viewed as highly fashionable at the time of construction.

Two styles in particular that preceded the Edwardian Neoclassical that influenced the design of the Truro courthouse are the Queen Anne style and the Colonial Revival style. The Queen Anne style was characterized by asymmetry, oversized windows with significant glazing unbroken by muntins or glazing bars, often with a covered verandah and usually with a turret or tower forming a significant decorative element extending from ground level into the roof line with its own roof. The Colonial Revival style was created in the United States at the time of the commemoration of the one hundredth anniversary of the American Revolution of 1775-1783. It was intended to reject the British formality of Georgian architecture and the American Federal style but retain the American colonial simple

Left: *The principal courtroom on the piano nobile has been remodelled in contemporary fashion but retains the original standards of courtroom layout.*

Right: *The floor of the entrance level has encaustic tiles in a popular late Victorian pattern.*

expression of that style. The Colonial Revival style was intended to serve as the American national house style and included many interior amenities not found in earlier styles. It was also applied in simple rural public buildings as well.

THE EXTERIOR

The Truro courthouse adopted a tower from the Queen Anne style which was constructed to the left side of the building. The tower served as an elegant formal staircase well and hall. From the Colonial Revival style, the Dumaresq design adopted the window scale and glazing practices: the windows are large in relation to the mass of the wall area and in the lower sash of the double hung windows no glazing bars (muntins) were used.

One of the significant characteristics of a formal Georgian public building is found in the configuration of the roof: the roof of the Truro courthouse is a hipped platform similar to that of Province House in Halifax (1819) and Province House in Charlottetown (1848), both designed in a neoclassical style.

The return to formality in the Edwardian Neoclassical style also allowed greater creativity in the design of the traditional decorative details around the

windows and doors. The building is truly neoclassical, but no true Georgian building would have had the same decorative details as the Colchester County Court House. It contains a simpler and more restrained range of details.

This detailed exploration of the architectural properties of the Truro courthouse is relevant to the theme of our book. The selection and use of this style was highly fashionable in major centres in Canada and Britain; it demonstrates the adoption of the principle that a courthouse is one of the three most significant civic structures in a city, town or village. The courthouse must be presented as a centre of authority and commitment by government and the people to the peace, order and good government of the community. The Truro courthouse is an exceptionally fine example of a courthouse designed to meet the appropriate contemporary standards of courthouse design, location and civic importance.

The architect of the courthouse deserves comment. He was J.C. Dumaresq, who was one of the most influential and significant architects in the Maritimes in the late nineteenth and early-twentieth century's. James Charles Philip Dumaresq (1844-1906) was born in Sydney, Nova Scotia and died in Halifax. He enjoyed exceptional success as an architect in both Nova Scotia and in New Brunswick. His architectural vocabulary included a wide range of styles, such as neoclassicism, which was employed in the Truro courthouse, the Second Empire style employed in various buildings in Saint John and Fredericton, New Brunswick and the Victorian Eclectic style employed in various buildings throughout both provinces. The most significant building Mr. Dumaresq designed was the New Brunswick Legislative Building located in Fredericton, construction

Left: The chair illustrated is one of the few surviving judge's chairs, which would have been located behind the bench on the dais. This locally crafted chair is an example of exceptional cabinetry.

of which was completed in 1882. It was designed in the Second Empire style that he employed in several buildings he designed in Saint John after a devastating fire in that city a few years earlier.

THE INTERIOR

The interior of the Truro courthouse conforms to the neoclassical standard of placing the principal rooms on the second floor (the *piano nobile*). The ground floor houses service areas and offices for support staff. The principal courtroom and judge's quarters are on the second floor.

The configuration of the internal spaces is unusual in terms of courthouse design as there are no dedicated passageways for the judiciary to get to their offices or to the courtroom, for an accused to be taken from a ground floor holding cell to the courtroom or to a secure dock (place of holding the accused during the trial), or for the jury to access the jury box in the courtroom via a dedicated passageway. The standards of courthouse internal layout prescribing such dedicated passageways are not an obsolete or esoteric tradition; they ensure personal and professional security and dignity for each of the participants in the courthouse. Without them, the justices enter the courtroom either from the public staircase or the recently installed elevator which they must share with counsel for the parties, the accused or the litigants and the jury. Justice must appear to be done; the participants in a trial must not be seen to be socializing or conferring with each other except as set down by the due processes prescribed by the Rules of Court or the statute under which a charge has been laid.

The Colchester County Court House is now a relatively little used component of the delivery of justice in Nova Scotia. Much of the day-to-day work in the ever expanding family law, civil litigation and criminal law areas are handled in one of the recently created justice centres located a short distance away from the Colchester County Court House in Truro. There are many similar new justice centres throughout Nova Scotia.

Above: The courthouse has an element of the Queen Anne style; this stairway is embedded in a hexangular tower that projects from the left side of the courthouse.

KINGS COUNTY COURT HOUSE
KENTVILLE, NOVA SCOTIA

The Kings County Court House located in the shire town of Kentville, in the Province of Nova Scotia, was constructed on Cornwallis Street to architectural plans prepared by Leslie R. Fairn, whose primary architectural practice was located in the nearby town of Wolfville. The building, completed in 1904, was one of Mr. Fairn's first commissions. The first court sessions were held in that year. As a county courthouse, issues falling within the jurisdiction of both county courts and the superior (Supreme) court were heard in this courthouse. A superior court, with the justices appointed by the Government of Canada, was first established in the town in 1874.

In Nova Scotia, as in New Brunswick, the legislature of the province delegated responsibility and legislative authority for the administration of justice to the county governments. It was the responsibility of the County Council to provide a courthouse and the necessary officials to adequately operate the justice system in the county. The standard of courthouse design was left to each county council, which led to a remarkable diversity in the exterior and interior configuration of courthouses. The county paid for maintenance of the courthouse. Staff, including the Sheriff, Prothonotary and the Registrar of Probate were appointed and paid by the government of the province and from the court fees paid for filings and registration of documents. The superior court justice's salary was paid by the federal government.

The decision to build the 1903-1904 courthouse in Kentville by the Kings County council was not inevitable. The former county courthouse was located there, but the Town of Wolfville presented a forceful argument together with a substantial financial commitment to have the construction of the courthouse in Wolfville. However, the final decision of the County Council was to leave it where it had been historically which honoured the fact that Kentville was the shire town (county capital for administrative purposes).

Right: The cupola surmounting the roof of the courthouse. It provided air circulation to the courtroom below.

Opposite page: The Kings County Court House is dominated by its central projecting bay and the prominent Romanesque entrance.

Above: The courtroom is located on the piano nobile as required in a building designed in a neoclassical style. The interior panelling, judge's dais panelling and bench are original. The judge's bench ending in two hexagonal witness boxes is found in some other southern Nova Scotia courthouses.

THE EXTERIOR

The exterior design elements of the Kentville courthouse are Romanesque. The building is a simple rectangle with a hipped roof, surmounted by a cupola. The most notable architectural feature of the front elevation is the entry, in the form of a Romanesque Arch which is in a shallow projecting pavilion. At the roof line it has a neoclassical pediment. The prominent entry has a large semi-circular, stone-faced arch and is similar to the entryway of the Digby County Court House, later designed and built by Mr. Fairn. The windows on the second floor have Romanesque round-headed top elements that are connected along the bottom of the windows with a belt course of stone which extends across the front of the building. It further extends around the sides to provide continuity and cohesion in the design. Another belt course of stone extends below the ground floor windows at the sill level. The lower belt course at the entryway follows the contours of the Romanesque arch over the double front doors.

The cladding of the building is local Kings County brick. The belt courses and decorative elements in stone are constructed of Cumberland County freestone. The roof was originally covered in Spanish tile.

The building has a raised ground floor enabling a full set of administrative offices in the basement. These included space for County Council officials and the registry of deeds for the county. The raised ground floor also contained various court-related offices, such as for the Prothonotary (chief court clerk) and court support services. The principal floor, which is located on the second floor, conforms to the principles of neoclassical architecture by placing the principal room (*the piano nobile*), the courtroom, on that floor.

The front entrance facing Cornwallis Street provides public access to the building. A dedicated separate entry on the side of the building was for the use of the judiciary but it was also used to take the accused to and from the courtroom in a secure manner. Small courthouses could not afford the luxury of segregated entrances and passageways exclusively for the use of the judiciary and a separate passage for the accused that larger buildings could provide.

The staircase from the first floor to the second floor is original and is constructed of quartered oak. The woodwork has been refreshed and displays the banister, balusters, treads and risers to their optimum appearance.

THE INTERIOR

There is one courtroom in the courthouse. It covers approximately one half of the second floor (the *piano nobile*) extending on the south side of the building from front to back. The woodwork in this room is local pine and grained to look like oak. The wainscoting extends from the baseboard at floor level to the dado rail (chair rail) and extends around three sides of the room. The judge's bench (desk and chair) is on an elevated dais on the Cornwallis Street side of the building. The bar of the courtroom is intact as are counsel tables. There are two witness boxes, one on each side of the judge's bench. This is similar to several other New Brunswick and Nova Scotia courthouses built in the nineteenth century. The accused's dock (location where the accused would sit or stand during the trial) has been removed.

A relatively modern theory now applied in this courtroom is to have no dedicated space for the accused so that there could be no appearance of guilt until after the final decision in the case, should that be the verdict. The accused sits with one or two security officials from the sheriff's office off to one side of the courtroom. The prisoner's dock was originally located directly in front of the bar dividing the public and private functional areas of the courtroom and between the clerk of the court and counsel tables. This was a design format used in several Nova Scotia and New Brunswick courthouses of that era. The public had a substantial tiered seating area behind the bar. The ceiling was originally a deep coved recess sheathed in pressed tin. The ceiling has been dropped substantially and covered with acoustic tile to allow for technical and lighting support.

In 1992 the Kings Historical Society acquired the building and has maintained it to a high standard. The Kings County Court House no longer is a venue for hearing superior court, civil or criminal trials. It is now styled the Kings County Museum.

DIGBY COUNTY COURT HOUSE
DIGBY, NOVA SCOTIA

The Digby County Court House located in the Town of Digby, in the Province of Nova Scotia, was constructed between 1908 and 1910 to plans prepared by Wolfville architect Leslie R. Fairn. The architectural style employed by Mr. Fairn was the Richardsonian Romanesque. The courthouse was built as a county administrative centre and all municipal offices were located in the building, including the Council Chamber.

The Richardsonian Romanesque style was developed by Henry Hobson Richardson, a Boston architect whose work in New York and Boston led to substantial commissions in Chicago and the Midwest. Mr. Richardson's designs were of great significance principally because they were copied widely by other architects which led to the style becoming one of the most prevalent styles for important public buildings in the northeastern and central United States in the late nineteenth century. The dominance of the style in Chicago was an influence on the selection of the Richardsonian-type architectural designs being employed in the Ontario Legislative Building, (Queen's Park), and in the old

Right: The courthouse facility in Digby combines a jail illustrated here, but is separate from the courthouse.

Opposite page: The Digby County Court House is designed in the Richardsonian Romanesque style characterized by fortress-like cylindrical towers and a monumental entrance. The jail lies to the right of the courthouse.

City Hall in Toronto. Both of the latter buildings were designed by a Toronto architect faithfully employing the standards of Richardson's architectural style.

The Richardsonian Romanesque style is an historicist style which, in an eclectic and free-spirited manner, adopted medieval French monastic architectural designs and adapted them to late nineteenth century practicalities. The selection of the style for so many public buildings was because of its monumentality and

Above: The judge's dais panelling contains the flags of Canada and Nova Scotia, a carved scales of justice and neoclassical swags below a swan-necked pediment.

Left: The monumental entrance typical of the Richardsonian Romanesque style.

Opposite page: The principal courtroom is located on the piano nobile and retains much of its original cabinetry such as the judge's dais panelling and the ceiling and wall decorative elements. The modern changes are complementary with the old.

overt declaration of the importance of the building giving prominence to the civic core of the city.

The responsibility for construction of county courts in Nova Scotia rested with the county government, which in this case was located in Digby. The selection of Mr. Fairn and the Richardsonian Romanesque style was made by the council which was dominated by members of the Masonic Order. There is a tradition in Digby that the selection of the style was made under Masonic influence. The Masons base much of their rituals and symbolism on medieval and older historicist sources; the tradition holds that the Richardsonian Romanesque style conformed to their vision of important civil architecture.

The Digby courthouse and its counterpart, also designed by Mr. Fairn and constructed in 1913 in what is now the City of Miramichi (formerly Newcastle) in New Brunswick, reflect the standards of the style. Those standards include the use of turrets capped by conical roofs, round-headed windows, a projecting central bay in which the elevated double-door entry with its imposing Romanesque Arch is framed by freestone and a dominant central gable surmounting the entrance bay. The Digby courthouse served as a model for the exterior and significant parts of the interior of the Miramichi courthouse.

THE EXTERIOR

The exterior building materials include locally crafted red bricks as the primary cladding, which is contrasted with grey freestone in the decorative elements of the Romanesque arch, in the entrance window details, belt courses and foundation walls. The overall effect, particularly as it is in an elevated position overlooking a body of water, is one of monumentality. The building speaks to the importance of the rule of law, the importance of the building in the town and to the maintenance of law and order. This is not a building designed to invite or host the public; it is designed to impress, if not intimidate and serves to remind the citizens of the discipline expected of a civilized populace. This is in conformity with nineteenth century British standards of courthouse appearance and purpose.

The roof of the building is original, sheathed in copper tiles which in their appearance resemble slate and would have been used in many Romanesque buildings. The use of such materials demonstrates the adherence of the architect and county council to the standards of the architectural style.

THE INTERIOR

The interior of the Digby courthouse is in an exceptionally fine state of conservation and maintenance. There are two courtrooms. The principal courtroom together with the judge's chambers, jury room and barrister's room are located on the *piano nobile*. Emphasis in this book is made to referring to the second floor as the *piano nobile* when it is the principal floor because it is technically the accurate term in a building based on neoclassical standards. The Richardsonian Revival style is a specialized expression of neoclassicism. The neoclassical elements speak to the intent of those designing and constructing the courthouse that it conform to the nineteenth century courthouse standards of presenting the face of justice as imposing, intimidating and of the highest dignity.

The interior decoration of the principal courtroom is similar to that of the Miramichi building. The most prominent feature of the courtroom is the elevated judge's dais and the handsome backdrop to the judge's bench on the back wall. The judicial dais backdrop has framed panels, the centre panel of which contains a carved scale of justice – a symbol of the purpose of the judicial system. The ceiling is a recessed cove sheathed with the original pressed tin. The decorative elements in the pressed tin are similar to those in the Miramichi courthouse.

The configuration of the principal courtroom is also virtually identical to that of the Miramichi courthouse. The woodwork in the Digby courthouse is original and displays its age with a beautiful patina that only age and appropriate care can give it.

The courthouse contains a small courtroom remodelled in a modern style in terms of the woodwork and facilities for the judge's staff, lawyers and litigants. This courtroom is much less imposing. It is used for family law matters among others and reflects the twenty first century philosophy of making the court facilities used for family purposes as friendly and as amenable to assisting in conflict resolution as the built environment can provide.

The Digby courthouse differs in its facilities in one fundamental aspect from the Miramichi courthouse. The Miramichi building combined jail and courthouse facilities (the jail being later expanded into an adjacent building) whereas the Digby building was not designed to serve as a jail. Jail facilities were constructed adjacent to the Digby courthouse in a separate structure. It included a designated outdoor space for the carrying out of death penalties by hanging. The public's curiosity and sensitivities were addressed by allocating an interior space in the jail for this purpose.

The Digby County Court House, like many county courthouses, has served many municipal functions including being a site for the county council meetings.

Right: This detail illustrates the public gallery at the back of the courtroom with the original pressed-tin ceiling and finely articulated cornice.

Opposite page: The judge's chair is original to the date of construction of the courthouse and was designed with symbols of justice specifically for the purpose.

LAW COURTS BUILDING
HALIFAX, NOVA SCOTIA

The Law Courts Building located at 1815 Upper Water Street in Halifax, the capital of the Province of Nova Scotia, was constructed in 1971 to architectural plans prepared by the Halifax architectural firm of Fowler, Bauld and Mitchell. The building contains the Nova Scotia Court of Appeal and the Nova Scotia Supreme Court which includes general trial-level courts, the Family Division Court, the Bankruptcy Court and the Probate Court. It also contains a dedicated courtroom for the Federal Court of Canada.

The Law Courts Building is a replacement for the Court of Appeal and Supreme Court facilities formerly located in the building known as the Halifax County Court House, which currently houses the primary Halifax area Provincial Court. The Law Courts Building is a successor as well to the Supreme Court facilities which formed one of the three principal functional components of Province House, the Legislative Building which opened in 1819.

In Province House the Supreme Court chamber serviced both the trial functions of the court and the Court of Appeal. It was located according to English constitutional traditions between the Legislative Council Chamber (location of the "throne" symbolizing the presence of the monarch in the legislature) and the House of Assembly. All three chambers were located on the *piano nobile* and were in sequence complying with the tradition of "handedness" governing the location of the three chambers: the chamber with the highest precedence was the Legislative Council chamber to the right of one's entrance into the passage or hallway connecting the three chambers, the Supreme Court in the middle and the House of Assembly to the left, at the opposite end of the building from that occupied by the Legislative Council Chamber. The proximity of the Supreme Court chamber to the throne was not happenstance. The theoretical legitimacy and source of ultimate authority as a court rested in its connection with the monarch (the "Crown"). Because the Crown was seen to be the fount of all justice, justice was and continues to be dispensed in the name of the Crown by the courts.

Prior to the Supreme Court having its facilities in Province House, it met in various locations after its establishment by the governor of the colony of Nova Scotia. The government acted under the authority and direction conferred on him by his Commission and Instructions, documents issued in London in the name of the monarch appointing the governor. The Commission and Instructions contained his powers and administrative directions. The Supreme Court of Nova Scotia was established in 1754. The first chief justice was appointed in that year. However, prior to 1754 judicial functions were performed in the colony of Nova Scotia after 1713 (Treaty of Utrecht) when mainland Nova Scotia was finally ceded by France to Great Britain. Between 1713 and 1754 judicial functions were performed by the governor and his council. The first court was based on a general court model used in the English colony of Virginia. That court was established in the Town of Annapolis Royal which was the first capital of the colony of Nova Scotia.

Opposite page: The Law Courts Building is located on the waterfront of Halifax Harbour. It is designed in the International Modernist style known as "Brutalism". This pedway bridge over Upper Water Street leads to the entrance of the courthouse.

Above: *The interior decoration and fittings of this courtroom used by the Federal Court of Canada are contemporary in style and similar to courtrooms in most new superior court courthouses in Canada. The symbolic presence of the monarch is seldom represented in recently decorated courtrooms.*

After the Treaty of Utrecht, the Supreme Court of Nova Scotia had jurisdiction over all of continental Nova Scotia, which included all of what is now the Province of New Brunswick but did not include Isle Royal (Cape Breton Island) or Isle St. Jean (Prince Edward Island). After the Treaty of Paris of 1763 which concluded the wars referred to historically as the French and Indian War, also known as the Seven Years War, the authority of the Supreme Court of Nova Scotia extended to and included Isle Royal and Isle St. Jean. That authority ("jurisdiction" in technical language) continued until the Supreme Court of Prince Edward Island was established in 1770, after the creation of Isle St. Jean as a separate colony of Great Britain in 1764 and until the creation of the Supreme Court of New Brunswick in 1784, after New Brunswick was separated from Nova Scotia as a separate colony in the same year. The laws in force in the new colony were the English common law and statute laws passed by the British Parliament having general application (referred to as "received law"). The legislature of the colony had very limited powers to create laws and those were restricted to matters of local interest.

THE EXTERIOR

The Law Courts Building was designed in a style that was prevalent in the 1960s and 1970s for public buildings, irrespective of function or purpose. The style was not intended to define or even suggest the particular activities that would be carried on in the building. There is a significant element of anonymity in the architectural features of the style employed. The Nova Scotia Law Courts Building is designed according to the international modernist architectural movement that has become known as "Brutalist".

Brutalism as a term does not have its origins in a pejorative opinion of the appearance of buildings in this style. It is derived from the French language term "béton brut", meaning raw concrete, a term used by the mid-twentieth century Swiss born architect i whose work achieved international fame and profound influence. Le Corbusier favoured the use of concrete in the exterior and interior finishes of his buildings. His architectural compositions and those of architects who were influenced by him, and who adopted his style, created modular units in the design which reflected the interior elements of the building in its external façade. Concrete was favoured by Le Corbusier and those who followed his design principles because of what they asserted were its raw and interpretative honesty. The surfaces of the concrete were often left with the wood used as framing into which the concrete was poured as a surface texture of the concrete.

The Law Courts building was designed by the architects in collaboration with the Halifax County Court House Commission. This Commission had representation on it from the Government of Nova Scotia, the municipal governments of Halifax and Dartmouth, and the Law Society of Nova Scotia. The Law Courts was owned by the Commission until it was transferred to the Government of Nova Scotia in about 1990.

The architects were instructed to place the building on the waterfront as a component of the rejuvenation of the waterfront and as part of a planned Harbour Drive. Harbour Drive was designed to extend from the only component actually built, the Cogswell Street Interchange eastward towards Point Pleasant Park as a boulevard containing several lanes of traffic. Harbour Drive was designed to be constructed over five feet above the natural grade.

The only building constructed in compliance with the plans for the proposed Harbour Drive (now known as Upper Water Street) is the Law Courts Building. The Law Courts Building was substantially elevated above street grade to accommodate the design of Harbour Drive and to enable underground parking. The building so elevated had its principal floor substantially above street level, cut off from the opposite side of the street. Because of the elevation of the first floor, the entrance of the building faces a plaza, which is the landscaped roof of part of the garage. Access to the plaza is by a pedway across Upper Water Street, connecting the Law Courts to the opposite side of the street.

The garage on street level has parking dedicated for the use of the judiciary and courthouse staff, as well as a secure entry to the building for police transferring prisoners to the courthouse for court purposes.

The exterior of the building is framed in a grid pattern as if the horizontal concrete belt courses were lintels and the vertical concrete posts were part of a post and beam framing, giving artfully exposed structural elements. The principles of a post and beam form of construction bring the design of the building into continuity with the earliest historical courthouses of the province, which were also constructed in the post and beam manner. That continuity is further expressed in the exterior elements of the building in its formality, symmetry and assertion of dignity. While the Law Courts Building does not contain neoclassical decorative features the building was designed to create the same statement of permanence, authority and prominence.

The severity of the concrete and glass is given texture and visual interest by panels of sandblasted concrete aggregate.

The overall character of the Law Courts Building owes more to the late nineteenth century presentation of a courthouse in terms of the standards and principles of design, than with twenty first century philosophical approaches to courthouses as public places for conflict resolution. The Law Courts building, like its Victorian prototypes both in its exterior and in its interior presentation, is a forbidding, authoritative, intimidating and uninviting structure.

As dissimilar as the Halifax County Court House and the Law Courts Building are in their architectural styles, they are remarkably similar in the philosophy of those who designed the buildings in terms of the presentation of the buildings to the public.

Left: One of the Nova Scotia Court of Appeal courtrooms. This courtroom is set for a panel of three justices. It can also be used by a trial level justice in a jury trial.

Supreme Court of Nova Scotia (trial level courts on floors 2 to 7, except 5). The 7th floor also houses the two libraries located in the building. One library is for the use of the lawyers and staff of the law courts building and the other is dedicated to the exclusive use of the judiciary and their clerks. Both Supreme Court justices and Court of Appeal justices use the same library. As there are clerks available, justices of the two levels have infrequent contact for research purposes, thereby preserving the principle of segregation between the two levels of the courts.

The interior was designed to accommodate and facilitate an efficient arrangement of courtrooms. The courtrooms were configured in their interior layout to conform to the historic courthouses

THE INTERIOR

The main entrance is identified by the words "The Law Courts". The entry doors lead into an entrance hall that extends across approximately one half of the front elevation. The exposed concrete elements of the exterior are continued on the interior. The concrete on the interior is unadorned by decorative detail. It is a narrow practical passage with a security desk at the south end and a bank of elevators in the middle of the east wall. Stair access to the basement level and to upper floors is also available from an internal staircase to which access is provided by a door adjacent to the elevators. Unlike nineteenth century courthouse reception halls, there is no attempt to impress the visitor with historic decorative details or the creative energy of designers intending to suggest the functions carried on in the building. This is a characteristic of Brutalism.

The building houses both the Nova Scotia Court of Appeal (5th floor) and the

of the province. The pattern and layout and design selected by the Halifax County Court House Commission was the historic Nova Scotia courtroom and courthouse. This Nova Scotia courtroom was highly influenced by the standards of English courthouse traditions and to a lesser degree by early American courthouse designs embedded in historic Nova Scotia courthouses. The actual use of space in the Law Courts building is not as noted unlike its predecessor on Spring Garden Road.

Standards of design for courthouses include a set of specific standards for courthouse libraries. The Courthouse and Law Society Library Management Group, a national association of librarians specializing in the operation, design and efficient use of libraries, established standards for law libraries as recently as 1998, although there have been periodic updates since that time. The Preamble to the Standards clearly expresses the significance of law libraries and the requirement for standards.

The law library is essential to the administration of justice in all jurisdictions. The quality of its legal services is dependent upon the quality of its law library. Legal information is the lifeblood of the legal system. The health of that system depends very heavily on the quality and accessibility of the information by which it is served. Any part of the system that is not adequately supplied is apt to fail in meeting the needs of those whom it is intended to serve.

Access to legal information is vital to the effective operation of the Canadian judicial system. Canadian courthouse libraries provide access to legal information resources for all citizens, either through direct access to those resources, or through judges and lawyers who rely on those resources.

The standards prescribed are intended to be used only by Canadian courthouse and law society libraries which service the needs of practising lawyers, judges, court officers and others who are directly involved in the process of the administration of justice. The standards should act as guidelines to ensure that Canadian courthouse libraries maintain collections, staff and services of the highest quality.

Each functional element of a superior court courthouse like the law libraries must have standards that have general application in the province and that conform to standards having national scope. No aspect of the functioning of a superior court courthouse in the Maritimes is without traditions and demanding standards designed to ensure the highest quality delivery of judicial services and preservation of law and order within its jurisdiction.

The Supreme Court courtrooms conform to the standards of segregation established by the third quarter of the nineteenth century in the English courtroom tradition. The courtrooms are characterized by light-toned wood fixtures including an elevated judicial bench, clerk's desk, jury box (in those courtrooms fitted for use in jury trials), counsel tables and public seating. Most of the courtrooms have the flags of Canada and the Province framing or behind the justice's bench. No portraits of the monarch, Queen Elizabeth II, are mounted in the courtrooms. In some courtrooms the Coat of Arms of Canada are mounted behind the justice's bench. The coat of arms of Nova Scotia is mounted on the wall behind the Court of Appeal justices' bench. Virtually none of the traditional symbols of justice, such as the portraits of the current monarch, the scales of justice, representation of Lady Justice, and one or more of the four virtues, have

been employed in the Law Courts Building. Indeed, very few coats of arms of Canada are installed as decorative elements in the courtrooms.

The Court of Appeal courtroom is similar to a Supreme Court courtroom in terms of style and decor, but as a full Court of Appeal bench includes all eight Court of Appeal justices, the bench has seating for eight Court of Appeal justices. However, the usual complement of Court of Appeal justices sitting on an appeal is three.

Handedness as a standard of the configuration of spaces and functions in working Supreme Court and Court of Appeal courtrooms is adhered to in the Law Courts Building. For example, the position occupied by counsel for the plaintiff/appellant and that occupied by counsel for the defendant/respondent is determined by the handedness tradition. Counsel for the plaintiff/appellant customarily sits at counsel table to the right of the justices as they face counsel, and for the defendant/respondent to the left. If counsel tables are parallel plaintiff/appellant counsel takes the front table and defendant/respondent behind.

There is a courtroom dedicated for the use of the Federal Court of Canada which is somewhat larger than all but the principal chamber of the Court of Appeal. As in the Court of Appeal chamber there are several counsel tables. It is not uncommon for numerous parties to appear in complex cases coming before the Federal Court.

The Nova Scotia Law Courts Building is an excellent example of one of the phases in the architectural styles, dignity and role of courthouses in urban design and delivery of judicial services in the Maritimes. It is a product of its time of construction as is each of the other courthouses profiled in this book. The variety in style, decoration and presentation used in law courts buildings is a reflection of the culture, traditions and attitudes of society at the time of their construction.

Above: The Sir Louis Henry Davies Law Courts.

THE HISTORIC COURTHOUSES OF PRINCE EDWARD ISLAND

PRINCE COUNTY COURT HOUSE
SUMMERSIDE, PRINCE EDWARD ISLAND

The Prince County Court House, which contains both a courthouse and jail, was constructed on Summer Street in the Town of Summerside in the Province of Prince Edward Island between 1873 and 1876 to a design created by master builder John Corbett of Summerside. In addition to the courthouse, a number of buildings in the town were also constructed by Mr. Corbett.

The Prince County Court House is a neoclassical building in a prominent location in the City with the principal courtroom conforming to the traditional standards of English courthouse design. It is an important visual reminder of the origins of the English and Canadian rule of law and the procedures applied

Right: The entrance has neoclassical elements suggestive of a Roman Triumphal Arch which adds dignity and importance to the building.

Opposite page: The Prince County Court House combines superior court and Provincial Court functions. It also has temporary jail facilities. The four tall Romanesque windows on the side of the building provide light into the principal courtroom.

in it. The origins of its design and construction link it to the history and importance of the building in the City and to the people of the City.

Summerside is now a city and the principal urban area in Prince County, Prince Edward Island. It was not always so. The provincial and county capitals were established by Captain Samuel Holland in his comprehensive survey of the Island completed in 1765. The capital of Prince County designated by Holland was Prince Town (later spelled Princetown) which is an area adjacent to the contemporary community of Malpeque. In the mid-eighteenth century, because of its harbour and apparent economic potential, Princetown warranted designation as the county capital. However, within a few years the harbour was substantially infilled by sand dunes migrating southwardly as they have historically all along the north coast of the Island. No public buildings were erected in Princetown. Although a settlement of early Scottish immigrants became established there, preserving the name for over a century – very little remains of Princetown.

The principal community in Prince County in the early nineteenth century was the village of St. Eleanors where a small wood-framed courthouse was

Left: *The principal courtroom contains most of its early 20th century cabinetry and fittings. The Coat of Arms in the judge's dais is a polychromic plaster cast of the Arms of Canada.*

it stands as bare and angular as a big barn." However, significant changes and improvements to the exterior design of the building were made in 1906 and 1938.

The courthouse is constructed of brick and is four storeys in height. The primary visual interest on the exterior is provided by the entrance and the exterior staircase leading to it. The staircase has a wrought iron railing with treads spreading as the staircase reaches ground level. The principal entrance is neoclassical in character as are the particular decorative elements of the façade. It is in the nature of a ceremonial Roman arch and has an entablature supported by pilasters. There is a belt course of stone through the brick work across the façade, including the entrance arch surrounding the double doors that lead into the building. There is a second belt course below the third storey windows broken by the remains of a Palladian window.

The Romanesque style of the front entrance is continued on both sides of the entrance by a round-headed window next to the entrance and adjacent to it is a double-sash window surmounted by a roundel window. All four windows have the same height and are carefully balanced and proportioned to the height and dimensions of the entrance.

Over the entrance is the remnant of a Palladian window partially infilled in the upper round-headed element of the window. A small double-sash window is located over the first floor round-headed Romanesque window on both the *piano nobile* level and the level above. The corners of the courthouse are given added definition through the use of quoins which run from the basement to a point below the eaves. It is unusual that the quoins would not link to an architectural feature such as an entablature; it is likely that during the renovations of 1938 the roof and adjacent areas were rebuilt and elevated leaving the quoins stranded from a traditional connection. The roof and interior were reconstructed in 1907 after a fire in 1906, and in 1938 a new roof, upper windows, doorway and brick were added to the building.

constructed. The advantages offered by the harbour nearby at Green's Shore, renamed Summerside in 1873, resulted in a shift in the development of the two communities. Summerside prospered and became a leading centre in shipbuilding, import and export of goods by seafaring vessels and a centre of the local agricultural and fishing industries. It was the advent of the railway that made the most dramatic improvement in the economy of the town. By 1873 it was apparent that the appropriate location for the principal county courthouse and jail for Prince County was Summerside.

In 1873 an act of the Legislature of the Province was passed "... to authorize the building of a jail, Supreme and County Courthouse in Summerside in Prince County." This Act also established Summerside as the county town of Prince County.

THE EXTERIOR

The exterior of the building in its original design was a simple rectangular block with a hipped roof that was otherwise quite plain. Both the *Patriot* and the *Examiner* newspapers in comments on the original design of the building were uniformly critical of the lack of architectural merit. The *Examiner* concluded "...

THE INTERIOR

The interior of the courthouse was destroyed by fire in 1906 but was rebuilt within the exterior walls which were left largely intact. It has an elevated basement which is used to house short term inmates, usually awaiting arraignment or trial. The elevated main floor contains the administrative support facilities for the Judges of the Provincial Court and Justices of the Supreme Court. For many years the courthouse has contained the Registry of Deeds for Prince County as well as the Registry Office for the filing and storage of court documents. The third level is the *piano nobile* (the principal floor) which contains the principal courtroom. In its design and decorative elements it dates to the post-fire 1907 re-construction. This courtroom is configured to have a segregated jury box on the north wall on a slightly elevated dais, a judge's bench (extended desk) on an elevated dais directly opposite the public entrance to the courtroom and a clerk's desk in front of the bench. Counsel tables are parallel to each other facing the dais; counsel for the Crown/plaintiff is at the table closest to the judge's dais and for the accused/defendant behind. The configuration of the Prince County superior court courtroom conforms to the traditions of English courtroom design.

Adjacent to the main courtroom is a small 1990s new courtroom used by superior court justices for non-jury civil litigation proceedings. Chambers for the justices and judges are located on this floor behind the two courtrooms. The third floor contains a jury room and barristers' library.

The only internal components of the building that could be considered compatible with the exterior design and created early in the life of the courthouse are the principal staircase which rises from the elevated first floor through the *piano nobile* containing the principal courtroom and up to the top floor. Both the principal courtroom and the staircase are in the late nineteenth century Renaissance Revival style with extensive woodworking. The staircase has been painted, obscuring the original stained and varnished finish. The principal courtroom has retained much of the original post-fire stained and varnished woodwork and contains fine examples of period woodwork and cabinetry.

The Summerside courthouse was typical of many late nineteenth century courthouses by including a jail as part of its functional components. The citizens of Summerside are reported to have been unimpressed, if not in opposition,

Above: The new superior court courtroom is in a contemporary style and is adjacent to the original courtroom.

to having a jail in what was one of the finer areas of the town. In August 1874 the *Charlottetown Patriot* newspaper expressed the view of many in an editorial which read *"Now, contrary to wishes of nearly every intelligent man in the place, the government are (sic) about to deform the principal square in the town by placing upon it an unsightly prison."*

The Prince County Court House has served the people of the city and the county for over one hundred twenty-five years. Modifications have been made to accommodate growing demands for court services and changes in the nature of the primary court services required. It is accepted as one of the two primary secular buildings in the city and has been the site of some of the city's most historical events.

KINGS COUNTY COURT HOUSE
GEORGETOWN, PRINCE EDWARD ISLAND

The Kings County Court House located in the Town of Georgetown, Kings County in Prince Edward Island was designed to serve both County Court and Supreme Court functions. The architect was William Critchlow Harris. This building was constructed in 1887 and became a necessity with the destruction of the original wood-frame building by fire. The fire was caused by arson, the perpetrator unknown.

Georgetown, Prince Edward Island was designated as the capital of Kings County in the Captain Samuel Holland survey of the Island of 1764-65. In the nineteenth century Georgetown was a small but modestly prosperous community with an economy based on shipping, ship-building, forestry, fishing and agriculture. By 1832 the legislature of the province was directed by Lieutenant Governor Artemas Young to make financial provision for and to arrange construction of a courthouse in the town. The lieutenant governor had the authority to give such direction as the province (then colony) had a form of government known as Representative Government in which extensive executive power was vested in the Crown's representative, the lieutenant governor. His Commission and Instructions empowered him to give direction to the legislature for the administration of the colony, including the construction of public buildings.

Opposite page: The Kings County Court House, while designed as a courthouse, is a finely conceived Anglican Rectory (left) and sanctuary (right) designed by a specialist in 19th century ecclesiastical architecture.

The original courthouse also served both county and Supreme Court functions. It was constructed in 1832 and was a wood frame structure which combined the functions of courthouse and jail. It was designed by master builder and architect Isaac Smith who was part of the design team which designed both Province House and Government House in Charlottetown. Adjacent to and at the back of the courthouse were accommodations for the prisoners. The rudimentary nature of the building is reflected in the story of an inmate, Tom Williams, who was incarcerated over a winter in an unheated cell. The jailer requested the attorney general to provide heat for the prisoner. The only response, one given half way through the winter, was to "provide Williams with a pair of shoes and two pairs of socks". The wood frame courthouse was replaced by the current courthouse in 1887 after the fire.

THE EXTERIOR

The vulnerability of a wood-frame structure being apparent, it was necessary that the new building would be constructed of a more fire resistant material. Wallace sandstone for the exterior walls and local sandstone for decorative contrast around the windows and doors were selected. Wallace sandstone was quarried from the same location in Nova Scotia as the stone used in the construction of Province House in Charlottetown and Province House in Halifax, among many public buildings in the region which used the material.

Left: The interior of the courtroom has a beamed ceiling supported by engaged columns in the Renaissance Revival style. They are original to the building.

Opposite page: The interior of the courtroom now has the judge's bench on the south end. The original configuration was the reverse. The judge's bench and dais panelling are part of the original decorative scheme relocated with the reorientation of the courtroom.

William Critchlow Harris' design for the courthouse s in the Romanesque style. It is typical of his non-ecclesiastical public buildings. His designs for churches were primarily neo-gothic in style. The composition of the interior spaces follows his practice in designing small churches.

THE INTERIOR

Georgetown courthouse in its external design is a church (the south end of the building containing the one storey courtroom) and an attached two and one half storey rectory. He had virtually no experience in designing courthouses and appears to have had little briefing on the standards and requirements of a courthouse. The exterior and interior decorative elements represent some of his finest work, but the impracticality of the arrangements of the interior spaces meant reconfiguration was required.

Regrettably, the Georgetown courthouse, built in 1887, is an excellent example of the consequences of failing to correctly apply the principles of nineteenth-century courthouse design. Those principles included segregation of the accused from the public and the judiciary, and segregation of the judiciary from the accused, the public and the barristers representing the accused. The layout of internal spaces also failed to provide security in the building. In its original planning, and as constructed, the 1887 courthouse placed the judge's bench, office and access to the building adjacent to and forming part of the passages used by the accused, the public and the lawyers to gain entry to the courtroom. The same passages were used by court officials including the sheriff and they provided an entrance to the building by the building caretaker and his family and to his apartment on the third floor. There was no segregation and little security. The building had to be reconfigured to conform to the appropriate

Above: The details of the fine Romanesque masonry and window are demonstrated above.

nineteenth century standards; remedying the design defects thereby brought into sharp focus what those standards were.

The courthouse was constructed by Lemuel A. Wilmot of New Brunswick at a cost of $8,000, remarkably $1,000 less than had been budgeted. The building was formally opened in 1888 with considerable pomp and ceremony as part of Georgetown's Jubilee Celebration commemorating the fiftieth anniversary of Queen Victoria's accession to the throne. A special train was arranged to bring the lieutenant governor and other dignitaries to Georgetown for the event. The opening ceremonies included, predictably, speeches by local worthies, band music and food. One would suspect libations of the stronger sort were also available.

During the opening ceremonies, Mr. Justice Peters made the following comments as reported in *The Examiner*, an Island newspaper, which expressed the pride, confidence and contentment of the populace in the new building:

> *"...the building reflected credit on the Government and on the County... Islanders, as a rule, are a strong healthy and well-to-do people, living in a salubrious climate and healthy atmosphere protected by a constitution superior to other countries; that our Canadian constitution embraces many and most of the benefits which appertain to the neighbouring Republic (USA) without including its vices... and (the building is) one of which a free people might well be proud."*

The Examiner also described the interior amenities of the building. The courthouse, it reported:

> *"... is a solid structure of Island sandstone, with grey freestone facings, and three entrances. On the first floor is the courtroom 51 feet long by 31 feet wide, well ventilated with a ceiling 15 feet high. On this floor are also the Judges' room, the Crown office, the Prothonotory's office with a vault... and the Barrister's room, all well lighted and comfortably heated by grates and stoves. On the second floor are the jury room with ante room for witnesses and the petit jury room; while above this (on the third floor) the caretaker has been comfortably provided for."*

The new courthouse did not have a jail connected with it, as did the former courthouse, but in or about the year 1915 when other renovations were made to the building a jail was added to and connected at the back of the courthouse.

The 1915 changes made to the interior configuration of the spaces on the ground floor of the courtroom included: 1) the main public entrance at the south end of the front façade was reconfigured to serve as the entrance solely for the judges; 2) the original judge's chambers to the north of the courtroom were relocated to newly constructed rooms connecting to the former public entrance at the south end of the courtroom – this ensured segregation of the judges from the accused and the practising bar; 3) the judge's bench which had been at the north end of the courtroom was relocated to the south end adjacent to the newly relocated judge's chambers to provide appropriate access by the judiciary to the courtroom; and 4) the entrance formerly dedicated for use by the judges, accused, barristers, officials and the caretaker and family now excluded the judiciary.

This brought the layout of the courtroom, judge's entrance and chambers into conformity with the prevailing standards of nineteenth-century courthouse design.

The Georgetown courthouse is a National Historic Site and is recognized in the Province of Prince Edward Island as one of the finest architectural compositions in its external appearance in the province.

Above: *The extension to the back of the building contains a jail added several years after completion of the courthouse.*

SIR LOUIS HENRY DAVIES LAW COURTS
CHARLOTTETOWN, PRINCE EDWARD ISLAND

The Sir Louis Henry Davies Law Courts located on Water Street in Charlottetown, the capital of the Province of Prince Edward Island, is the seat of two distinct levels of federally appointed superior courts: the Supreme Court of Prince Edward Island (essentially the trial-level court) and the Prince Edward Island Court of Appeal (the highest superior court in the province). While the two courts share the same roof, walls and many of the same support facilities, they operate as separate and independent courts. They are segregated as to space and maintain a functional independence.

Who was Sir Louis Henry Davies? Sir Louis Henry Davies,

Right: The redecorated entrance to the courthouse with the name highlighted on a serpentine metal decorative element that serves to connect the columns across the front of the building.

Opposite page: The interior of the ground floor courtroom. The courtroom is configured to serve as a jury room, a court for criminal trials, and for non-jury civil trials.

PC, KCMG, QC was born in Charlottetown on May 4, 1845 and died on May 1, 1924. His family roots go back to one of the founding families of the province. He was a descendant of the Honourable Peter Stewart, the second Chief Justice of the Province and was educated in Charlottetown and then studied law at the Inner Temple in London. After being called to the bar in London in 1866, he returned to Charlottetown where he soon became a leading member of the Prince Edward Island bar. Like many lawyers, before him and since, he was attracted to politics and was elected to the House of Assembly. In 1876 he became premier and attorney general after forming a coalition of Liberals and Conservatives. His government was defeated in 1879. He then developed a legal practice which included acting successfully for the British Government in a major dispute with the Government of the United States on certain fisheries-related matters. In 1882 Davies was elected in the Sir Wilfred Laurier government in the Parliament of Canada. Davies became Minister of Marine and Fisheries in Laurier's government.

Above: The original elements of the building are the two storey, hipped-roof segment to the right and the extension is the steeply pitched segment at right angles to it on the left. Virtually nothing remains of the original warehouse.

In 1901 he was appointed to the Supreme Court of Canada and in 1918 was elevated to Chief Justice of Canada. An extraordinary Islander and Canadian: the only Islander to be appointed to the Supreme Court of Canada.

The Court of Appeal has three members who sit as a panel when hearing appeals. The trial level has five justices who sit independently when presiding on litigation coming before the court.

All superior court justices must have at least ten years as a member in good standing of the Law Society of Prince Edward Island (or Nova Scotia or New Brunswick) to be eligible to be appointed as a superior court justice. Very few lawyers elevated to either the Supreme Court or the Court of Appeal have less than twenty years of active practice either in government or private practice. Men and women are equally eligible to be appointed as justices and as chief justices.

The courthouse serving both superior court levels was constructed in 1978-79 to architectural plans prepared by Halifax architects Cochrane and Forsyth. The building is comprised of a much older building and a purpose-built addition. The older building was a wholesaler's warehouse which was considered at the time to have merit for preservation because of the hand-hewn posts and beams

used in its construction. It had no architectural value in terms of its design, builder or history. The building, when adapted for use as a courthouse, was gutted and the new courthouse in a simple contemporary design was created around the posts and beams. The warehouse section is that portion of the building situated to the right (west) of the front entrance. The new structure is devoid of earlier warehouse structural elements and includes the entrance, the ground floor security and reception hall, and areas adjacent to it to the south and east (to the left of the front door), and the five courtrooms which are located in the east wing of the building.

The attraction to the posts and beams of the former warehouse quickly dissipated when dust and debris from the old exposed wood kept falling onto all exposed surfaces in that part of the building rendering maintenance difficult. A more serious problem occurred when the debris clogged the computers and technological equipment in that area. The care taken to preserve the posts and beams was rendered redundant when it became necessary, soon after the courts moved into the building, to have all the old wood sandblasted and in places, sealed.

The front of the courthouse is much the same as it was in its original configuration, but in 1998-1999 the exterior and the interior were both modernized and the architectural design elements improved following architectural plans prepared by the Charlottetown architectural firm of Bergmark & Hammarlund. During the modernization several changes were prompted by the Chief Justices and the Prince Edward Island Department of Justice applying new approaches to the use of courthouses by the public. The changes also reflected a philosophical change in the approach of the judiciary to the delivery of its services to the public. Changes in technology and increased security problems required changes as well.

The 1998-1999 changes in the architectural configuration and decoration of the courthouse were a deliberate expression of the late modernist architectural movement known as post modernism. It was a design movement defined by its questioning of long established social and architectural conventions: traditional dark decorative elements were replaced with light, for example, to demonstrate a fresh approach to openness and inclusion.

The colour selections for the public spaces were carefully chosen to create a warm, secure and welcoming environment. The decorative elements of the

Right: The ground floor lobby with post-modern decorative brackets and a stairway leading to four of the five courtrooms.

buildings were enhanced considerably from their original austere and unadorned design to give visual interest and attractiveness.

The philosophical changes in the delivery of judicial functions in the Sir Louis Henry Davies Law Courts were subtle but marked a substantive shift in the use of courthouses by the public and the approach of the judiciary to those using the facilities and their interaction with the public. Courthouses in the twenty-first century share little in the concept and use of courthouses as applied in the late nineteenth and for most of the twentieth century. Courthouses ceased to be places to intimidate and impress the public with the power and authority of the Crown, government or the judiciary. Courthouses had come to be viewed in the twenty-first century as spaces required for conflict resolution in its many forms. They were to provide a forum for conflict resolution – not just in the traditional trial and judicial decision format.

The redesign created spaces that are intended to enable judge-led conferences with litigants and their lawyers in a setting, other than in a courtroom, having an atmosphere as non-adversarial as the system could allow. In this setting the parties could communicate in a controlled and civil but structured environment. During these conferences the objective is to move litigation forward to resolution as quickly and efficiently as possible and at the same time actively exploring possibilities for settlement. Justices, litigants and lawyers are all equal participants in the new approach to conflict resolution. Cases move forward to trial only when settlement through discussion and mutual agreement fail. Even when the parties are unable to resolve their differences during these preliminary stages, the parties can now agree to alternate conflict resolution techniques.

The most prevalent alternate conflict resolution techniques are: 1) third party mediation; 2) judicial settlement conference; 3) arbitration; 4) negotiations between the parties assisted by their lawyers; and 5) collaborative law procedures.

The only one of the alternate procedures that must take place in a courthouse is that of a judicial settlement conference. It can take place only if the parties mutually agree to the procedure and a justice accepts the matter as one which is appropriate for judicial settlement. It must be a proceeding where it would be

Above: *While this is identified as courtroom number 4, its principal use is for pre-trial conferences, judicial settlement conferences and similar processes designed to enable conflict resolution outside a conventional courtroom setting.*

useful in reaching a settlement on the issues with those particular parties. The justice would have to be satisfied the parties are genuine in their commitment to settlement and that the Justice's role would be one that could bring out-of-court resolution to the type of problem dividing the parties.

THE EXTERIOR

The exterior of the courthouse is designed to provide a recognizable image of a government building to which the public is invited. It achieves this by clear signage that identifies it as a courthouse and presenting a façade that is not intimidating and is of a scale and decoration that is inviting to access and use by the public. Unlike nineteenth and early twentieth century courthouses, there is nothing in the exterior appearance to identify the building specifically as a courthouse other than the signage.

A decorative element was added to the front of the building in the 1998-1999 renovation in the form of a polished stainless steel panel, on which the name of the courthouse is incised. It wraps its way, in a curvilinear fashion, among the post-modernist style columns. This design element adds a visual interest to the building and serves to connect the elements of the two wings of the building containing the new and old sections of the building.

THE INTERIOR

The 1998-1999 renovations created new openings in the interior of the building which provided additional light and a sense of attractiveness necessary for an atmosphere removed from the austerity and hierarchal standards of traditional courthouse designs. Circular windows with broad architraves highlighted by four keystone design elements located at the top, bottom and sides give a sense of playful decoration one would expect in a modern home. These add to the sense of invitation and inclusion the new post-modern philosophy required.

The Sir Henry Louis Davies Law Courts contain the following important design elements inherited from English courthouse traditional design: 1) Segregation: the judiciary are segregated from the public spaces and from the lawyers. There are separate entrances for the judiciary and passages to and from their chambers to the courtrooms. The judiciary has a separate library removed from the barristers' library. The reasons for this segregation were addressed in the Introduction but in summary the reasons include the judiciary's independence from external contact and influence (it must appear to be real as well as theoretical) and modern security standards designed to protect the judiciary. Because the courthouse contains the two levels of superior courts in the province, namely the trial level and the separate appeal court level, the principles of segregation also apply by physically dividing the spaces in the building where the two levels have their chambers and support staff; and 2) the principal courtrooms are located in the *piano nobile*: the principal rooms in a neoclassical or traditional public building were placed on the second floor. The first floor contained the administrative and support facilities. This courthouse has most of its principal courtrooms on the second floor.

The Law Courts building is one of the most successful courthouses in the Maritimes in terms of compliance with the English and now prevailing Canadian standards of segregation of spaces, people, and functions. It is a relatively small structure which combines two levels of courts and various administrative and professional uses. It does so with efficiency and with a clear message to the public – that it is a public building to which the public is invited for conflict resolution.

Above: Queen's County Court House, Gagetown, New Brunswick.

THE HISTORIC COURTHOUSES OF NEW BRUNSWICK

SAINT JOHN COUNTY COURT HOUSE
SAINT JOHN, NEW BRUNSWICK

The Saint John County Court House located on King Square in the City of Saint John, in the Province of New Brunswick, was built between 1824 and 1829 under the supervision of Saint John architect, John Cunningham who also designed the building. The courthouse on the front elevation and the side facing King Square is constructed of sandstone brought to Saint John from England. It is the first courthouse constructed of stone in New Brunswick.

The courthouse is a fine example of late Georgian neoclassical architecture. Several examples of late Georgian architecture most in the Greek Revival style were built in New Brunswick in the early-to-mid-nineteenth century. Most were wood framed structures heavily influenced by New England construction practices and architectural styles. The Saint John County Court House on the other hand is thoroughly British in its exterior architectural design.

Right: The Belvedere surmounting the roof of the courthouse. It contained an internal staircase that leads to an observation platform outside the Belvedere.

Opposite page: The Saint John County Court House is one of the finest neoclassical buildings in Canada.

The allusion to the Saint John courthouse being late Georgian in its neoclassicism is confirmed by the period of its construction which was during the reign of King George IV (1820-1830). The elements of the architectural composition of the exterior conform to the neoclassicism prevalent in Britain at that time. Its location on King Square in Saint John is a further reference to the monarchial connections between the city's origins, the naming of the principal streets of the city and the high style selected for the courthouse by the local county council. Saint John became the shire town of Saint John's County in 1826. The term shire town may appear archaic in today's vocabulary but it is relevant to the placing of such an imposing courthouse in Saint John. Shire town means the "town of the sheriff", the latter being the chief law enforcement officer in the county. It is in the town of the sheriff in the English tradition, and as such the principal town of the county and the appropriate place where the courthouse would be built.

The Saint John courthouse served as a county council chamber and seat of the King's Bench Court (a superior court) in addition to its role as a city magistrate's courtroom and as a courtroom for the enforcement of city bylaws. King's Bench Court

Above: Detail of the Georgian architectural details on the front elevation, particularly the fluted Doric columns, the triglyphs and metopes in the architrave, and the pediment.

Left: Detail of the fluted Doric columns, window detail, the architrave and pediment.

justices would go on circuit at prescribed times during the year visiting county courthouses such as that in Saint John. It served as the principal civil building in the city hosting visiting dignitaries such as royalty, and after confederation, governors general and lieutenant governors. To commemorate the visit of Edward VII when he visited Saint John in 1860 as Prince of Wales, the coat of arms of the city was crafted by local artisan F.X. Swift and installed in the principal courtroom located on the *piano nobile*.

Right: The judge's segregated spiral staircase that leads from the ground floor to the judge's chambers on the piano nobile. The balustrade is wrought iron believed to have been forged locally.

THE EXTERIOR

The front elevation of the building, above the ground floor, is faced with sandstone. It is finely finished in a form referred to as ashlar. The ground floor level is rusticated sandstone meaning it is finished in regular rectangular blocks roughened and chamfered to give an appearance of solidity, permanence and importance. The ashlar are in blocks of the same size giving a uniform surface and one that appears heightened by the rustication of the ground floor masonry. The back of the building is constructed of local igneous rock and sandstone mixed haphazardly, generally referred to as rubble. The back of the building originally faced the county jail and made no pretentions as to style.

The front elevation of this highly accomplished Georgian neoclassical building is dominated by the three centered second storey windows (on the *piano nobile*). These are framed by Tuscan Doric columns and an engaged balustrade below each window extending to the belt course of masonry dividing the rusticated ground floor from the finished ashlar above. The fluted columns extend upwards into the attic storey. At that level the columns meet and give the appearance of support to a Greek Revival frieze. Above the frieze there is a pediment inset into the hipped roof. There is a space above each of the three windows and below the frieze into which are inset neoclassical carved stone swags. The composition of the three windows and Tuscan Doric columns is designed as a neoclassical triumphal Roman arch. This element rests on a shallow projecting segment of the building called a pavilion which serves as a base for the triumphal arch.

The windows on the ground floor are recessed in a round-headed arch with articulated voussoirs, each of which is a simple neoclassical arch. The recessed areas contain a double-sash window in the Georgian style each sash having six lights or panes of glass. The Georgian windows are also located in the second and attic storeys; those on the second storey are identical to those on the ground floor being double-sash windows with each sash having six lights. However, in the second storey the windows are not recessed but are on the face of the building with architraves and a capital in the Greek Revival style. The attic storey

Above: The principal courtroom on the piano nobile. The Georgian style of the exterior is continued with accuracy and accomplishment in the interior of the courtroom. The judge's dais and part of the jury box are original elements of the courtroom.

The front door is recessed in a round-headed arch. The doors are replacements for the original doorway and now are paired with glazing. The originals would have been Georgian panel doors.

The overall architectural composition of the front elevation is an elegant, well designed and proportioned late Georgian building that would be a complement to and dignified presence in any county town in England, Scotland or Ireland. The building is now abandoned, deteriorating and its fate uncertain.

THE INTERIOR

The front entrance leads into a spacious entry hall. It is sheathed in a grey and white marble, resembling federal post offices built in the 1950s. Off the central hall is the principal stairway leading to the *piano nobile*. The stairway is a spiral staircase with a central newel which rises through all three floors of the building similar to those embedded in medieval Scottish castles. However, unlike Scottish examples, which always turn clockwise, this staircase runs counter-clockwise. Clearly the architect was not worried about the sword arm of the users of the building. This staircase is original to the building and has been little altered. On each side of the staircase enclosure is a brass handrail.

There is a secondary staircase located at the back right hand corner of the building. This was the segregated staircase for the judiciary enabling them to gain access from their dedicated entrance at the back of the building to the justice's chambers adjacent to the principal courtroom on the *piano nobile*. This staircase is a celebrated feature of Saint John's built heritage. It is often referred

windows are directly above those on the ground and second storeys except in the area of the triumphal Roman arch which features an entablature containing decorative modillions in the Greek Style. The attic storey windows are the size of a single sash in the windows now, but they are divided into two sashes each having three lights.

to as "free standing". It is not free standing; it is securely affixed to the sidewalls and is vertically supported by the stone treads interlocking from top to bottom and laterally embedded in the adjacent wall. There is a traditional story in Saint John that when the building opened in 1829 the sheriff of Saint John County did not believe the staircase would support human activity. He therefore decided to test its strength before he might be challenged by the family of a judge whose death could be attributed to the collapse of the staircase. He is reported to have taken fifty prisoners from the adjacent jail and placed them on all the steps that rise three storeys from ground level to the attic, and for at least half an hour made them jump up and down continuously. The prisoners no doubt enjoyed the exercise and while they may have been as worried as the sheriff they all survived as did the staircase. The staircase is referred to architecturally as a "cantilevered" staircase and is similar to that constructed as the principal staircase in the 1878 Legislative Building located in the provincial capital Fredericton. No harm has come to those using either staircase. The staircase has a balustrade constructed of wrought iron in an elegant Georgian style typical of such staircases.

The *piano nobile* is the location for the principal courtroom. It is a large chamber with windows facing the front and the back of the building – (those on the right hand side of the building referred to in the description of the exterior second storey of the front elevation). The windows have neoclassical wood framing with the architraves designed as fluted Tucson Doric pilasters rising to a pedimented capital which has a dentillated frieze. Each window presents the appearance of a neoclassical triumphal arch. The theme of neoclassicism and dentillated detailing extends throughout the chamber.

The courtroom has been largely disassembled. What is left is only suggestive of the grandeur and importance the chamber had in the life of the city for over one hundred eighty years.

The Saint John courthouse, as an architectural composition, is one of the most significant neoclassical buildings in the Maritimes. Given its age and the quality and integrity of its architectural elements it is deservedly a National Historic Site and a building of exceptional architectural significance, in the Province of New Brunswick.

Above: The back of the courtroom with the bar and public seating. Most of the original fittings have been removed as part of dismantling the building as a courthouse.

OLD CARLETON COUNTY COURT HOUSE
UPPER WOODSTOCK, NEW BRUNSWICK

The Old Carleton County Court House located at 19 Court Street in Upper Woodstock, in the Province of New Brunswick, was constructed in it its first phase in 1833. An extension to the original building was added in 1866 which created the current dimensions of eighty feet (length) and sixty feet (depth). The County of Carleton was created by statute of the legislature of the colony of New Brunswick and assented to in London by the United Kingdom parliament in 1832. It formed part of the County of York.

The location of the courthouse in Upper Woodstock was the result of a strenuous campaign led by one of the leading figures in the community, Mr. Richard Ketcham, of Loyalist stock, to have Upper Woodstock designated as shire town (county capital). His fight to have Upper Woodstock designated as the shire town resulted in the name "Hard Scrabble" being applied to it informally. With the designation of Upper Woodstock as shire town, a seat of county administration which would include a courthouse became a necessity. Mr. Ketcham donated six acres on which the courthouse was built; the donation was one of the factors that led to its designation as shire town. Between 1833 and 1852 meetings of the general sessions of the court were conducted in the courthouse by the magistrate. It also served as the site of the county government.

Right: The porticoed entrance to the courthouse. The windows, doors, and external cladding conform to the original Greek Revival style of the courthouse.

Opposite page: The Old Carleton County Court House has been rescued from its use as a horse barn and has been meticulously restored to its form as a courthouse, now as a courthouse museum.

Right: Detail of the wrought iron chandelier, originally a gasolier.

Opposite page: Interior of the two storey courtroom. The pipes are part of the 19th century heating system sourced originally from wood burning stoves. The balustraded enclosure in the centre of the courtroom is where counsel for the parties would have had their places.

The designer of the Old Carleton County Court House is unknown, but its origins are clear. The form of the building is that of a New England meeting house. The influence of the substantial Loyalist population in this area is evident in the design. The building is in the Greek Revival style which was prevalent in the 1820s and 1830s in New England. It was, in fact, a national style in America and dominated the architectural design of most public buildings there at that time. The oversize double-sash windows are also characteristic of American Greek Revival architecture of this period. The meeting house concept of the building meant it was to be used for several community purposes: as a courthouse, as the centre of county administration and as the location of county fairs and other special events.

The courthouse remained in active use as a courthouse until 1909 when the current Carleton County Court House was constructed. The old courthouse was then sold and used as a barn for almost fifty years. Apparently the building was sold complete with its courtroom fittings and furniture. There is a tradition in the community that the judge's bench (desk) was to be left in the building while it served as a horse barn and while in that use the horses were prone to gnaw on the bench. In fact, the remnants of the judge's bench with cavities created by the horses are an exhibit in the building.

In 1960 a dedicated group of conservationists formed by the Carleton County Historical Society undertook the restoration of the Old Carleton County Court House. Their dedication extended to retaining expert conservationists to assist in reconfiguring the courthouse as a museum. The restored museum courthouse was officially opened on June 25, 1986. The building now stands very much as it was after the 1866 renovations and extension. Every detail of the exterior and interior was researched and accurately replicated. The restoration visibly starts with a rail fence enclosing the front and side yards of the courthouse. Adjacent to the entrance gates in the rail fence are two hitching posts for horses. The

attention to detail is also evident in the hardware used in the hinges and gate opener. The attention to hardware was also applied to all the hinges, locksets and latches used in the interior of the courthouse.

THE EXTERIOR

The exterior of the courthouse, as noted, is in the Greek Revival style. That style has the following characteristics employed in the design of this building: classical symmetry, proportions and decorative elements common to late Georgian architecture in the Greek Revival fashion. The building is framed at its edges by wood framed quoins; quoins were part of the stone work of a Greek Revival building. In this building they served as a corner framing for the exterior architectural design elements and as a transition from one face of the building to the next.

The exterior cladding of the building is locally obtained and milled clapboard which would have been whitewashed (now painted). When this style was popular in America in the early nineteenth century it demonstrated America's dedication to Athenian principles of democracy and justice. It was then believed that the original Greek buildings were white. This arose from the fact that the ancient Greek ruins visited during the nineteenth century were believed to be in their original colour. This was incorrect. Ancient Greek temples like the Parthenon were polychromatic; that is, multi-coloured. The belief in the democratic principles of ancient Greece led to a commitment to white as the colour in which to express the dedication to democracy and justice.

The windows have a simple narrow architrave or external framing. The top of the windows continues the stone-like effect of the quoins through the use of voussoirs constructed in wood with a central vertical keystone, also in wood.

The front door is neoclassical in its design. The doors are late Georgian which was the design employed in Greek Revival meeting houses. The paired doors have a fan light surmounting them. There is a simple pedimented open porch with Doric columns providing a covered entry to the building. The porch is also neoclassical in its design. The front doors, as with the internal doors, are eight-panelled doors called double cross doors, referring to the fact that the configuration of the panels suggests two crucifixes, one over the other.

THE INTERIOR

The courtroom was and remains a two storey chamber with a balcony around three sides supported by Tuscan Doric columns mounted on plinths. The interior configuration of the chamber is that of a classical peristyle hall. This does not conform to British standards of nineteenth century courthouse design. The balcony, while convenient for a community meeting hall or a church, provides little security or segregation of the principals who must carry out their court functions in the chamber. This too reflects the American influence in this building.

The interior of the courtroom has an elevated judicial bench (desk) which has a witness box built into the end, to the judge's left. The clerk of the court was

Left: A 19th century judge's chair with a scales of justice carved into a medallion surmounting the upper edge of the chair bordered by foliate symbols of the British settlers.

Above: The original iron-forged lockset mounted on the interior of the front doors.

also on an elevated dais (lower than that of the judge) facing counsel into the courtroom. The conservation expert engaged in the restoration of the building concluded from his research that the positioning of the judge's bench was originally reversed from its current position.

Behind the judicial chair on the wall above the judge's chair is a portrait of Queen Victoria who was the reigning monarch when the courtroom was reconfigured in 1866. Queen Victoria's coat of arms is mounted above her portrait. The presence of the royal portrait and coat of arms are an English convention that demonstrated the nexus between the monarch as the fount of justice and the place where justice is administered by a person who indirectly is her delegate.

Facing the judge and clerk in a balustraded enclosure in the middle of the courtroom is a segregated space for counsel for the parties.

There is a jury box within a segregated balustrade enclosure to the left of the judge as the judge faces the lawyers. This space is configured for a petit jury – a jury that would be the decider of guilt or innocence in a criminal matter (or in a civil matter of the facts in a civil matter). While not in place at this time, it is

probable that there would have been an enclosure for a grand jury on the wall opposite to the petit jury.

A significant achievement in the restoration of the courtroom was the discovery of pieces of the original wallpaper. The wallpaper was meticulously reproduced and remounted on the wall behind the judicial bench. The wallpaper contains a blue pattern which is highlighted in the centre of each repeat with a dark rose decorative element. The courtroom walls are painted in the same rose colour but in a lighter tone. Plaster was replicated from the original. The floor contains some original pine boards but the majority are replacements complementary to the originals.

The 1866 renovation included the installation of chandeliers to provide addition light to the courtroom. The original light source would have been kerosene lamps. There were also several wall mounted candle sconces.

The chamber was heated by wood-burning stoves similar to Franklin stoves. The stoves obtained for the restoration were made by Enterprise in the town of Sackville, New Brunswick, which was noted for high quality stoves used extensively throughout the Maritime Provinces.

The panelling in the judge's bench, clerk's desk, witness box and prisoner's dock were reproduced faithfully in the restoration as a museum. The wood is locally obtained and wood-grained to resemble one of the finer woods such as mahogany.

The courthouse also contains a dedicated judge's chamber, jury room, barrister's room, guard's room and clerk's office. The stairs from the front hall to the second storey gallery are original in form and design, with replacements for some of the elements.

The Old Carleton County Court House is an interesting example of a nineteenth century blending of British and American courthouse standards. The restoration of the courthouse as a museum is a testament to the importance the courthouse had to its builders and to their successors in the twentieth and twenty first centuries.

For a small town such as Upper Woodstock to have expended the initiative and expense required for this restoration is an exceptional achievement, particularly given the accuracy and attention to detail in the restoration.

QUEENS COUNTY COURT HOUSE
GAGETOWN, NEW BRUNSWICK

The Queens County Court House located at 16 Court House Road in the former shiretown of Gagetown in Queens County, New Brunswick was completed in 1836 and was occupied as a courthouse in 1838. The building was constructed to architectural plans prepared by Saint John architect John Cunningham and construction was carried out by local builder John Glass.

Mr. Cunningham had been engaged as the architect of the Saint John County Court House (1824). He also designed the Charlotte County jail in St. Andrews (1837).

THE EXTERIOR

The Queens County Court House is virtually identical to the Charlotte County Court House. Both are modelled architecturally on ancient Greek temples and are of wood frame construction and are based on a New England meeting house plan which usually included one or more courtrooms. They share a façade designed in the Greek Revival architectural style employed in American early nineteenth century meeting houses. The façade featured a prominent portico centred on the front elevation extending across approximately one half of the front rising from the foundation level to the eave line of the roof.

Opposite page: Queens County Court House is an American meeting house in form built in the carpenter Greek Revival style. It has been carefully restored and now serves as a courthouse museum.

There is, however, a difference in the quality of the architectural details of the St. Andrews and Gagetown buildings. The St. Andrews building was constructed by master carpenters who were thoroughly familiar with the American prototypes on which the building was modelled. The Gagetown building was constructed by carpenters who were less sure of the purpose and function of some of the Greek Revival elements of the design. The Gagetown building was constructed two years prior to that of St. Andrews. It would be speculative to state that the Gagetown building was the prototype for the St. Andrews building. However, it can be accurately stated that they both have the same source – namely a New England meeting house/courthouse designed in the early nineteenth century Greek Revival style.

The Gagetown courthouse is little changed on the exterior from its original form. It remains, in a Gothic Revival style known as Carpenter Gothic – an impressive and elegant example of local vernacular construction and interpretation of the architectural style.

The building is perched on a sharply falling slope which adds to its imposing presence. This setting was used to good advantage by Cunningham and the local craftsmen. Today it is undisturbed in this setting by the intrusion of urban growth and development.

The courthouse has been viewed by the citizens of the county as its most significant civil building. Citizens in almost each generation have produced advocates for and conservators of the building. Its current condition, in a somewhat remote and isolated location in New Brunswick, has been carefully preserved and maintained. It stands as a credit to the people of the region who have devoted the interest and

Above: *Forged iron lock and latch set mounted on the interior of the front doors.*

Left: *Portico with Greek Doric (unfluted) columns.*

support to enable the conservationists under the leadership of the Queens County Historical Society and Museum to do their work.

The courthouse served, in the nature of an American court/meeting house, a number of civic functions: courthouse, community meeting hall and as a symbol of the origins and culture of its original British settlers. They were Loyalists, who immigrated to the area from New England both during and after the American Revolution (1775-1783). The settlers while loyal to the Crown and rejecting the principles of the revolution brought with them many of the cultural expressions with which they were familiar in New England; the most obvious of which were the architectural styles and uses of public buildings. These were replicated in their new country.

THE INTERIOR

The interior of the courthouse differs in its layout from the St. Andrews building but only in its specific allocation of space for customary uses. The two buildings conform to the principles of early English and contemporary American courthouse/meeting house design and use, but as with most locally

Right: Prisoner's dock; forms part of the bar of the courtroom adjacent to the public seating.

Far right: Interior of the restored courtroom modified to enable public exhibitions, lectures and entertainment.

built courthouses they were modified to meet local needs or preferences in the use of secondary spaces.

The difference between the Gagetown courthouse and the St. Andrews courthouse in their interior configuration lies, for example, in that the St. Andrews courthouse front doors open directly into the courtroom, whereas in the Gagetown building there is a large entrance hall from which the courtroom is accessed. The reason for the difference can only be guessed as there is no record of the reason; however, given the severity of the winter weather in this area and the need to provide shelter before entering the courtroom, the entrance hall was a sensible variation in the design. There is a difference also in the location of the courtroom. In the Gagetown building the courtroom is at the back of the building with its axis parallel to the front elevation, whereas in the St. Andrews building the courtroom occupies all the space between the front and back walls except for the lateral offices, passages and stairs.

The configuration of the courtroom is similar to that of St. Andrews: the placement of the judge's bench, dais, prisoner's dock, counsel table and public seating is similar to those in the St. Andrews building. Of particular note is the counsel table which was a single table at which both counsel were placed, facing each other at right angles to the judge. When the presiding judge was addressed by either counsel, they stood facing the judge. Each counsel had a small table in front of him (there were no female lawyers at that time) designed as an adjunct to the counsel table. The original tables remain in the courtroom. Many of the original fittings also remain.

The furniture, including the tables and chairs, was crafted locally from a base wood such as pine which was then grained to resemble quartered oak. Quartered oak was highly fashionable but very expensive at the time of the construction of this courthouse.

Lighting in the courtroom was by candles inserted into wall sconces and chandeliers.

At the back of the courtroom an elevated gallery provided additional public viewing of court or community activities. The local traditional understanding of this gallery was that it was for the use of Afro-American Loyalists who received land grants in the area. They were provided with seating segregated from the white Loyalists, whose seating was at the back of the courtroom on the main floor level.

The Queens County Court House served as a courthouse continuously between 1838 and the mid-1960s when it was abandoned as a venue for the purposes for which it was built. Having served as a courthouse for over one hundred twenty five years, it was left vacant until it was taken over by the local historical society. It is now a community museum and a designated Provincial Heritage Site. In its current role it is a courthouse museum, theatre, art gallery and community hall. It is one of the most significant and informative historic buildings in New Brunswick.

CHARLOTTE COUNTY COURT HOUSE
ST. ANDREWS, NEW BRUNSWICK

The Charlotte County Court House located at 123 Frederick Street in the Town of St. Andrews, in the Province of New Brunswick, was constructed in 1840 and continues to serve both Supreme Court and Provincial Court functions, making it one of the oldest functioning courthouses in Canada. There are older courthouses extant but not serving the purposes for which they were built. The Charlotte County Court House is a blending of New England and English courthouse standards of courtroom layout and function. Its exterior architectural design owes its origins to the English neoclassical architectural tradition known as Palladianism.

The courthouse was designed by local architect Thomas Berry. He was so committed to creating a building that would serve as a dignified monument honouring the town and its people that he undertook much of the extensive decorative enhancement of the building at his own expense and hoped to be reimbursed later by the county council. After litigation on the matter he received partial payment only. As the result of Mr. Berry's enthusiasm for his town, its people and the Loyalist roots of most of its citizens, he created one of the finest – some commentators assert *the* finest – wood-framed and clad neoclassical courthouses in Canada of the first half of the nineteenth century.

Opposite page: Charlotte County Court House.

THE EXTERIOR

The exterior of the courthouse is designed in a specialized architectural form of Palladianism known as the Greek Revival style. This was a highly fashionable style then prevalent in New England. Indeed the Greek Revival style in the 1820s, through the 1840s, was considered in the United States to be a national architectural style because of the origins of its architectural elements in ancient Greece, believed to be the source of the philosophy and practice of nineteenth century American democracy.

The Greek Revival style was used elsewhere in the Maritimes in significant public buildings, some of which like the Charlotte County Court House, could trace their origins to the New England model of the style. Other examples such as the legislative building Province House, in Charlottetown (1848), which also contained a superior court, owed its origins to British sources. Several other early Maritime courthouses share their New England influences with the Charlotte County Court House.

The extensive use of the Greek Revival style and its identity as the National American style in early-nineteenth century American public buildings was largely the result of the personal taste, influence and political prominence in the revolutionary period of Thomas Jefferson. Jefferson was a knowledgeable and gifted amateur architect whose most celebrated buildings are on the campus of the University of West Virginia and his personal residence known as Monticello, also in Virginia. Each of these buildings conformed to the Greek Revival style.

Left: The judge's bench on an elevated dais and the balustrade segregating the judge from the rest of the courtroom. The petit jury box is on the right and counsel would have been located in the middle balustraded area.

Below: The double front doors, an interior view.

architecture in giving expression to democracy and the delivery of justice in America's public buildings. He viewed the Greek Revival style as a means of teaching the citizenry the nature and forms of government and the administration of justice. The courthouse, in its architectural style and internal configuration, served both those ends. Pedimented temples in the Greek architectural tradition came to be the norm in both the United States and in early Nova Scotia and New Brunswick for courthouses and for their expanded community uses.

He was also directly engaged in the design of courthouses in Virginia. They became the standard of exterior architectural design and interior layout, both in Virginia and elsewhere in the evolving United States of America. The most visible expression of the influence Jefferson had on courthouse design was in New England. This is primarily because in the late eighteenth and early-nineteenth centuries it was the most populous area of the new country, with a density of population and established legal traditions (English common-law based) which created a need for enforcement of laws, courts, and courthouses. Jefferson was committed to the principle of democratic government and was convinced of the role of

Dominating the front elevation of this temple-like courthouse is the substantial portico covering approximately one half of the front. The classically proportioned pediment is supported by four Tuscan Doric columns which rise to a frieze comprised of a simple layered detailing which encircles the building. Giving much emphasis and interest to the pediment is the polychrome coat of arms of Queen Victoria which covers most of the tympanum. The coat of arms was carved from local wood by a St. Andrew's craftsman and painter, Charles Kennedy, in 1858. The locating of a coat of arms in a pediment in a building associated with the Crown or a government is a tradition having its roots in British architecture. While the Charlotte County Court House in its neoclassical composition would be of outstanding importance without the carved and coloured coat of arms, it gives the building a dignity and presence second to none in its depiction of the Greek Revival style and the use for which the building was constructed.

The main building is a simple rectangular block having balance, harmony and classical proportions in its elements and composition, all of which have their origins in British Georgian architecture. The immediate source of the design elements is found in New England, but the source of the American standards was pre-revolutionary Britain.

The courthouse can be viewed as a perfect Canadian architectural composition encapsulating in Canadian fashion a mixture of American and British influences. The Charlotte County Court House is therefore a thoroughly Canadian structure. It was constructed in the pre-confederation era when the Colony of New Brunswick was part of British North America; even then the adoption and mixing of British and American influences was common in the Maritimes.

The front elevation is comprised of vertical boards at the edges of the building on all four sides. These are called pilasters. They are not only a decorative detail complementary to the columns in the portico; they also serve as a reminder that the origin of the design is Greek temple architecture, which had columns across the front of the building. Pilasters are vertically applied thin non-structural columns in the same style and external dimensions as the columns in the portico.

The dimensions of the windows are of a New England scale. They are double-sash windows, each having twelve-over-twelve lights. They are substantially larger than a Scottish Georgian inspired building of the period. For example, there is a nearby comparison to the Charlotte County Court House – the Greenock Presbyterian Church a few blocks away. The Church was completed in June 1824 following Scottish Georgian architectural traditions. Among other differences, the size and proportions of the windows differ. The Scottish-sourced windows in the church are much narrower and, while substantial, are more compact. The shutters on the courthouse were an original component of the design and are a further influence from the New England origins of the courthouse.

The centre of the front contains the paired eight-panelled entrance doors with a transom light surmounting them. The transom is the same size as one of the sashes in the adjacent windows, thereby providing an even line and continuity to the architectural composition. The eight-panelled doors are often referred to as "double-cross" doors, not because a former accused was guilty of nefarious behaviour, but because the panels are configured to resemble two vertical crucifixes.

The cladding of the building is narrowly spaced clapboards painted white. The colour white would have been an original part of the decoration of the building.

Above: Witness box.

Right: Prisoner's dock connected to the bar of the courtroom, inside the functional area of the courtroom is adjacent to the public seating on the other side of the bar. The carved hole in the seat was to enable the prisoner to be chained in place.

Above: Public seating at the back of the courtroom. Windsor bench seating locally crafted.

THE INTERIOR

The interior of the courthouse is as impressive as the exterior.

The layout of the building divides the internal space into three units: a central space, virtually square, occupying half of the building containing the courtroom, and segments of one quarter of the width of the courtroom on both sides of the courtrooms. The spaces on either side of the courtroom contain offices and secondary access.

The courtroom is a space into which the front doors open directly. The public seating area was in this space and extended forward to the "bar" of the courtroom – the bar is a balustrade separating the public space in the courtroom from the functional space into which the public could have access only with the permission of the presiding judge. This would occur if a person were charged with an offence such as under *The Criminal Code of Canada* or if a person were a party in a civil litigation. The configuration of the space is primarily American in origin. But it should be noted that American courtroom standards had their origin in eighteenth century English courtrooms. The American standards were a variation reflecting colonial legal experience and traditions. It does not fully comply with nineteenth century standards of England courtroom design which required segregation of the principals functioning in the courtroom: the judge from everyone else, the clerk and court officials such as the sheriff from the public, the lawyers from the judge and court officials, and the accused from everyone but his lawyer. English courtroom standards also required a secure segregated access to the courtroom by the judge from a secure dedicated entrance. The Charlotte County Court House provided a segregated entrance and dais for the presiding judge but not to the degree that provided much security for the participants in a court proceeding – particularly in the placement of the accused.

The clearest example of the lack of security in this courtroom is the placement of the prisoner's dock adjacent to and in front of the "bar" which as noted was directly in front of the entrance. Recently, the prisoner's dock received an addition in the form of a plexiglas screen on the back of the dock, which theoretically would prevent an accused from simply jumping over the back of the dock and the bar and exiting through the front doors.

The judge's bench is on the opposite wall from the front entrance and is located behind a balustrade which extends on an elevated dais across the full

It is now painted but originally it probably was whitewashed. The selection of white as the body colour of the courthouse reflects the early-nineteenth century belief that ancient Greek temples were devoid of colour. However, the stones forming the structures were bleached almost white by the intense Greek sun. In fact, the Greek temples were polychrome in their decorative elements; bright vibrant colours were used. The strong colours used by Mr. Kennedy in the coat of arms in the pediment are fully in keeping with the original decoration of Greek temples.

The courthouse rests on a substantial basement constructed of local igneous rock, most of which is granite. The basement originally contained a holding cell for temporary incarceration of an accused while awaiting trial. The courthouse was built adjacent to an existing granite jail which served as the place of incarceration for serving a sentence after a verdict of guilt.

width of the courtroom. This balustrade segregates the judge from the rest of the courtroom. Behind the judge on the back wall are two windows of the same size as those directly opposite, on the front elevation adjacent to the double front doors.

The courtroom has two jury boxes, one on each sidewall, both enclosed in a balustraded space. The larger box was for a grand jury and the smaller for a petit jury. This is an American adaptation of the English courtroom standards.

An interesting enclosed space, original to the construction of the courthouse, is a witness box used for the trials of persons accused of criminal offences. This witness box, located at the end of the judge's dais, is unusual because there is no seat for the accused: the accused was expected to stand during the trial, hence the term used, even to this day, of an accused "standing trial". Tradition at the Charlotte County Court House has it that the accused's box for giving testimony was directly in front of a vent which piped hot air into the box. It was believed that a little aggravation would encourage honesty and an admission of guilt. This practice would be frowned upon today, although some Crown counsel (prosecutors) might be tempted to employ it in certain cases.

There is a second witness box to the left of the judge, opposite to the location of the accused's box. This is for all other witnesses. It has space for a chair and provides some degree of comfort to a witness giving evidence.

Another interesting element of the design of the courthouse is the arrangement of the space dedicated to counsel. The lawyers for the parties are not allocated separate tables. They sit at the same table facing each other and at right angles to the presiding judge. This may appear to some twenty first century lawyers and judges as a strange configuration, but it conforms to one of the basic principles of the exercise of judicial authority and the relationship of counsel to the judge. The single table with counsel facing each other is a reminder and demonstration of the principle that lawyers are officers of the court and have a high ethical duty to the court of honesty, integrity and serving the objective of achieving justice. It also serves as a demonstration that all counsel have the same purpose and that it is their role to seek the truth and to put the law and facts fully and accurately before the judge. Counsel tables of this type are found in several other early nineteenth century Nova Scotia and New Brunswick courtrooms.

The courthouse has a dedicated entrance on the side of the building for the judge, but it is a door also used to bring the accused into the courtroom.

Therefore, timing of the entrance of the principals in a proceeding was important in keeping the security of the judges intact. This courthouse had an additional practice that reflects the principle of justice appearing to be done. The accused is brought into the building through the side door from the jail in shackles, but before entering the courtroom the shackles and other visible restraints were removed so that when the accused entered the courtroom there was no appearance of presumed guilt. The accused was escorted to the prisoner's dock described above. The momentary freedom from shackles ended when the accused was seated in the prisoner's dock. The shackles were reinstalled on the accused and affixed to tear-drop like openings in the accused's seat in the dock. The sides of the dock are panelled and sufficiently high so that the shackles cannot be observed by those present in the courtroom. However, the reaffixing of the shackles in the courtroom must have defeated the appearance of innocence.

The courtroom has a portrait of Queen Victoria above the petit jury box which is appropriate given that the courthouse was constructed in the early years of her reign. The portrait also serves as a reminder, as with the coat of arms in the pediment, of the connection between the Crown as the fount of justice in the English and Canadian judicial systems.

On the wall opposite the portrait of Queen Victoria, above the grand jury box, is a collection of portraits of King George III, his consort Queen Charlotte and their thirteen children. While King George is not specifically relevant to the Charlotte County Court House, the Town of St. Andrews was settled during his reign, primarily by Loyalists. The Loyalists immigrated in the late 1700s from the town of Castile in what is now the State of Maine. These portraits are a reminder of the origin of the names of the streets of St. Andrews that run at right angles to the harbour – the name of each child is recorded in a street name, together with a King and Queen Street. While the courthouse has American origins, the town and courthouse were British and are now a blend of American and English courthouse standards.

The Charlotte County Court House remains an active court serving both Supreme Court and Provincial Court functions. It maintains its reputation as one of the longest serving courthouses in Canada – certainly one of the most elegant and interesting courthouses in the country.

KINGS COUNTY COURT HOUSE
HAMPTON, NEW BRUNSWICK

The Kings County Court House located at 648 Main Street in the Town of Hampton in the Province of New Brunswick was completed in 1872 with the first court sessions held in that year. The architect who designed the courthouse was a resident of the town, J.T.C. McKean. The builder is not recorded.

The Kings County Court House was typical of late nineteenth century courthouses inasmuch it also served a number of civic functions including the registry of deeds and various municipal and county offices. It has been abandoned. The interior has been largely gutted and allowed to deteriorate while decisions are yet to be made by the responsible officials as to what its future should be.

The courthouse is in two primary architectural styles: the mansard roof defines it as having a Second Empire influence and the fenestration and portico give it an Italianate character. It was not uncommon for late Victorian architects to mix more than one architectural style in the same building. There are, in addition, three Romanesque design elements. The overall composition of the building is symmetrical, well-proportioned and harmonious in its use of decorative detailing.

Right: Detail of the interior of the portico.

Opposite page: The Romanesque architectural style of the courthouse, with its flaring hipped platform roof, created an elegant and dignified centrepiece for the Town of Hampton.

THE EXTERIOR

The two most prominent features of the exterior are the one storey portico sheltering the front door and the attic storey clock tower with an embedded pediment.

The portico, as with the facing on the remainder of the courthouse, is constructed primarily of locally-cast red brick, finished smooth to the face of the building. Giving highlights to the front elevation are belt courses in sandstone.

Above: The tower roof with its inset medallion contains the timeless motto "let justice be done, though heavens fall".

Right: The bracketed eaves and the cornice containing wood and brick decorative elements add to the architectural composition of the courthouse.

The portico contains fine Romanesque arches on each of its exposed three sides. The roof of the portico is edged with copper, which gives a complementary highlight to the brick and sandstone.

In the attic storey above the portico, in the embedded pediment in the clock tower, is the Latin motto found in the St. John's Anglican parish hall in Lunenburg, Nova Scotia: "*Fait Justitia ruat coelum*" which means "let justice be done, though heavens fall". This motto is a reminder to all who were to use the building of one of the precepts of the administration of justice. No building in the Maritimes more prominently displays this motto. It defines the primary use of the building as a courthouse and the location of the building in the centre of the town broadcasts that motto as a commitment to justice being served.

The windows are round-headed Italianate windows with a keystone at the apex of each window giving verticality to the design further complemented by the tower.

The mansard roof is in a hipped platform configuration which means that the top of the roof is basically flat. The roofline from the platform to the eave

line flares gently giving movement to the design. The edges of the roof as it transitions from one plane to the next are also decorated with copper.

Below the eave line are brackets known as corbels, which are similar to projecting floor joists.

The architectural composition, while containing two primary architectural styles and a third supplementary style, is a coherent and pleasing design that gives prominence and dignity to the building and the purposes it was designed to serve.

THE INTERIOR

As noted, the interior has been largely gutted but the principal courtroom on the *piano nobile* contains some of the original fittings. These are primarily neoclassical in style and give a consistency between the exterior architectural elements, all of which are in a modified form of neoclassicism.

The Kings County Court House remains the single most significant architectural creation in the town. It deserves to be preserved, at least on the exterior and a new use found for the interior which would reflect the history, dignity and architectural integrity of the building.

Above: The prisoner's dock with finely turned balusters.

Left: The concave-domed ceiling provided enhanced acoustics in the courtroom. The brackets, cornice and connecting elements originally would have been dark varnished wood similar to the prisoner's dock.

VICTORIA COUNTY COURT HOUSE
PERTH-ANDOVER, NEW BRUNSWICK

The Victoria County Court House located at 1135 West Riverside Drive, in a prominent position on the Saint John River, in the Village of Perth-Andover, New Brunswick was constructed by the municipal council of the county in 1878. The selection of this location for the courthouse reflected the position of Andover as the shire town of the county. A shire town was the designated capital and principal centre of the county. This building was designed for the purpose of a courthouse and temporary lock-up, but as the principal civil building in the county, it was fashioned with great pride and commitment to the importance of the community.

THE EXTERIOR

The designer and the builder of the courthouse are unrecorded. The three storey wood-framed structure is now disused and abandoned. The exterior design incorporates some Second Empire and Italianate architectural elements. The Second Empire architectural elements include a mansard roof and a projecting central tower, which at the ground floor level contains the entrance with a simple double-door configuration surmounted by a transom.

The Italianate aspects of the design are found in the windows located in the projecting tower which rises up to the ridge line of the principal roof of the building. The paired windows on the second and third floors are framed

Opposite page: The Victoria County Court House is a late Victorian adaptation of the Second Empire style of architecture.

with typical broad architraves and a broad mullion separating the windows. The windows are capped with wood-framed hood mouldings.

The neoclassical elements are characteristics of the Italianate style and the Greek Revival style. They were added to the decorative composition of the front elevation as well. They are included in the tower and front elevation of the building in the form of pilasters or corner boards, which have their origin in Greek Revival architecture. The corner boards extend from ground level to a plain deep frieze below the eaves. A porch was a later practical addition to the building. The pediment of the porch is supported by Tuscan Doric columns and a shallow pitched roof.

The windows of the front elevation are tall double sash windows with each sash having two lights or panes of glass.

The exterior cladding of the courthouse is clapboard.

The overall design of the courthouse is a combination of architectural styles typical of the Victorian era, probably created by a local master builder. All of the elements of the design were well established at this time and were available to a skilled carpenter from pattern books readily accessible to him and through visiting larger communities in the province.

THE INTERIOR

The skills of the local craftsmen who constructed the building are expressed in impressive fashion in the stairway leading to the main courtroom on the second floor. That the courtroom was located on the second floor is in recognition of

Above: The courtroom has been dismantled, but some of the original fittings remain such as the segregated balustraded area where counsel would have been placed.

Left: The courtroom contains fine craftsmanship in the woodworking and cabinetry.

the nineteenth century courthouse design standards. The principal chamber in a neoclassically-inspired building should be placed on an elevated level – the second floor, which in classical architectural language is referred to as the *piano nobile*. It waas so placed in this courthouse.

The main stairway leads from the public entrance hall to a second floor landing from which access to the courtroom is provided through double doors. The balustrade of the staircase is constructed of local wood. The builder displayed skilled joinery and woodturning techniques in the balusters. There is a second staircase as one would expect which provided segregated and secure access to the courtroom for the judges. It leads directly to the judge's bench from the ground floor.

The courtroom is clad in tongue-and-groove boarding in various configurations. These were designed to demonstrate the skills of the craftsmen who constructed the room and to demonstrate the importance of the courtroom in the life and administration of justice in the county.

The chamber is almost a cube, two storeys in height. There is a balcony around three sides of the courtroom which provided public viewing to both court and council activities. In classical terms it would be known as a peristyle hall. This configuration is not British; it owes its origins to traditional eighteenth century American architecture. The ceilings are in their original condition with pressed tin decorative panelling.

The Victoria County Court House served several roles: courthouse, jail (primarily as a temporary lock-up, located in the basement) a meeting place for the county council, the registry of deeds and storage of court documents. The building also provided a residence for the jailer.

As noted, the courthouse has been abandoned and appears to be available for sale. This is unfortunate. Its use as a courthouse may no longer be practical but it is one of the more significant civil buildings from the 1870s in this county, demonstrating as it does the extraordinary craftsmanship and pride of the people. It is unfortunate it cannot be preserved for a complementary contemporary use as have many other similar courthouses in the Maritimes.

Above: The courtroom retains the original judge's bench, balustrades and prisoner's dock. The future of this building is uncertain.

JUSTICE BUILDING
FREDERICTON, NEW BRUNSWICK

The seat of the New Brunswick Court of Appeal and the Supreme Court of New Brunswick, which include the Court of Queen's Bench, Trial Division and Family Division is located at 427 Queen Street in the capital of the province, Fredericton. The building is known as the "Justice Building" reflecting the several levels and layers of judicial and support services available in the building. In addition to the Court of Appeal and trial level superior courts the building also contains one of the several provincial courts in the province which deal with entry level criminal and quasi-criminal offences.

The Justice Building is located in a building constructed in 1876 for the Provincial Normal School – a school for student teachers in which elementary school students were enrolled. After several fires which resulted in the interior of the building being largely gutted, the building was vacated as the Normal School in 1973 and rebuilt as a courthouse to accommodate the superior courts and the provincial court. The building was spatially reconfigured on the interior and expanded with lateral wings to accommodate the various courts.

Right: A granite column with a finely carved Corinthian capital, part of the tripartite pointed arches forming the entrance to the courthouse.

Opposite page: The front elevation of the Justice Building comprising the original segment in the centre extending to the outer line of quoins, with later additions on both sides.

THE EXTERIOR

The primary exterior architectural elements are found in the original Provincial Normal School section of the building. The wings contain elements complementary to the original normal school that in their simplicity neither add to nor detract from the original design.

The building is a four storey brick clad structure with stone detailing around the windows and in the principal entrance. Three of the floors of the building are above an elevated base. The third floor is created out of the attic space. The elevated base contains a semi-basement, housing provincial court facilities. There is no *piano nobile* as in a classical or neoclassical building. Each of the upper three floors contains superior court facilities.

Above: The New Brunswick Court of Appeal principal courtroom. Counsel tables in the foreground.
The bench is set for a panel of three justices. The painting on the wall behind the justices is highly
significant. It is described in the text. (see also p.19)

The Justice Building is in a prominent position in the capital. It is on the same street as several of the principal buildings in the city including the Legislative Building which houses the legislature of the province. Government House is nearby on Woodstock Road and provides a residence for the lieutenant governor. The Justice Building is situated in a park-like setting bordered by an elegant curvilinear wrought iron fence anchored at regular intervals by granite piers. The prominent position of the Justice Building in the capital city and its imposing presence as one of its three most significant civil buildings conforms to the principles of colonial urban design and the British legal traditions of justice being visible and accessible. The character of the Justice Building asserts its role as performing one of the most substantial duties of government – the administration of justice.

The architectural elements of the front elevation of the Justice Building reflect the period in which the Provincial Normal School was constructed. The 1880s was a time when Victorian architects found challenge and satisfaction in taking several architectural styles and combining them, almost randomly, into a confection of the architect's imagination. The centre block of the Justice Building is typical Victorian architecture. It combines several distinct styles. It does so with panache and a conviction that the building must speak to the importance of the activities that are performed in the building. When the Normal School was established in the late nineteenth century, there was a prevalent conviction held by the people and government of the province that education was one of the primary keys to a productive future for its citizenry and for the economy of the province. The combination of styles employed in the design of the building, while eclectic, successfully represents that conviction.

The architectural elements in the design include neoclassical, Gothic Revival, Renaissance Revival and Romanesque styles. The most prominent aspect of the front elevation is the recessed entry with a Gothic Revival arcade on the same plain as the face of the building. The arcade, with its pointed arches, is supported by neoclassical granite columns which have capitals in the Corinthian order. The proportions of the columns are eccentric being more in the nature of stout Romanesque columns used in contemporary interpretations of the Romanesque Revival style. The columns rest on granite piers. The arcade and entry are

Above: The New Brunswick Court of Appeal recently created a second courtroom set for a panel of three justices. The courtroom contains some fine panelling and cabinetry.

approximately mid-level between the basement and first floor.

Above the Gothicized arcade is a belt course of sandstone which contains three plaques. The two outer plaques have the dates 1876 and 1930 carved into them. The dates relate to the use of the building as a normal school. The central plaque has had the Normal School identification removed. It was in high relief similar to the dates. Also above the arcade and the two lower side pointed arches, are two medallions in high relief which appear to be symbols or crests of the Normal School. After the building was adapted to a courthouse, the belt course was revised to remove the name "Normal School" and incised with a word to identify the building and its new usage as a courthouse: "Justice".

The fenestration is modern. The current glazings of the windows are inserts into the original window openings – practical and efficient – however, some window openings have been expanded to enable enhanced light and air circulation.

Above: The New Brunswick Court of Queen's Bench, one of the trial level courtrooms.

THE INTERIOR

The interior of the Justice Building conforms to the contemporary concept of the delivery of judicial services and justice-related support services, particularly as required in family law matters. The building effectively offers "one stop shopping" for resolution of conflict. Two Provincial Court courtrooms are located on the first floor with offices for court officials, a police office and holding cells. Judicial services provided in the Court of Queen's Bench in civil and criminal matters are located on the second and fourth floors along with offices for the court officials and justices. The building also contains the Probate Court and a barrister's robing room. The third floor houses the New Brunswick Court of Appeal as well as the law library. The Family Law courtrooms are located on both the second and fourth floors.

The traditional English concept of segregation of spaces for justices, court officials, members of the bar and litigants/accused has not been applied in the layout and design of the Justice Building. It is conceptually possible to have all levels of the court services integrated in one building, but it is essential that the principle of segregation be preserved and manifest.

There are other continuing functional adjustments required among the judiciary and support staff to compensate for the configuration of the spaces and uses of the building. An excellent example is the location and use of the one law library in the Justice Building. It is on the second floor across the hall from the Court of Appeal and adjacent to Queen's Bench courtrooms and staff. The very real and practical issue that arises from this arrangement is that justices of the Court of Appeal must do their research for an appeal in the same space as that used by the justice whose decision has been appealed. It is also used by the barristers and litigants, if self-represented, who are engaged in the litigation.

The reason the proximity of judges and justices of the various levels of courts can create a problem arises, for example, where a Queen's Bench justice who is anxious to make a decision in a problematic case that he or she wishes to survive an appeal could wish to approach a justice of the Court of Appeal even in a seemingly casual way and discuss the case. While the etiquette of the courts prohibits such discussions, proximity and shared facilities make casual discussion difficult to control.

Proximity also raises the issue of justice appearing to be done. A litigant who has failed in a case before a Queen's Bench justice and has filed an appeal, seeing that trial justice talking in the courthouse to a Court of Appeal justice who will sit on the appeal, may suspect discussion on the litigant's case, irrespective of whether there has been. Justice must appear to be done. It is difficult to establish that standard in a totally integrated facility that does not have clearly segregated areas.

The traditional English standards of courthouse design of space, function and segregation, while open to twenty first century interpretation, are as relevant and significant in the twenty first century as they have ever been.

The Justice Building in Fredericton works well, but adjusts its services and activities to compensate for the lack of some of the traditional principles of courtroom and courthouse design. On the other hand, as an integrated facility, it has been well ahead of the contemporary trend to have fully integrated justice-related facilities in one building.

The New Brunswick Court of Appeal has two courtrooms on the second floor of the building. The larger of the two is the original created during the renovations made to convert the building into a courthouse. It can accommodate all seven of the Court of Appeal justices or a smaller panel as may be determined

Above: The New Brunswick Court of Appeal viewing from the bench to the public seating behind the bar. The front row counsel table is referred to as the "inner bar" (for Queen's Counsel) and behind it the tables for non-Queen's Counsel, referred to as the "outer bar".

Above: The tripartite pointed arches are the entrance to the Justice Building.

by the chief justice. The courtroom contains a novel feature not found in any other superior court courtroom in the Maritimes – namely, an "Inner Bar" and an "Outer Bar". The Inner Bar is the first row of seating and desks for lawyers representing clients appearing in an appeal. It is a segregated area for Queen's Counsel. The Outer Bar is the second row behind the Inner Bar which is designated for the use of juniors – members of the bar who are not Queen's Counsel. The Inner Bar desks are distinguished by red baize coverings and have lockable drawers beneath the sloped platform desks. The Outer Bar desks are covered in a green baize covering. The colours are traditional representations of precedence.

The Court of Appeal also has a recent addition to its facilities: a second courtroom for its use has recently been created adjacent to the justice's chambers on the second floor. It is a compact space sufficient for hearing an appeal by a panel of three. The desks, cabinetry and decorative elements are finely crafted in dark-stained wood, creating an elegant and dignified chamber.

CARLETON COUNTY COURT HOUSE
WOODSTOCK, NEW BRUNSWICK

The Carleton County Court House located at 689 Main Street in the Town of Woodstock in the Province of New Brunswick was constructed in 1909 as a successor to the Old Carleton County Court House built in 1833 in Upper Woodstock. The 1909 building was constructed in a prominent position ("Greek Village") facing the Saint John River in the middle of the three Woodstock communities. The shift of economic and political power resulted in the shire town being relocated and with that relocation a new courthouse was required. The new courthouse was designed to conform to the prevailing standards of English courtroom designs, but an American influence reflected in the Old Carleton County Court House remained.

Right: The Romanesque entrance to the Carleton County Court House. The masonry is skillfully designed and crafted. The front elevation is balanced, dignified and harmonious in its elements and composition.

Opposite page: The Carleton County Court House; the courts are located in the right hand side of the building.

THE EXTERIOR

The 1909 courthouse was designed by F. Neil Brodie as an addition to an existing building housing several municipal offices such as the registry offices. The registry section was designed by J.G. Fletcher in the Romanesque Revival style. Mr. Brodie simply expanded the Fletcher building retaining Fletcher's design elements. The resulting building has two equally prominent front entrances. An imaginary line drawn vertically through the middle of the building would see both halves equal in size and detail.

The Romanesque Revival style is articulated in the cluster of three round-headed windows on the second floor above the Romanesque arrangement of three windows below. The roof is a hipped platform roof with a dormer inset into the roof on each side of the building. The dormers are constructed of the sandstone used in the window trim and belt courses. They have an interesting architectural feature expressed in the outside walls of the dormers flaring outwards as they approach and meet the roof.

The two entrances to the building are located in projecting pavilions which extend to a pediment in the roof. Each pavilion has a Romanesque entry in

Above: The prisoner's dock; now relegated to a back corner of the courtroom.

Right: The principal courtroom located on the piano nobile contains some exceptionally fine panelling and cabinetry as is evident in the jury box and wainscoting behind it.

Opposite page: The Carleton County Court House; interior of the principal courtroom.

the form of a simple Roman arch. The Romanesque arches framing the two entrances have a carved foliate design at the transition point between the arch and the vertical architrave elements. The outside section of each doorway buried in the foliation is the carved head of an owl. It is not obvious and must be sought to be observed. It is unknown whether this is the result of whimsy on the part of the mason, or whether it speaks to the wisdom ascribed to owls – suggesting that in this building wisdom is practised. The entrance doors are recessed in an open porch; each of the two entrances has a pair of doors with a transom.

The exterior cladding of the courthouse is red brick sourced locally. The brick is complemented by the local grayish sandstone used in the decorative detailing. The grounds at the front of the building contain a cenotaph originally installed as a memorial to the First World War (1914-1918) with later inscriptions added after conflicts such as the Second World War and a conflict as recent as Afghanistan. The presentation of the building is that of the most significant civil building in the town. Its elevation, size and the presence of the cenotaph assert that standing in the community.

THE INTERIOR

The interior of the courthouse contains numerous spaces for public offices, the most significant of which is for the courtroom. The courtroom is a full two storeys in height and approximately a cube in volume (equal height to the length of the walls). There is a balcony over the public entrance into the courtroom. The courtroom contains fine wood panelling and decorative wood trim. The

Above: At the back of the principal courtroom there is public seating on the floor and in a balcony.

panelling is constructed of local wood and stained to resemble highly important wood such as mahogany. The decorative elements in the interior are in a Georgian Revival style called "Edwardian Neoclassical". The principles of Edwardian neoclassicism are followed strictly: absolute balance, harmony, proportion and the application of Georgian decorative details. The cube-like space is entirely classical. In classical architecture a cube was considered to be a perfect form for an interior space. The principle of balance is reflected in a pair of doors on the right side of the back wall on which the judge's bench is located. The doors are decorative only. They are a blind "bay" on the wall placed to balance functional doors on the left end of that wall.

The most emphatic decorative element of the room is a recessed apse behind the judge's seat on the bench. The apse is proportioned well to the dimensions of the wall. It provides an effective framing and focal point for the presiding judge. There is a door immediately behind the judge's chair which gives access to the judge's chambers behind. The decorative elements feature dentilled friezes in the pedimented over-door treatments and in the frieze surrounding the room. The ceiling is a deep coved recess adding an additional sense of space, elegance and acoustical enhancement to the room.

The internal layout of the courtroom is also interesting as it is part of the tradition in older courthouses in Nova Scotia and New Brunswick to have a balustraded grand jury box and a separate petit jury box on opposite sides of the chamber. The position of the "dock" is also a curiosity found in a few of the courthouses of a similar age in Nova Scotia and New Brunswick. The accused's dock originally, and until recently, was located inside the functional area of the courtroom abutting the bar (that is the balustrade separating the public and the functional areas of the courtroom). This is unlike the English tradition of placing the dock in a more secure segregated space.

In accordance with modern philosophical changes in the application of the principle that "justice must be seen to be done as well as be done" and its corollary that an "accused is innocent until proven guilty", a prisoner's dock is no longer used in this chamber. The balustraded structure remains in the courtroom but is tucked away in a corner of the chamber. The furnishings are original, but the judge's throne-like chair is not present. Judges, it seems, are prone to back problems. An orthopedically corrective chair is in use for the presiding judge in this chamber, as in virtually all courtrooms in the Maritimes. The high style judge's chair, as constructed for the Upper Woodstock courthouse, is missing from the contemporary courtroom. Its absence can be lamented by those with traditional values but not those required to sit through proceedings that can be tiresome and seemingly interminable.

This courtroom in its state of preservation is a reflection of the high standards of conservation one can observe in the Old Carleton County Court House Museum and in other buildings such as Connell House, also in Woodstock.

The Carleton County Court House is a worthy successor to the older courthouse in Upper Woodstock. It is as respected and conserved as the other building, to the credit of the citizens of Woodstock who clearly value their built heritage.

Above: A bird's-eye view of the principal courtroom.

NORTHUMBERLAND COUNTY COURTHOUSE
MIRAMICHI, NEW BRUNSWICK

Built on an elevated position overlooking the Miramichi River, the Northumberland County Courthouse was constructed at 599 Prince George Highway in the Town of Newcastle (now together with the Town of Chatham, renamed Miramichi) in the Province of New Brunswick. It was built between 1912 and 1913. The courthouse was designed by Wolfville, Nova Scotia architect Leslie R. Fairn in the Richardsonian Romanesque style. It is modelled on the Digby County Court House in Nova Scotia, built three years earlier. It is now disused as a courthouse and awaits a buyer to give it a new use, probably of a commercial nature.

The 1912-1913 building was a replacement for a wood frame Georgian style courthouse built in 1829 across the Miramichi River in Chatham (now part of the amalgamated City of Miramichi). While the 1829 building remains standing with its exterior largely intact,

Right: The two ashlar corner circular towers with conical roofs, and the massive ashlar masonry entrance define the architectural style.

Opposite page: The Northumberland County Courthouse is in the Richardsonian Romanesque style, similar to the Digby County Court House, the former faced in ashlar, the latter in brick.

the interior has been gutted and turned into apartments. None of the 1829 courthouse internal layout, fittings or decorative elements survive.

The 1912-1913 Northumberland County Courthouse combined the functions of a courthouse and a jail. Holding cells, said to be haunted, remain in the basement of the building.

THE EXTERIOR

Fairn applied the Richardsonian Romanesque style – a style which originated with Henry Hobson Richardson, an American, who was born in 1838 and died at the age of 47. His architectural practice was at first centred in Boston, then New York. He designed numerous significant buildings in his highly distinctive style in Chicago and in the Midwest of the United States. His style came to represent the highest standards of architectural design for public buildings such as courthouses, churches, city halls and legislative buildings in the United States in the late nineteenth century and early-twentieth century. American architectural designs were highly influential in Canada. Old Toronto City Hall and the Ontario legislative building, (Queens Park) in Toronto are both in the Richardsonian Romanesque style, although neither was designed by

Left: The judge's dais panelling in the principal courtroom. One of the few fittings left in the courthouse as it is being renovated for other uses. The "scales of justice" and dais panelling are also similar to the Digby courthouse.

The primary surviving elements of the courthouse are found on the second floor where some of the panelling, ceiling details, balustrades and the judge's bench remain intact.

The layout of spaces in the courthouse conforms to the standards of late nineteenth century courthouse design, namely segregation of the participants in the conduct of legal proceedings. There is a justice's

him. His influence on domestic architecture was also profound. There are houses having this style in Charlottetown and Halifax, for example.

The Richardsonian Romanesque style was perfectly suited to the late nineteenth century concept of a courthouse, which was to powerfully establish the might, dignity and authority of the law and the justices administering the law. The courthouse was intended to serve as a visible and dramatic reminder to the citizens of the area of the maintenance of law and order. It was not intended to be inviting. It was designed to intimidate and to serve as a statement that the rule of law and good conduct prevailed in that community.

One of the defining characteristics of a Richardsonian Romanesque design is omitted from Fairn's composition. Romanesque architecture was asymmetrical. Mr. Fairn, in his design for the Northumberland County Courthouse, chose to have a symmetrical front, but otherwise conformed to the architectural standards established by Richardson.

THE INTERIOR

The interior of the courthouse was designed to have two similar courtrooms, one on the first floor and one directly above it on the second floor. Since the building was closed as a courthouse and sold, it has been substantially altered on the inside preparing for adaptation to contemporary commercial purposes.

dedicated entry on one side of the building which through a series of passageways leads to the justice's chambers on the first floor. There is also a separate dedicated stairway for justices that leads to the second floor courtroom. The first floor passageways also led to a secure access to the first floor courtroom.

The interior decorative elements are in oak stained and varnished to continue the theme of medieval castle-like solidity. The second floor courtroom retains its original oak double doors that lead from the stair hall into the courtroom. The doors open into an area that was allocated for public seating. That area is segregated from the functional area of the courtroom by a balustrade in oak known as the "bar" of the courtroom.

The justice's bench is directly in front of the double doors but on the far back wall of the courtroom. The bench is on a substantially elevated dais and has an extensive panelled oak backdrop which rises to the ceiling. On this backdrop one of the central panels, the most prominent, has a carved scale of justice, similar to one in the Digby, Nova Scotia courthouse. This is one of the most prevalent symbols of justice, particularly in American courthouse design. It serves as a reminder that this building is fundamentally American in its design elements, but fully conforms to late nineteenth century English courthouse layout and segregation principles.

The jury box was to the left of the presiding justice and the dock where an accused sat during trial was on the wall to his right which was opposite the jury box so the accused and jury could face each other.

Left: Detail of the ceiling displaying the original pressed tin ceiling. Note the fleur de lis embossed in the metalwork.

Right: The juxtaposition of the conical roof of the tower and the angularity of the main roof provide an interesting contrast.

The lawyers representing the parties (the Crown or plaintiff and the accused or defendant) sat at a common table in front of the justice and in between the parties.

An expertly installed and elegant pressed tin ceiling remains in its original form. One decorative element in the elaborately decorated pressed tin is worthy of note: the fleur-de-lis, a medieval symbol of France. The origins of the Romanesque (including the Richardsonian style) were primarily from southern French medieval castles, monasteries and cathedrals. The fleur-de-lis was also a popular decorative element in late nineteenth historicist decoration because of the fashion for all things French in terms of interior design in both America and Great Britain. However, the presence of the fleur-de-lis has particular relevance in the Miramichi region which has a substantial Acadian population, whose origins were in France. Whether the design element was selected to honour the Acadians is unknown, but it is clear that its presence as a decorative element in the courtroom has a particular significance and relevance in this area of New Brunswick.

While the former 1912-1913 Northumberland County Courthouse is no longer in service, it remains an important historical and architectural monument that has served the people of Miramichi region well and remains one of the most significant architectural achievements in the Province of New Brunswick.

The use of the Richardsonian Romanesque style is also a reminder of the significant influence the United States has had on Canadian culture.

APPENDIX:
PRIMARY LEGAL PROCEEDINGS HEARD IN COURTROOMS

The courtrooms examined in this book extend in time from the earliest extant Maritime courthouse – the Argyle County Courthouse in Tusket, Nova Scotia – to the newest Superior Court courtrooms which are in the Sir Louis Henry Davies Law Courts in Charlottetown. The standards of design and the layout and placement of fixtures to accommodate those performing court-related roles in them have been described in some detail in the preceding text.

It may be helpful in understanding the use of courtrooms to describe the three basic legal proceedings that are conducted in a contemporary Superior Court courtroom and to connect those proceedings with the courtroom layout, fixtures and personnel engaged as part of the process of conducting the proceedings.

The descriptions given below are generic in nature: each province has its own rules of court and procedures for the conduct of trials but underlying any differences there are substantial similarities. It is the similarities that establish the generic descriptions.

CONDUCT OF A CIVIL TRIAL

A civil claim is one that is not conducted under *The Criminal Code of Canada* or under a statute creating a quasi-criminal offence (criminal-like, such as a breach of a federal statute prescribing sanctions for breaches of its provisions).

A civil matter is typically a claim for money owed by one person to another for example, or a claim for money damages arising from the negligent operation of a vehicle in which bodily injuries are sustained by someone as the result of the negligence of another person or there is damage to property which results from the incident.

Civil claims fall into one of four categories in most provinces:
  a)   Small claims for which most provinces have a specific court procedure and rules of court. These claims are limited as to the maximum value of the claim. Discoveries are not held in small claims matters;

  a)   Simplified procedure – designated in most provinces for claims having a prescribed maximum set monetary amount, and while within the Supreme Court are subject to rules simplifying the procedures to be followed (for example, removing discoveries as part of the procedure);

  a)   An unrestricted claim in the Supreme Court;

  a)   Family law related litigation.

Starting a Claim – by filing an originating document: it identifies the claimant (Plaintiff) and the Defendant and the particulars of the claim. Examples of which are: Statement of Claim; Application; Petition (a specialized form of an originating document used, for example, to commence divorce proceedings).

Filing a Statement of Defence: usually within thirty-days but can be longer depending on whether the Defendant resides outside the province or is a body corporate in which case the limitation period for filing is extended.

Filing a Reply: the Plaintiff has the right to file a reply to allegations in the Statement of Defence not dealt with in the originating document.

Place of Filing: the Supreme Court of each province has a clerk's office in which all documents used in a particular litigation are filed. The principal clerk in some provinces is called the Prothonotary. There are specialized clerks responsible for various categories of legal proceedings who review the documents submitted for filing to ensure compliance with the rules of court. If in compliance, the document is filed and then the litigation is monitored throughout the proceeding to the conclusion. The purpose of the monitoring is to bring the litigation forward as efficiently as possible.

Monitoring by the Court: after the pleadings have closed (originating document, defence and reply have been filed) the court clerk responsible for this category of proceeding periodically schedules case-management conference calls with the lawyers for the parties to track and record the current status of the file.

A justice of the court will conduct an office or telephone conference when required, and after a pre-trial conference.

While no decisions on the merits of a case are made during the monitoring process, the justice can give directions as to management of the file that the lawyers are wise to accept and comply with.

Interim Relief: the court has authority to hear preliminary submissions on the Plaintiff's pleadings after a motion requesting an order to dismiss the pleadings on technical grounds or to grant a summary judgement order on the merits of the case. Both are extraordinary remedies and given only when the rules of court specifically allow the remedies.

In particular family law matters interim relief is permitted, usually in emergency matters such as child support, spousal support, custody and day-today care and control of a child. Such interim relief extends only until a justice makes a final decision after a trial. In many such cases, the interim order is accepted as the final adjudication and the parties often enter into a mutual settlement agreement based on the interim order.

Discoveries: this pre-trial procedure not held in a courthouse. Discovery enables the lawyers/parties to examine under oath the principal witness for the other party to determine the evidence that person would give at trial, thereby enabling the interrogating party to determine the strength or weakness of their case.

Pre-trial Conference: after all preliminary matters have been finished including exchange of documents and discoveries (if required by any of the parties) either the Plaintiff or the Defendant can request a pre-trial conference. This conference is a required step before the case is set down for trial. A justice presides at the conference and after reviewing the documents required of the parties for the conference, the justice meets with the parties and their lawyers (if represented by counsel) and the justice decides whether the case is ready for trial. The justice may decide additional steps are required and if so sets a time within which the task is to be preformed. Many justices will take the conference as an opportunity to attempt to mediate a settlement. If settlement is not possible and all preliminary matters are completed the justice sets the matter down for trial. The pre-trial conference is held in a conference room configured to facilitate discussion and exchange of opinions around a table. The conference in most courthouses is recorded.

Trial: The parties prepare a pre-trial document setting out the relief sought, the core evidence and any relevant case law they intend to rely on. The document is intended to prepare the justice for the hearing of the matter and to focus the argument for the opposite party. The trial is held in a courtroom chosen by the chief justice or an administrative official delegated to make the selection. The parties appear at the time designated in a court-issued notice of the trial. The Plaintiff is required to prove its case; the Defendant is not required to prove that it is not liable.

The Plaintiff leads first with its witnesses. After direct examination of each of the Plaintiff's witnesses by the Plaintiff or its counsel, the Defendant or lawyer cross-examines the witness. The process of direct and cross examination tests the relevance and veracity of the evidence. At the conclusion of the Plaintiff's case, the Defendant can move to request the court to dismiss the case because the Plaintiff has not met a reasonable standard of proof. This is very rare. If there is no motion for termination of the proceeding or if such a motion fails, the Defendant then advances whatever evidence it chooses to support its case.

Conclusion of the Evidence: after the parties have concluded examining the witnesses and examination of the documentary evidence through the witness verbal or written closing submissions are made by the parties to the presiding justice… at the conclusion of which the justice may request supplementary submissions on one or more particular points.

Decision: The presiding justice at the conclusion of the evidence and submissions may choose to give an oral decision or reserve judgement. If the latter, the justice takes the matter under advisement to give time for the justice to formulate a written decision. The written decision must be made within six months of the conclusion of the trial. The decision is released to the parties in a printed judgment. All judgements of a Supreme Court are recorded and available to the public. Many are printed in law reports.

Jury: if the matter is a jury trial, the jury hears the evidence and makes a decision on the evidence, ultimately on whether the Plaintiff's facts advanced or those of the Defendant are believed by the jury. The jury is the decider of the facts and ultimately on the liability of the Defendant.

The jury is selected by the parties from a much larger panel of jurors called by the sheriff. The jurors sitting on a particular trial are subject to questions from all the parties. Each party has a set number of challenges which is applied to a particular juror; a challenge eliminates that person from the panel. Once the selection of jurors has been made the presiding justice calls the Plaintiff to commence with its evidence.

The Configuration of the Courtroom: is designed to facilitate all aspects of a civil trial – and by extension all of the courthouse and its staff. The courthouse provides segregation and security for all participants in a trial.

CONDUCT OF A CRIMINAL TRIAL

The conduct of the trial of a person or corporation charged with an offence under *The Criminal Code of Canada* is similar to that conducted in a civil trial but the procedure that precedes the trial is different and some of the rights, privileges and duties of an accused standing his or her trial differ from those of a litigant in a civil trial.

A person or corporation rarely appears in a Superior Court to answer a criminal charge as the court of first instance. The trials of criminal matters are usually held in a provincial court before a judge appointed by the province. Virtually all charges under *The Criminal Code of Canada* involve an appearance before a provincial court judge to enter plea and to stand trial. There are rare exceptions to that process and they arise where *The Criminal Code of Canada* expressly authorizes the accused to elect trial by Superior Court justice with or without a jury. The most prominent situation in which an election would arise is in a murder charge.

Summary Convictions/indictable offences: all charges under *The Criminal Code of Canada* are styled either a summary conviction or an indictable offence. Some offences may be prosecuted as either summary conviction or as indictable procedures at the choice of Crown Counsel. These are called "dual procedure" or "hybrid" offences. Summary conviction offences are, generally speaking, less serious offences than indictable ones.

Before Plea: before entering a plea an accused is not usually kept in custody until trial but may be taken into custody and held pending trial if the Crown has reasonable and probable grounds for believing the accused would pose a threat to the public or a specific person or persons. In cases where there is any concern about the accused having further contact with the alleged victim or attending at a particular place, the police require the accused to enter into an undertaking to keep the peace and stay away from certain people or places pending trial. If the police are seeking to have the accused detained pending trial certain procedures have to be followed. Upon arresting and charging the accused the police have to bring the accused before a Justice of the Peace within a prescribed time-frame and have a "Show Cause Hearing." Subject to some exceptions, the burden is usually on the Crown to show cause why an accused should be detained until dealt with according to law. The procedure in *The Criminal Code of Canada* regarding this is entitled "Judicial Interim Release." It used to be more commonly referred to a "bail". The posting of money called a "surety" is seldom a condition of release; the grounds for detention and focus is instead on whether the detention is necessary to ensure the accused's attendance in court or prevent the continuation of commission of offences – to protect victims or witnesses or generally to maintain public confidence in the administration of justice. The request for posting of a surety is usually confined to cases where the accused ordinarily resides in another jurisdiction.

The accused's first court appearance: for all charges whether summary conviction or indictable involves the accused attending at the indicated time, which is usually on a regular "Docket Day" in provincial court. Every charge, whether summary conviction or indictable is presented at this time only on an Information.

The indictment is read and the accused is asked to enter plea. At this stage the Information and the indictment are one and the same. The accused is entitled to enter either a guilty or a not guilty plea. In the Canadian legal system an accused is innocent until proven guilty and as such may enter a not guilty plea putting the Crown to the burden of proving guilt. The presumption of innocence has been a fundamental principle of English law since the middle ages and was part of Canada's received law from England codified as a fundamental right in *The Criminal Code of Canada*.

After the first court appearance: the Crown as represented by Crown Counsel, proceeds with the conduct of the trial in much the same manner as counsel for the Plaintiff would in a civil matter. The procedure is the same whether the trial proceeds in a Superior Court or a provincial court. The Crown must disclose the evidence it has against the accused before trial after a request by defence counsel and must provide copies of documentation in its possession. Unlike in a civil litigation the accused, as a party to the proceeding has no duty of disclosure or production of documents

The Trial: the accused, if in custody, is taken by the sheriff's officials from the detention facility to the courthouse and taken by one or more of those officials to a segregated holding area in the courthouse and up a segregated staircase (if one is part of the courthouse) to a prisoner's dock where the accused sits during the trial. If the accused is considered to be at high risk to create a disturbance or to be a risk to anyone in the courtroom the accused is held in a secure area of the courtroom. If the accused is not considered to be a security risk the accused is entitled to sit with defence counsel (if represented, by counsel); if not represented the accused can sit at the table in the operational area of the courtroom designated for the use of defence Counsel. The Crown is required to prove its case to the high standard of "beyond a reasonable doubt". The Crown examines each of its witnesses. The accused cross-examines after direct examination of each witness. At the conclusion of the Crown's case, if there is no motion for a mistrial by the accused, the defence is entitled to advance its case but the accused is not required to give evidence and may choose to remain silent. After the evidence has been introduced by the Crown and the accused, submissions on the law and the facts from both are advanced. The trial judge makes a decision on the facts and on guilt.

The modern approach to criminal trials: in most jurisdictions, it is to ensure the appearance of innocence is maintained throughout the trial. That means that the accused, unless there is compelling reason to do otherwise, enters the courtroom escorted by officials from the sheriff's office and is usually free from any form of obvious physical restraint; however, on Prince Edward Island, if the accused is in custody and enters the courtroom in shackles the accused may remain in shackles during the trial. Nineteenth century prisoner's docks which were balustraded boxes with or without seats are seldom used in the twenty-first century.

Where a criminal trial is conducted by judge and jury: the number of jurors is prescribed by provincial statute. The jury's role is to serve as trier of facts.

The presiding judge's role: is to conduct the trial in an open, objective, fair and civil manner instructing the jury on the law and answering such questions as are raised by the jury and deciding objections or procedural points raised by counsel or the jury.

After a verdict of guilty or not guilty by the jury: the accused is released if the jury's verdict is one of not guilty and if the verdict is guilty the presiding judge decides the sentence appropriate in the interests of public order, the facts of the case and according to the requirements for sentencing prescribed in *The Criminal Code of Canada*. Consideration of earlier decisions of courts rendered on the same offences is also part of sentencing.

The Crown's duty in a prosecution: is neither to obtain a conviction nor to represent the victim; it is to objectively conduct the Crown's case in a manner that will enable the truth of the matter to be found.

The enforcement of *The Criminal Code of Canada* in the name of Her Majesty Queen Elizabeth II: arises under the Royal Prerogative as the monarch is deemed to be the fount of justice and that is confirmed by statute – it goes to the nexus referred to in this book between the monarch and the administration of justice. The monarch as the fount of justice necessarily has the corresponding obligation to enforce the law, hence the charge being brought in the name of the monarch.

At the conclusion of the trial: the accused is entitled to appeal the conviction and/or the sentence to a justice of the Supreme Court (trial level) or in some situations to the provincial Court of Appeal. If an appeal is filed the sentence is not stayed pending appeal but the accused may apply for release from custody until the appeal is heard and a decision rendered on the appeal. However, where the accused is perceived by the presiding justice to pose a threat to the public or a particular person (to reoffend) or is perceived to be likely to abscond, the accused can be ordered to continue to be held in custody until the decision of the Court of Appeal is released.

The configuration of the courtroom: is designed to facilitate all aspects of a criminal trial. The courtroom provides segregation and security for all the participants in the trial and ensures the accused is not presented or perceived during the trial as having been found guilty. The rights of the accused are preserved.

APPEAL TO A PROVINCIAL COURT OF APPEAL

Appeals: can lie from any judicial decision rendered irrespective of which court. Some appeals may also lie from an administrative tribunal; the appeal would be to a single justice of the Supreme Court. An appeal from a provincial court judge in a criminal matter lies either to a justice of the Supreme Court or to its Court of Appeal depending on the section of *The Criminal Code of Canada* under which the conviction was made. An appeal from a Superior Court justice lies to the Court of Appeal.

There is a limitation period within which appeals can be filed: all of which are prescribed by statute. Other than in *The Criminal Code of Canada* matters where the terms and conditions for appeals are prescribed by *The Criminal Code of Canada*, each province has a statute called the *Appeals Act, the Judicature Act,* or a statute having similar provisions which prescribes the conditions governing appeals. Generally speaking most appeals must be filed within thirty days from the date of the court Order perfecting the judgement of the lower court.

An appeal is a matter of right in most situations: however, an appeal will be filed only if the losing party believes it has reasonable grounds on which to base the appeal and also believes it has a reasonable prospect of success. Failure to win the appeal results in significant costs against the appellant in favour of the respondent (the winning party at the lower level court). Costs awarded to a losing party at an appeal are added to the costs invariably awarded against that party at the lower level and collectively would constitute a very substantial expense to the losing appellant and one that must be factored in deciding whether to appeal. Costs are not awarded against an individual convicted of a criminal offence who loses an appeal. Some appeals required leave or permission of the court of appeal.

An appeal is commenced: as prescribed by the provincial statute and rules of court governing appeals. A notice of appeal (or equivalent) is filed with the Court of Appeal. The grounds or challenges to the lower court's decision are set out in sufficient detail to establish in appropriate language the errors made in the lower court's decision, and the remedies sought by the appellant from the Court of Appeal.

Most appeals request: a reversal of the decision made by the lower court and costs. However, an appeal can be to vary only some parts of the lower court's decision.

Documents the appellant must file with the court: First, a Notice of Appeal and a certificate issued by the appellant, second an Appeal Book within thirty days or some other period prescribed by the rules of court from the date of filing the notice of appeal. It is served on all other parties to the appeal. The Appeal Book must contain a transcript of the evidence adduced at the lower level if required by the appellant and copies of exhibits filed in the court from which the appeal lay. The appellant must also file a Factum which is served on all other parties. The Factum sets out the appellant's submissions to the court on the facts and the law supporting the appeal. The appellant completes the pre-hearing procedure by filing a Certificate of Completion.

New evidence at the appeal hearing: none is admissible without the leave (permission) of the court. That is rarely requested and when it is, it is usually a highly contested request by the opposite party.

Testimony by witnesses during a Court of Appeal hearing: none, unless the court has received a specific motion to admit such evidence and issues an order granting the request.

Composition of a Court of Appeal: an uneven number of justices. A majority of the justices sitting on an appeal make the final decision. A justice of the Court of Appeal who disagrees with the majority decision may "dissent" which means that the justice can issue a separate decision differing from that of the majority. The actual composition of the bench in a Court of Appeal matter is the decision of the chief justice of the court. Nova Scotia for example has eight Court of Appeal justices. Three of those justices are the customary panel but the chief justice may direct that all five sit on the panel hearing the appeal. The actual number of Court of Appeal justices who sit on an appeal in New Brunswick is seven. Three of the seven Court of Appeals Justices make up a customary panel, similar to Nova Scotia. On Prince Edward Island where there are only three Court of Appeal justices all three sit – if there is a conflict of interest or a justice is unable or unavailable to sit, a justice of the trial level is called on to fill the vacancy for that hearing.

The actual appeal hearing is a relatively simple procedure: the panel of justices take their position on the dais and the chief justice invites the appellant to proceed with the appellant's submissions. At the conclusion of the appellant's submissions the chief justice invites the respondent to make its submissions. During the hearing any one of the justices can, and frequently does, interrupt the submissions being made by counsel to ask a question or a series of questions or challenge submissions on the law or the facts. Counsel may raise objections to representations made on the facts and the law made by opposing counsel. Where that occurs the chief justice decides on the merits of the objection.

The decision of the Court of Appeal is, under limited circumstances, appealable: to the Supreme Court of Canada. An appellant who wishes to appeal a decision of a provincial Court of Appeal must apply to the Supreme Court of Canada for "leave" (permission) to appeal. The submissions on the issue of leave are in themselves a procedure involving extensive documentation and written submissions. In making a decision whether to grant leave to appeal the Supreme Court of Canada must be satisfied that the case is not one of a local matter and that the case raises a substantive issue of law of national interest requiring clarification or adjudication.

The decisions of the courts of appeal are available: on line and printed in law books published to distribute decisions of the court as are the decisions of the trial level Superior Courts. Access to the decisions of the Superior Courts is essential to ensure the public has the opportunity to keep itself informed of the law, as ignorance of the law is no defence.

Just as the public has a right to access decisions of all Superior Courts so too the public has the right to sit in and witness proceedings in all Superior Courts, including Courts of Appeal. The only exemptions are where national security or public policy establishes that access should be denied for established reasons.

GLOSSARY

alcove: a recessed area behind the primary surface of a wall in the interior of a courtroom, but open to the courtroom, forming part of it giving visual emphasis or highlight to the area of the room in which it occurs, usually forming a backdrop to the Judge's bench.

arcade: a sequence of arches each separated from the next by a column; occasionally blind.

architrave: either the lowest section of an entablature, directly supported by columns or a pilaster, or a moulded decorative frame around a door or window.

archivolt: the curved band of ashlar blocks forming decorative details of an arch often found framing the curved top of a semi-circular or ovoid arch.

armorial bearings: the coat of arms and heraldic features of a person of high estate or of a country or municipality.

ashlar: dressed stone facing on the external or internal surface of a building, either structural, or surface mounted as a decorative element.

asymmetrical: the opposite of symmetrical; the left side of a surface being of unequal size or detail to the right side.

balustrade: a row of balusters topped by a cornice forming a handrail usually ending in a newel post or volute.

bar: the bar of a courtroom is a balustrade dividing the segregated functional area from the public area, the functional area being reserved for the justice, court staff, litigants and lawyers.

barristers: persons trained in the law at an accredited law school, who have passed exams prescribed by a law society and who have been admitted to the practice of law by an order of a justice of a superior court.

base block: a square or rectangular base for a column, pilaster or architrave.

belt course: an alternative term for a string course of masonry.

bench, judge's: the table and chair located on an elevated dais at the front of a courtroom, segregated for the use of the presiding judge.

blind: as in a blind door, window or arch, the space usually occupied by the door, window or open arch is infilled and not a void, designed to maintain symmetry in the decorative and functional elements of the wall or surface area in which it is located.

British: having origins in the culture, history, architecture, law or decorative elements of England, Ireland, Scotland or Wales.

brutalism: a term derived from the French language term "bréton brut", meaning raw concrete, applied to le Corbusier-inspired modern architecture.

canopy: a roof-like structure, overlaying another structure often of a different material, in an interior decorative scheme, usually to create a ceremonial focal point in a room; in the context of the interior of a courtroom, forming the upper element of a dais panelling.

capital: the top of a column or pilaster supporting an entablature.

chambers: a justice's office which is used occasionally, for meetings with lawyers for litigants, but only on invitation of the justice, but in the context of a "chambers" hearing, a request made in open court at a predetermined time to a justice on a narrow point of law for a specific remedy in open court.

chandelier: a ceiling mounted ornamental branched support to hold candles or lights which can be a central feature of a courtroom.

civil architecture: architecture for a public building that is not of a religious or private nature.

civil litigation: court proceedings in a Superior Court that are not of a criminal nature.

code of conduct: a statement of the ethical standards to which lawyers must adhere in their dealings with clients, fellow members of their profession, the judiciary, and court staff, prescribed by the law society of each province.

colonial revival style: an architectural style created in the United States at the time of the commemoration of the one hundredth anniversary of the American Revolution of 1776. It was intended to reject the formality of British Georgian architecture and the American Federal style but to retain the American colonial simple expression of that style, utilizing all the modern conveniences available.

colonnade: a row of columns, either outside or inside a building, supporting a number of arches or a flat entablature.

column: an upright pillar or post, whether free standing or providing support outside or inside the building, made of stone or wood usually in one of the classical orders with a base below, and a capital above carrying the entablature.

common law: the law developed by superior courts in England since the medieval period based on common customs and usages which when accepted and applied by superior court justices attained the status of law, ever changing to meet new situations or changes in community standards or morals.

commutation of sentences: termination or reduction of the effect of a justice-made sentence issued after a conviction of a criminal or quaisi criminal offence.

corbel: a bracket or block designed to be weight bearing usually mounted on a wall supporting a ceiling or other structural element, often decorated and sized to compliment the over-all architectural style of a building.

corner block: square relatively flat decorative element usually made of wood, placed at the upper corners on each side of the architraves around a door or a window.

cornice: either the upper projecting portion of a classical entablature, or a decorative moulding where ceiling and wall meet.

counsel: an alternative term for a lawyer representing a client.

Corinthian order: the third classical Order of columns having their origin in ancient Greece or Rome.

Crown: a generic term used to denote the administration and enforcement of criminal law; the term arises from the role of the monarch as the fount of justice.

crown moulding: any moulding forming a crowning or finishing member of an interior decorative element that may contain design elements based on concave or convex forms and often with a bead, ribbon or rope.

cupola: a roof-mounted decorative structure with its own roof having no practical function such as providing light (a lantern) or a viewing platform (a belvedere).

dado rail: a wall-mounted moulding often set at the top of panelling protecting the wall from damage from chairs, sometimes referred to as a "chair rail".

dais: an elevated platform in a courtroom used to segregate the judge from others.

dentil: a small rectangular block set within a row of closely but equally spaced similar blocks to decorate a cornice, hence dentilation which means a decorative pattern containing dentils such as in a frieze.

dock: from the Dutch usage, a segregated space in which an accused is located in a courtroom during most of his or her trial.

domed ceiling: a ceiling, or a portion of a ceiling which is concave either forming a shallow dome or one that is a hemi-dome, a half dome.

Doric Order: a column in the form and style of the oldest and simplest of the three classical Greek architectural orders.

dormer: a window and adjacent roofed structure housing it installed on the slope of the roof.

entablature: in classical architecture the entablature is located above the columns, set horizontally between the capitals and the roof, and is comprised of the architrave, frieze and cornice.

fanlight: a semi-circular or ovoid shaped transom above a door or window frame, usually divided into separate lights in a geometric pattern.

Federal Style: a style of architecture developed in the late eighteenth century in the United States based on, but a modification of the architectural and decorative neoclassical styles developed by Scottish architect Robert Adam; this style became the first recognized national American style.

fenestration: windows.

finial: a vertical decorative element in the shape of a neoclassical urn or other neoclassical form such as an acorn, or pineapple, with a bulbous or pointed top, usually forming a pinnacle as part of a neoclassical decorative scheme.

foliate: decorated patterns of foliage such as leaves, vines, or flowers, forming part of a decorative scheme.

frieze: the horizontal part of the classical entablature that comes between the architrave below and the cornice above.

gallery: an open sitting or viewing area on the mezzanine level of a courtroom overlooking the courtroom.

gaol: is an obsolete spelling of the word now commonly referred to as a jail.

gasoliers: a lighting fixture designed to transmit natural gas or other gaseous substance to a device on the fixture in which combustion occurs thereby generating light, often in the form of a chandelier or a wall sconce.

glazing: glass for a window or door frame; if in smaller units than the frame, individual units are anchored by muntins.

graining: the simulation or imitation of wood or marble on an inferior wood or stone surface for decorative purposes, usually through the application of paint or tinted shellac, or similar material, applied to the surface by use of a comb.

handedness: the ancient tradition of the placement of spaces, objects, and people according to right and left hand, the right hand having greater precedence.

Ionic order: a column in the form and style of the second of the classical Greek orders, also the second in the Roman orders, having a capital with curved volutes, a moulded base and a shaft longer and narrower than in the Doric Order, but not so much as in the Corinthian, with entasis.

joinery: cabinetry and woodworking created by highly skilled and specialized craftsmen.

judgement: reasons for a judge's decision given at the conclusion of a civil or criminal trial.

keystone: a central stone voussoir at the apex of the curve of a vault or arch (archivolt).

lantern: a structure mounted on a roof designed to provide natural light or ventilation to the interior of a building, not designed as a viewing platform

litigants: parties to a civil legal proceeding in a superior court usually a plaintiff or a defendant.

lunette: a semi-circular space or window.

mansard roof: a roof in which the angle of slope is broken, usually at half its height, and is on all sides of the building, the upper angle being much more gradual than the lower angle.

mezzanine: an intermediate and partial floor level between the primary floor and ceiling of a room.

modillion: a small bracket under the projecting part of a cornice, either carved or plain, usually rectilinear in shape.

mullion: a structural support dividing two windows or doors.

muntin: a glazing bar used to anchor glass in a Georgian style window or door.

newel post: a decorative post at the start, finish, or intermediate landing of a staircase.

oculus: a circular opening in a wall or roof that provides light to an interior space.

Palladian window: a tripartite window with the centre window usually containing a round headed element, and two flanking windows being narrower and flat headed, also called a Venetian or Serliana.

panelling: a wall covering comprised of a series of framed panels, usually made exclusively from wood, the panels often being chamfered but can appear in various shapes.

panel door: a door constructed of wood with rails and stiles comprising a frame, with inset panels usually chamfered at least on one side.

paterae: circular or ovoid decorative ornaments in bas-relief which are applied to prominent external or internal surfaces as part of an over-all neoclassical design scheme, usually part of an architect's personal interpretation of neoclassicism.

pavilions: distinct structures, secondary to the principal architectural composition, often forming part of and complementary to that composition, for example as end sections to a long façade.

pediments: triangular gables surmounting an entablature and colonnade, all forming part of a portico.

peristyle hall: an enclosed area having an arcade of columns on two or more sides, in northern neoclassical buildings often roofed forming one of the principal rooms.

piano nobile: the floor on which the principal rooms in a building are located, in an 18th and 19th century neoclassical building, the second floor.

pilaster: a column or rectangular shaft that projects slightly from the wall to which it is attached, and often includes a base, shaft and capital that conform with the classical order of the primary columns of the structure involved.

portico: a roofed open structure usually projecting from the front of a neoclassical building supported by neoclassical columns containing architectural elements inspired by ancient Greek or Roman architecture, intended to give importance, dignity and a focal point for the building, usually engaged to the wall of the building and giving a covered entrance to it.

rectory: the living quarters of Anglican clergy usually adjacent to the church.

Romanesque: an architectural composition containing design and structural elements originating in ancient Roman architecture.

rosette: a foliate-designed ceiling mounted decorative element, often the point from which a chandelier is hung, and the word can also be used to describe a decorative element based on the form of a rose.

roundel: a round flat ornament or a small circular window.

Royal Prerogative: the remaining personal discretionary powers and authority exercisable by the Queen forming part of the Canadian constitution.

rustication: roughened ashlar blocks dressing the external surface of a building, usually on the ground floor or basement level, so as to give deep shadow lines and texture to the surface, also giving contrast with the ashlar in the upper storeys.

sash: a frame, usually of wood, fitted with one or more panes of glass and forming part of a window.

sash-window: a window containing one or more sashes in the traditional Georgian style, which usually has two sashes that overlap slightly and slide up and down inside a wooden or metal frame, which may also contain weighted pulleys and cords to enable vertical movement.

sill: the horizontal ledge at the base of a door or window frame.

sidelight: a vertical light flanking a doorway, usually one on each side.

storey: the separate floors or stages that constitute a building.

string: the sloping member, or raking beam, that hold the ends of the treads and risers of a staircase, either in open string or closed string form.

stringcourse: a continuous horizontal band, either plain or moulded, thinner than a belt course, often projecting from the face of the building and usually demarcating the division of the structure into units such as storeys.

transom: a window across the top of a door or window forming part of it.

tread: the flat surface of the top level of a step in a staircase.

tread end: decorative fretwork or scroll applied to the end of stairway tread in an open string configuration.

Tuscan Doric: of the five classical Roman orders of columns the Tuscan, adopted from the Doric, was the simplest of the orders, with fluted or unfluted columns, a plain entablature and unadorned capitals and bases.

tympanum: the triangular space in a pediment enclosed by the eaves of the roof of the pediment.

urn: the shape of a Roman vase which is used as a decorative element to enhance historicist detail.

vestibule: an entrance hall immediately inside an external entrance to a building, usually the principal door, leading to the primary hallway or corridor.

volute: a spiral scroll forming the most ornamental part of the Ionic capital, used as a component of a Georgian Style staircase.

voussoir: wedge-shaped blocks forming part of a structural external band that follows the soffit of a masonry arch forming part of the archivolt.

wainscoting: a form of wooden paneling at the lower part of a wall, below a dado rail.

SELECT BIBLIOGRAPHY

_____. *Province of Ontario architectural design standards for court houses/...* 1v. (various pagings): ill., plans; 22-28cm. Toronto, Ontario: Queen's Printer, c1999.

N. Blomley, D. Delaney and R. Ford (eds.). *The Legal Geographies Reader.* Blackwell, Oxford, 2001

Bulmer, Jane. *The Royal Courts of Justice, London.* Peterborough, UK: Jarrold Publishing, 2014

Calloway, Stephen. *The Elements of Style: An Encyclopedia of Domestic Architectural Details.* Revised by Alan Powers. Buffalo, NY: Firefly Books (US) Inc, 2012.

Carter, Margaret, (compiled by). *Early Canadian Court Houses: Studies in Archaeology, Architecture and History.* National Historic Parks and Sites Branch, Parks Canada, Environment Canada, 1983.

Chalklin, Christopher. *English Counties and Public Buildings 1650-1830.* London & Rio Grande. The Hamledon Press, 1998.

Clark, Andrew Hill. *Three Centuries and the Island: A Historical Geography of Settlement and Agriculture in Prince Edward Island, Canada.* Toronto: University of Toronto Press, 1959.

Cole, Emily. *The Grammar of Architecture.* Lewes, England: The Ivy Press Limited, 2002.

Curl, James Stevens. *Oxford Dictionary of Architecture.* London: Oxford University Press, 1999.

Douzinas, Costas and Nead, Linda (eds). *Law and the Image: The Authority of Art and the Aesthetics of law.* Chicago: University of Chicago Press, 1999.

Field, John. *The Story of Parliament: in the Palace of Westminster.* London: James & James (Publishers) Ltd., 2006

Foucault, M. *Discipline and Punish: The Birth of the Prison.* Harmondsworth, London: Penguin, 1977

Girard, Philip; Phillips, Jim and Cahill, Barry. *The Supreme Court of Nova Scotia, 1754-2004: From Imperial Bastion to Provincial Oracle.* (Osgoode Society for Canadian legal history). Toronto/ Buffalo/London: University of Toronto Press, 2004.

Graham, C. *The history of law court architecture in England and Wales; The institutionalization of the law.* Pp 36-37 *SAVE Britain's Heritage, Silence in court: The future of the UK's historic law courts,* London: SAVE Britain's Heritage. 2003.

Graham, Clare. *Ordering Law: The Architecture and Social History of the English Law Court to 1914.* Aldershot, Hampshire, England: Ashgate Publishing Limited, 2003

Haigh, Christopher, (ed.). *The Cambridge Historical Encyclopedia of Great Britain and Ireland.* New York/Port Chester/Melbourne/Sydney: Cambridge University Press, 1985.

Hale, C.A. *The Early Court Houses of New Brunswick.* Manuscript Report Series No. 290. Ottawa: Parks Canada, 1977.

Hale, C.A. *The Early Court Houses of Nova Scotia.* Manuscript Report Series No. 293. Ottawa: Parks Canada, 1977.

Haliburton, Justice Charles E. *The Judges of Nova Scotia 1754-2004, Biographical History.* Kentville, Nova Scotia: Gasperaux Press, 2004.

Hodgson, Judy (ed.). An Anthology, various contributors. *The English Legal Heritage.* Oyez Publishing, 1979

Gowans, Alan. *Building Canada: An Architectural History of Canadian Life.* Toronto. Oxford University Press, 1966.

Jacob, R. *The Historical Development of Courthouse Architecture. Zodia* 14:30-43, 1999.

Kalman, Harold. *A History of Canadian Architecture.* Don Mills, Ont: Oxford University Press, 1994.

Lawson, Simpson; Jordan, Fred; Tunnicliff, Robin. *Courthouse Design: The First International Conference.* Washington, DC: The American Institute of Architects, 1983.

Lounsbury, Carl. *From Statehouse to Courthouse: An architectural History of South Carolina's Colonial Capital and Charleston County Courthouse.* Columbia, South Carolina: University of South Carolina Press, 2001.

Lounsbury, Carl R. *The Courthouses of Early Virginia: An Architectural History.* Charlottesville and London: University of Virginia Press, 2005

MacKinnon, Frank. *The Government of Prince Edward Island.* Toronto: University of Toronto Press, 1951.

Macnutt, James W. *Building for Democracy: The History and Architecture of the Legislative Buildings of Nova Scotia, Prince Edward Island and New Brunswick.* Halifax, Nova Scotia: Formac Publishing Company Limited, 2010.

MacNutt, W.S. *New Brunswick, A History: 1784-1867.* Toronto: Macmillan, 1963.

MacRae, Marion and Adamson, Anthony. *Cornerstones of Order: Courthouses and Town Halls of Ontario 1784-1914.* Toronto, Canada: Clarke Irwin, 1983.

McNamara, M. *From Tavern to Courthouse: Architecture and Ritual in American Law 1658 – 1860.* Baltimore/ London: Johns Hopkins University Press, 2004.

Miele, Chris. *The Supreme Court of the United Kingdom: History, Art, Architecture.* London: Merrell Publishers limited, April 2010.

Mulcahy, Linda. *Architects of Justice: the Politics of Courtroom Design.* Birkberck University of London, UK: Vol. 16 No. 3 383-403. Social Legal Studies Sept., 2007.

Nead, L. *Visual Culture of the Courtroom: Reflections on History, Law and the Image.* Visual Culture in Britain 3(2) Pgs. 119-41.

Osler, Stephen. *Courthouses in Ontario.* pp 117-136. Toronto, Ontario: Carswell, 1979.

Philips, James and Simon Stern. *Anglo-Canadian Legal History,* Volume 1.

Ramsey/Sleeper. *Architectural Graphic Standards, 11th Edition.* The American Institute of Architects. March 2007. (Justice facilities).

Risk, R.C.B. *The Development of Canadian Law and Legal Institutions.* Toronto: The Faculty of Law, University of Toronto Libraries, 1974.

_____. *The Royal Courts of Justice.* London. Jarrold Publishing, Peterborough, England, 2014.

Scully, Vincent. *Architecture: The Natural and the Manmade.* New York. St. Martin's Press, 1991.

Taylor, C.J. *The Early Court Houses of Prince Edward Island.* Manuscript Report Series No. 289. Ottawa: Parks Canada, 1977.

Weisberg, Ruth. *The Art of Memory and the Allegorical Personification of Justice.* ' Yale Journal of law & Humanities': vol. 24: Iss.1, Article 12. 2012.

Willcocks, Gray V. *The Court of King's Bench in Upper Canada, 1824-1827. Gray v. Willcocks: an old cause célébre.* University of Toronto Libraries: Riddell, William Renwick, 1852-1945.

Willcocks, Gray V. *The Early Courts of the Province.* (microform). University of Toronto Libraries: Riddell, William Renwick, 1852-1945.

Winter, A.G. and Porter, S. *The Law Court 1800-2000: Development in Form and Function.* London: English Heritage. Zodiac 14:30-43. 1994

Woodcock, Thomas. *Legal Habits: A Brief Sartorial History of Wig, Robe and Gown.* London. Produced for Ede and Ravenscroft Limited. Good Books (GB Publications Ltd., 2003.

INDEX

COURTHOUSES LISTED BY DATE OF CONSTRUCTION